Mud, Sweat 'n' Beers

Mud, Sweat and Beers

Craig Stevenson and John Mackay

Cheapwayround Publishers
East Kilbride

*This book is dedicated
to the committees and supporters
who organize and
follow Junior Football
with such dedication
and madness*

and
our premier league team
Irene and Kate

First Published in 2014 by
Cheapwayround Publishers

ISBN No; 978-0-9570252-4-0

Typeset in East Kilbride by
Cheapwayround publishers

Edited by Ian Baillie

Printed and Bound by
Bell and Bain Ltd.
Burnfield Road, Thornliebank,
Glasgow, G46 7UQ

Cheapwayround Publishers
22 Balfour Terrace
East Kilbride, G75 0JQ

cheapwayroundpub@yahoo.co.uk
www.cheapwayroundpub.co.uk

Books by the same authors:-

The Cheap Way Round

Still Goin'

Goin' Roon the Edge

Inn Aff the Bar

Contents

Introduction

After the success of our last book, 'Inn Aff the Bar', we decided to follow up with a look at junior football. Arguably there is just as much passion and fanaticism attached to the junior game as that of the seniors. In fact it could be argued that because of its truly local nature, the junior game has a greater connection with its fan-base.

In this book we visit a number of junior clubs, not just to sample the ale houses around the grounds but to record the stories of interclub rivalry.

In our last book we visited all 41 senior clubs in Scotland (Berwick Rangers is in England, so we didn't go there.) This time we thought we would do the same with the juniors. However, a quick count, using the A to Z of junior clubs, gave us a total of 160 clubs in the country.

Even with our exceptional abilities there was no chance of us managing to visit all 160 clubs, so we had to prioritise. The decision to visit junior clubs was made at the end of a long session in one of our favourite pubs. The first thing we had to do was convene a meeting (between the two of us) when we were both completely sober, and come up with a workable plan.

We discovered that Scotland's junior teams are split into three regions West, East and North, there is no South Region. John assumed that's where the posh people and farmers play rugby. It was important for us to cover as much of Scotland as possible, not only to get a good cross-section of different teams and experiences, but to allow us some really good jaunts on the buses. We do enjoy a nice day out using our bus passes.

What we decided to do was to pick some of the best-known clubs from the three regions, pair them with their closest rivals, and listen to their stories of past triumphs and disasters on the field of play.

Very quickly we discovered that almost every junior club has a close rival, some may be from the same town, others might be from neighbouring towns and in some cases the rivalry may stem, not from the closeness of the teams but, from success or the lack of it in acquiring that end of season silverware.

Surely nothing is more likely to create a deep-seated rivalry between two teams than a much disputed cup winning goal scored against your favourite team.

Our ceaseless quest for perfection sees us not only interview committee men, and women, but also the ordinary fans in the team social clubs and adjacent pubs. The result is a great collection of humorous football tales from the past and present.

Larkhall Thistle V Royal Albert

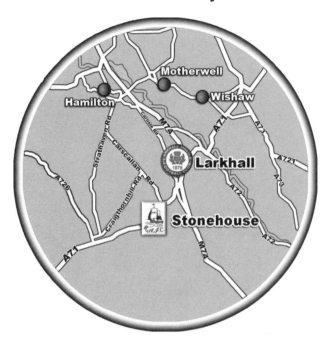

Club Name	Founded
Larkhall Thistle	1878
Ground	*Colours*
Gasworks Park	Red and White Stripes
League (2014-15)	*Selection of Honours*
Cen. League, 1st Div.	Jun. Cup 1907-08; 1913-14
Club Nickname	
The Jags or The Larky	

John: Today's trip was a local affair, two very old teams within spitting distance of East Kilbride. I don't know where this chapter will be in the book, but it was the first trip we carried out.

'Spitting Distance' reminds me of my pal in Rothesay, Robin Patrick's dad Harry, a great and very funny guy whom I met one day years ago in Rothesay just after he had moved house. On enquiring where his new house was he said, 'it's within spitting distance of the chapel'. 'How do you know that'?, I replied, 'I've tried it', he said. As you can guess, Harry was a Rangers man. I thought this story would be appreciated by 99% of the Larkhall population.

These two teams are as close rivals as you can get. Both were formed in Larkhall about the same time, although Larkhall Thistle lay claim to being the oldest Junior Football Club in Scotland, founded in 1878. One of Royal Albert's claims to fame is that they were the first team in Scotland to score from a penalty. It happened during a friendly match against Airdrie, the scorer being none other than the legendary Jimmy McLuggage. What a great name and a great piece of information for our readers. I hope more of these gems will follow.

Up until the end of last season the two teams shared Larkhall's Gasworks Park, a good name for a football ground. This season Royal Albert have moved to Tileworks Park in Stonehouse, where Stonehouse Violet used to play. I have no idea how this will pan out. I fear the worst, but hope for the best. As at every Junior team, the Secretaries and Committee members do a fantastic job in the background, keeping their clubs in business.

How many supporters will travel the two miles between Larkhall and Stonehouse to watch their beloved Royal Albert is anybody's guess. I doubt if City Link will have to alter their timetable to accommodate the crowds.

The weather in the weeks leading up to today's matches had been awful and during that time most of the Junior calendar had been wiped out, or the games had been called off.

I had spoken to Royal Albert's secretary Peter Higgins on the Friday and he had been doing everything he could to get their match played. Unfortunately, on Saturday morning he called me to say that the referee had cancelled the match. This meant that we had only Larkhall to visit. We will return to catch up with Royal Albert at a future time.

Larkhall's nickname is 'The Jags' or sometimes 'Larky', both not too bad, so I won't interfere and attempt some crap alternative like I usually do, although 'The Gasworks Gang', or 'The Prods', would fit the bill!

Our first trip of this book started with a walk down to the EK Bus station to catch the Number 254 EK to Stonehouse bus. Being out of training at the start of a book season, I had forgotten about my pieces until Kate (the luckiest woman in the world), asked if I was taking pieces with me. Of course I was. Although there was none of my favourite filling, corned beef, in the fridge, there was Sandwich Spread Light and plain bread to hand. By the way, the word Light added to Sandwich Spread, or anything else means light on taste, or crap.

I didn't want, or was feart, to complain, so off I went with Craig on our trip with the alternative pieces. As it turned out, the pieces were great and I ate the lot before we arrived at Larkhall.

Craig:At long last we are back on the road again. This time around it is junior football we will be concentrating on. By that I mean the pubs and clubs in and around Junior parks. Today's first target was the colourful town of Larkhall and, in case you don't know the town's background, the predominant colours are red, white and blue.

After that we intended to check out Royal Albert, over in Stonehouse. Up until this season both the teams we wanted to look at actually shared the same park.

Travelling with John can be like going on a trip with a big wean. He gets very excited, makes a lot of noise and if you don't keep an eye on him he will eat all his pieces long before lunch. This time we were barely out of East Kilbride before he had scoffed the lot.

It's not that I mind when he eats all his pieces early but I always feel obliged to share mine with him later. His wee eyes fair light up when I get the chocolate biscuits out.

13

There is a positive side to this of course. Like the younger traveller John gets really tired later on in the day and tends to sleep all the way home on the bus.

Larkhall Thistle and Royal Albert fit the bill as classic football rivals. From talking to some of the Thistle supporters it would seem that being so close to each other over the last few years has done nothing to inject any friendliness into that rivalry.

It has been decided that John will be doing all of the journey planning from now on, not because he is particularly good at it but because I like to have someone to blame when things go pear-shaped.

Even before we started out, things started going wrong. The game at Stonehouse between Royal Albert and Glasgow Perthshire was called off. However we were not going to be deterred. Having visited Stonehouse a couple of years ago I felt confident in stating that we would not be missing much. Given there is only one pub in Stonehouse, and that the locals have taken it upon themselves to hide it up a side street, I couldn't see too many of the faithful making the journey there for a pint or two.

Royal Albert is really a Larkhall club so I reckoned that most of their support would be taking their refreshment in the pubs and clubs of their old hometown.

John, the navigator, had a master plan. Rather than depending on getting directions to the Thistle's park or even reading the map I had
drawn for him, with the location marked by a cross, John chose to use his own natural cunning. His idea was that we should sit on the bus until we saw a pub, then get off.

All football clubs are built close to pubs he claimed. I hate to admit it but he was right. We were spoiled for choice. I did get a wee bit concerned about his navigating abilities when he immediately chose the wrong road down to Gasworks Park, but I gave him the benefit of the doubt since he was getting a bit desperate for a drink by this time.

14

John with Larkhall secretary Fiona

John: Because we thought we would be going to Stonehouse first, I had arranged to meet Larkhall's Secretary, Fiona Tierney, after the game in the social club at the ground. As usual, plans change and we found ourselves in one of Central Scotland's most famous wee towns, Larkhall, a bit earlier than planned.

It was cold, but bright when we got off the bus, and the sight of about a hundred pubs within spitting distance of the bus stop was a welcome sight. There I go again with spitting distance, I think it's because I have a bit of a cold, or just talk rubbish. I know I am exaggerating slightly about the number, but there must be more pubs per person in Larkhall than any other town in Scotland. If I'm wrong, I'd like to know which town has more. From the corner where we got off, there were at least five bars close by. If you don't believe me they were: *'The Commercial'*; *'The Raploch'; 'The Royal'; 'The Tavern'*; and *'Curleys'*. The sign outside 'Curleys' claimed it to be the number one Rangers Supporters Bar in Larkhall, which means 'the world'.

The sight of all these watering holes fairly cheered Craig up. He had been a wee bit quiet during the bus journey and I was wondering if he was getting too old for all this enjoyment. When I mentioned this to him he replied with all his Auchinleck finesse that he was a '*******' lot younger than me. Thank god I hadn't reminded him that his beloved Auchinleck Talbot were already out of the Scottish Cup. A few pints were needed to cheer him up!

Before enjoying ourselves too much, we decided to wander up to the park to check out if there was a real bar in the Social Club and to see if Fiona, the secretary, was about.

There was a sign at the side of the social club where you enter the ground which said, 'Welcome to Gasworks Park'. It's a great sign and a great welcome we got when we went in!
Although it was early and the place was almost empty, Chris Lenson, the President (not the American one), introduced himself and made us most welcome. When we told him why we were visiting today he said we must stay and meet all the committee, supporters and have a few pints. He sounded like our type of guy.

Before we could start to enjoy ourselves in this oasis, we said we had to go back into town to check out a few of the pubs. Not to enjoy ourselves you understand, but purely for research purposes, so we can let you all know the best pubs to visit when you are all following in our footsteps!

We wandered back down Raploch Street and crossed the main road and into 'The Royal'. We had a quick one there then crossed the road for another quick one in 'The Tavern'. Both were very busy and the type of pubs we like, men's pubs, and they really were men's pubs, not a woman to be seen in either of them. We checked, except behind the bar, where they should be-sorry, I meant to say where they do a great job!

The Larkhall Thistle committee had put signs up in all the pubs in town telling the locals the game was on. I spoke to a lot of locals who were all going to the match, the one at Ibrox! Mind you, it is Larkhall.

As we went back up towards the ground, two Rangers supporters buses were leaving 'Curleys' to head for Ibrox. Just think of the crowds local teams would have if it wasn't for the 'Old Firm'. Mind you, if it wasn't for them there probably wouldn't be the same number of nut-cases interested in football.

Craig: *Down at the park we met some of the club officials and, more importantly, made sure there was a bar in the clubhouse.*

Just to prove how professional we have become, I set out some of our leaflets on the bar before we left to check out some of Larkhall's pubs.

Instead of turning right as we got out of the gate, John confidently marched round to his left and headed into rural South Lanarkshire. I toyed with the idea of letting him lead us into no-man's land, but only for a few seconds. I was getting a wee bit drouthy as well.

We chose The Royal as our first stop of the day. I think the clock stopped in this place halfway through the last century. The bar is decorated in various shades of broon, and the barstools, tables and other fixtures and fittings wouldn't be out of place on the Antiques Roadshow, except of course they were too well worn for that. The alcohol prices seemed to be from a bygone age as well but neither of us was complaining about that. Only the flat-screen telly gave away the fact that this pub was not operating in the 1950s

After a quick pint we made our way over to The Tavern, another great bloke's pub, no frills or fancy trimmings, just a good basic and busy boozer. We only had time for a quick drink as John was getting a bit agitated.

He wanted to get back down to Gasworks Park as he was fairly certain that the beer was even cheaper down there. On the way we noticed a place called Curly's. I thought it might be a down-market hairdressers but it turned out to be another pub. There were two buses outside and that really should have been a clue, but then again some barbers can get really busy on a Saturday afternoons.

John: Back inside the social club we were introduced to a great crowd of people who work behind the scenes for the club in various ways, including supporters.

Stevie Johnstone, who was working behind the bar doing an excellent job, introduced us to a fantastic group of mad guys including John Coats, Jim Tallis Stuart McKechnie and his dad Malcolm.

17

John, Chris, Jim, Stevie, Stuart, Malcolm

Among other things, these guys run the supporters club, head up the committee and keep the playing surface in great condition, we also met up with Fiona Tierney, who had little time to talk to us as she was busy the whole day. What a woman!

We had a brilliant time, which included a great buffet of sandwiches and pies and seeing a bit of the game during which one of Larkhall's six goals were scored. What a day!

I had two copies of our previous book with me which I sold for a fiver each. One of the blokes who bought one was an old guy called Willie Parkinson, better known as 'Rooster'. I was keen to find out if his nickname was something to do with loose skin in his neck or a cock, but it was just because of his red hair when he was a boy, like a Red Rooster. Another piece of local trivia.

Craig was mad that I sold the books for just a fiver each, but cheered up when I said the money would just go into the kitty. He's easily pleased.

An added bonus was meeting up with an old friend of mine, Colin, who is a mad bus driver from Larkhall and watches the Thistle when he can escape from Sandra, his long-suffering wife.

Craig: By the time we got back into the lounge down at the park the place had filled up a bit. After finding a good spot at the bar we were introduced to our barman, Stevie.

Barman Stevie with two glamorous assistants

For some reason he looked a wee bit guilty when the reason for our visit was explained to him. Eventually he confessed. He said "I take it those leaflets I found on the bar were yours? I thought they had come oot of somebody's newspaper, so I flung them in the bin".

So much for professionalism, not to mention the power of advertising!

After a beer, or possibly two, I asked Stevie if he had any amusing tales to tell us about his favourite team. He thought for a minute or two then told me about an incident which happened a few years back. Apparently, in the first year of the West of Scotland Super League, Larkhall was playing against Auchinleck Talbot. Thistle scored an early goal and during the ensuing celebrations Stevie's big pal hugged him so hard that his ribs were cracked.

We were still laughing when he added, "Aye an then the Talbot went oan to hump us 7-1."

I nearly spilt my beer!

One of the reasons we are visiting junior clubs was to take a look at the rivalries between local teams. With that in mind I asked some of the guys at the bar about Royal Albert. I expected a few good stories but no one seemed to want to talk about them at all.

We eventually decided to wander out to take in a bit of terracing banter. While we were there I was told that the bloke standing just along from me on his own was actually a Royal Albert fan. This was my chance to get some info on that elusive team. Or so I thought.

He looked very nervous when I asked him a couple of questions but when I took out my note book I thought he was going to keel over.

There is definitely some bad feeling between these two teams but I decided to stop torturing the poor bloke and headed back indoors to finish my beer.

We eventually made our way back up Raploch Street towards The Tavern but we couldn't possibly pass by Curly's without checking it out.

To be honest it looked like a really scary place, from the outside at least. We couldn't believe our eyes when we went inside. It was well laid-out, bright and modern.

Within a couple of minutes we had pints in our hands and a group of interesting characters to talk to. Everybody had a story to tell but, to be honest, the majority of them would get us into big trouble if we ever printed them.

I had expected a great story behind the name of the pub but one of the lads assured me that it was named after a previous owner, Curly Jones. He told me that the name goes back about seventy years.

I always try to get a name when I take a picture so I asked my new pal what his was. Without the slightest hint of irony he told me that he was called Joseph O'Donnell. Obviously I had to ask him how he managed to survive in Larkhall with a moniker like that He just laughed.

I expect you need a good sense of humour, or a black belt in Karate, to live the quiet life in Larkhall with such an unusual name,

It reminded me of that old Johnny Cash song, 'A Boy Named Sue'. You would either have to quickly toughen up or find yourself a new post-code.

John: Before we left Larkhall, we had to visit 'Curleys', the mad Rangers Bar. Craig had imagined that it would be a real dive.

It was nothing to look at from the outside, but inside it was a lovely bar with great company. These were the ones remaining after the supporters buses had left. It just shows you that you have to go through the doors of pubs before you make judgements. Don't know what brought that on.

The Curly Crew

We had a lovely time in the bar talking to the locals as well as the girls working behind the bar. Now remember, we had had a good few by now and my memory is not as good as it used to be, but I think the barmaids' names were Fiona and Julia, a mother and daughter. One of them told the story of when she was the physiotherapist at Larkhall Thistle and was still running on to the park with the magic sponge when she was eight months pregnant.

That sums up the superb Lakhall women: do anything for a quick feel! Only kidding.

We had promised to meet up with my pal Colin in '*The Tavern*' after the game, and that is where we had our last couple of pints before leaving Larkhall on the number 254 bus to Hamilton. No direct bus to EK after about five. I am proud to say we did not have a pint in Hamilton but headed straight for the 201 to EK where we did go into the '*Lum*' for just the one nightcap.

I had a feeling all day that Craig, although acting fairly normally, for him, was not at his best, and this was confirmed when he ordered a diet coke in the 'Lum'. What's that all about? I think he may be dying, or it might be more serious than that.

We finished our drinks, soft in Craig's case, and wandered up the road with Craig mumbling about feeling his age. Hope he picks up for our next trip.

As far as the pubs in Larkhall are concerned, they are all great, especially if you don't have the wife or girlfriend with you, although I know from previous visits that there are plenty of 'burd' friendly bars as well.

We had an enjoyable day with the Thistle faithful. At first I was delighted that my spend for the day was just about £20, but then I remembered that I had put the tenner from the books into the kitty. That, linked to the fact that the drinks in the pubs in Larkhall were very reasonable, and in the clubhouse, where we had most, the prices were very very reasonable. On top of that we had a few rounds on the house. We must have had a real skinful. I'm really going to cut back. Who am I kidding? Certainly not the wife!!!

Craig: We had arranged to meet John's pal Colin up in The Tavern for a final drink before we headed home. Colin told me that when he wasn't supporting Larkhall Thistle he was a bus driver.

I'm not sure if I believe him! The evidence suggests that he was probably having me on. For example, he smiled a lot and he spoke in coherent sentences while maintaining eye contact. I rest my case!

The journey home was uneventful. By the time we arrived back in East Kilbride I was ready for an hour or two in front of the telly. John however had other ideas, having rested his eyes for quite a while he was ready for another refreshment.

I think he was kidding himself on a bit. He had checked the remaining kitty money and decided that we had not had our usual quota of beer.

Of course he had forgotten three important pieces of information. One, he didn't take into account the lower than usual price of beer in Larkhall. Two, we had met some very generous people who had insisted that we accept several free drinks from them. And finally three, John, 'the keeper of the kitty', had forgotten about the two books he had sold, so cheaply, to a couple of punters in the supporters club.

He had managed to put the meagre proceeds of the sale into the kitty pocket thereby giving the false impression that we had not spent a lot of cash.

The obvious result of all of this nonsense was John could hardly bite his own lip by the time we reached the bar of our local, 'The Lum'. That didn't stop him from knocking back a double vodka.

Since I was the responsible adult I settled for a diet Coke.

Royal Albert

Club Name	Founded
Royal Albert	1878
Ground	**Colours**
Tileworks Park	Black and White Stripes
League (2014-15)	**Selection of Honours**
	Jun. Cup; Semi-Final 1930;
Cen. League, 2nd Div	1940
Club Nickname	
The Berts	

John: It had been a long time since our visit to Royal Albert's rivals, Larkhall Thistle, but we had not forgotten about our need to visit one of the smaller clubs in the Junior Leagues. All Clubs are the same to us through the bottom of a glass. I know that makes no sense, but there you are. At the time of our original planned trip, the game, like most other junior games, was off because of the weather.

From Glasgow to Stonehouse, home of Royal Albert, you get the same buses that go to Larkhall. It's just a bit further on.

As most of our readers will know, we live in East Kilbride. So although the information at the end of this chapter describes the journey to the park from Glasgow, we went directly from EK to Stonehouse. The Whitelaw's No. 254 did the business.

We arrived on the main street in Stonehouse without any problems and after walking down the wrong road, eventually found Tileworks Park. The buildings are new looking and more functional than atmospheric. We walked round to have a look at the park, which is very nice, and flat. I always have a look at the flatness of the pitches as some of them are bumpers, the slopes are all over the place. But Tileworks Park is snooker-table flat.

Craig: First time around, our visit to Stonehouse to see Royal Albert had to be cancelled due to adverse weather conditions. This time everything was perfect. Perfect but for the fact that we couldn't find the stadium that is. I suppose it would have helped our cause if we had actually bothered to check the name of the place.

There is a fairly prominent sign, located in the centre of Stonehouse, pointing the way to Tilework Sports Ground. But if the person who had planned the visit did so in such a half-arsed fashion that he forgot to write down the name of the place, it is hardly surprising that we got into difficulties.

Now, I am not blaming anyone for what might be described as a gross dereliction of duty, but it wisnae me!

The clubhouse at the ground is quite new and is a lot larger than we thought it would be. In fact, for a few minutes I managed to convince myself that such a large modern building must have an equally large and modern bar in it, despite the lack of any brewers sign above the doors.

John: We spotted the secretary Peter Higgins right away. We knew it was him by the PH on his tracksuit. Peter introduced himself and asked us to go into the reception where he would join us in a couple of minutes, which he did.

Ross, Billy and Peter

Like almost all secretaries, he is rushing about all the time trying to do everything to keep the club going, but he made time for us and was great company. He even presented Craig and me with club ties. He then introduced us to the president, Ross Steven, and the club Physio, Billy Milson. Billy must be one of the most senior physios in the game. By that I mean he is a good age. All the Albert players know to get injured on the touchline Billy's standing at, or they might wait a while.

Oh no! I'm too late, again.

The guys told us some great stories which Craig was recording on his machine and, if it works, may even relate one to you. Just a wee note about the dedication of these guys. Peter and Ross (everybody calls him Steven) have 43 years service to the club between them. I doubt if the next generation will match this.

Today's game was against Lanark and Peter introduced us to four of their committee men. Mark McKenzie, Russell Hunter, John Galbraith and Tom Anderson, who is a past president of the SJFA as well as having served six years as president of the West Region. All the people who run the various clubs are great friends and appreciate the problems each other's clubs are facing. They also have great stories to tell. One of the Lanark guys told of the day they got lost trying to find Camelon's Park. Eventually they stopped the bus and one of the committee got out and asked a boy how he got to the park. 'My Dad takes me', was his answer. You couldn't make it up.

Mark, Russell, Tom and John

Royal Albert are just getting by. The players are only paid their travelling expenses. However, the boys have the chance, if they are good enough, to be picked up by a bigger junior club and eventually they might get the chance to play on the big stage. Or even Firhill, where I was once a ball-boy.

Kick-off time was approaching so we said our farewells to our Royal Albert and Lanark friends and said we hoped it would be a draw. Which it was, 2-2. We had a great time with them and hope they can survive in today's 'nobody can be bothered playing football' world. The Lanark guys have invited us to visit their club in the future. We would love to and hope we can fit it in. If not, we wish them all the best for the rest of the season and beyond.

Craig: It soon became obvious that my luck was very definitely out. There was a foyer with vending machines for hot and cold drinks but this didn't really strike me as much of a substitute for a thirst-quenching pint of ice cold lager so I gave them a miss.

Since there was no chance of sensible refreshment in the clubhouse we decided to wander down to the football pitch to check out the playing surface.

John has become a bit obsessed about this sort of thing recently. I half expected him to whip out a spirit level to check for any slope on the pitch.

We have seen a few grounds on our travels which really should have gradient warning signs posted on them. According to John, Royal Albert's ground is as flat as a snooker table in comparison with most others we have visited.

Being the secretary of a junior team doesn't sound like hard work, but if you were to watch Peter Higgins preparing for a home game you might change that view. When we met him he was manhandling the two sets of portable team benches on to the side of the park. He had already put up the goal nets by this time. After all this activity he had to set about completing all the team sheets.

Fortunately for us he found a few minutes to talk to us. That being said, he was still filling out his paperwork while we talked. Peter told us that his team were mostly all young boys, just starting out in the junior game. There was no money to be had playing for the Albert but they knew that if they showed any promise they could be picked up by one of the bigger-name teams. Keeping really good players is always going to be difficult but Peter and his committee are in it for the football not the silverware.

While we were talking we were joined by Ross Stevens, the club president. I asked if it would be alright if I took their picture but they insisted that we should wait for the team Physio to join them, although Ross did say that might take a little while as Billy Milson, their Physio, could well be the oldest still working in junior football. I thought it was a bit unkind to suggest that he was getting on for a hundred years of age, but Peter insisted that if a player was unlucky enough to be injured on the far side of the pitch gangrene could set in before Billy reached them.

While all this slagging was going on the opposition committee arrived and immediately joined in. Tom Anderson is a former president of the SJFA and is now on the committee of Lanark JFC. He told us that he had once been to a game at Petershill where two players clashed in a very tough tackle. Both were injured and lying a few feet apart on the pitch. As the Physio, a gentleman with many many years of experience, was attending to one player someone in the crowd shouted words to the effect that if he didn't get a move on the other player's cuts would have formed a scab. Apparently you have to be thick-skinned to be a Physio in the junior game, or maybe just hard of hearing.

We were very impressed by the friendliness shown between the two committees, even if it was not exactly what we had been hoping to find. I toyed with the idea of stirring up a bit of rivalry between them, but in the end I took the cowardly way out and said to each committee that I hoped they would win today's match. Of course I did this out of earshot of the other club. I found out the next day that it had been a score draw so I didn't feel that I had let either of them down.

Before we left the clubhouse I asked about sponsorship, and it turns out that the clubs main sponsor is the Village Tavern. For a few wonderful seconds I thought that Stonehouse had a nice wee pub that we had somehow missed but, it was not to be. The Tavern is actually in Larkhall.

John: We walked back up the road-across the main street-round a wee corner-up a back road-and into Stonehouse's only pub, called 'The Back Road'. These Stonehouse publicans have some imagination!

This might be the only pub in the town. But if there were another ten, I bet none would be better than 'The Back Road'. As we always say, it's the staff that make the pub. The Landlady Margaret McInnes, and Sarah Crown, one of the barmaids, were brilliant company and made us feel right at home. The pub is also a very nicely laid out place and has a lounge were they do food. As long as it's not at the bar, we're ok with that. We had a great time there and would recommend it to anybody passing through Stonehouse.

Margaret and her girls even took a photo of one of our books and some of the leaflets and are putting it on the pubs Facebook Page. We might be famous yet.

We found out from Margaret that there was a Social Club on the outskirts of the village, which is the old Stonehouse Violet Club. We had to visit it as it was old.

29

Margaret and Sarah

Craig: *As we came out of The Tilework Park it occurred to us that we did know where to find a bar within walking distance of the park. The Back Road, formerly known as The Cross Keys, is on Queen Street. You can't miss it as it takes up half the street.*

It is a bar and restaurant and it is bright and spotlessly clean. Usually we wouldn't have been too keen on such a modern pub but we decided to make an exception this time.

As soon as we got an elbow on to the bar the young girl, who was serving another customer at the time, called over to us to say that she would be right with us.

I could see John mentally ticking the good service box in his pub appraisal spreadsheet. He makes spreadsheets for everything else so I'm fairly sure he must have one to rate customer service. A wee bit of good manners goes a long way with us.

Sarah Crown turned out to be a good laugh as well as an excellent puller of pints. She explained why the pub had changed its name. It seems the new owners wanted to put their own stamp on the place and realised that the locals always referred to going to the back road when they were talking about going to the pub. So they changed the pubs name, from Cross Keys into The Back Road, and cleverly avoided confusing any of the locals.

The pub was doing a roaring trade but we still managed a wee chat to Margaret McInnes, the landlady. She told us that occasionally Royal Albert uses the pub for hospitality and that on match days a few supporters can be expected to sample a pre-match drink or two.

Just to do a thorough job of assessing the pub we decided to have another drink; nobody can ever accuse us of not going that extra mile. I'm happy to say The Back Road passed with flying colours.

While we were chatting something was said about a social club in the town. I wasn't too sure that I had heard Margaret correctly but by the way John's face lit up I knew there was another drink to be had.

The club she had been talking about was the old Stonehouse Violet Club. Violet, another junior club, had gone out of business a few years back but it seems that the old social club is still in action.

Margaret didn't seem too enthusiastic about telling us too much about the place. It seems that the club is a bit rough and ready, and while we might have been more than ready neither of us could ever pass for being rough. She was probably just trying to save us from making fools of ourselves but, as the saying goes, that ship sailed a while ago.

John: So we said our goodbyes to a fantastic pub and five minutes later found ourselves outside what looked like the most run-down club in the country. The land round about the club looked like a scene from a Spaghetti Western, just the sort of place we knew we would like.

Inside, it was just like the outside, a fantastic wee bar with a few old worthies who, you know right away, always sit in the same seats at the same time each day. We felt right at home.

We got talking to one of the old regulars, Gibby Young, who travels from Larkhall to this club. Now, as you know from earlier in this chapter, Larkhall has about a hundred pubs. But Gibby is a man of tradition. This is his club, so this is where he drinks, and that's the end of it.

Gibby filled us in on the history of the local club and all the old players from the past. It was very interesting to listen to him with a drink in hand, wouldn't like to do it without. We were enjoying his company, but our time was coming to an end and we said our goodbyes to the club and Stonehouse.

We had a great time at both of the clubs in this chapter of the book and all the pubs and clubs visited.

Craig: Armed with precise directions to the club we only got lost the once on our way there. Even when we got there we were not convinced that it was still a going concern. It looked derelict. If it hadn't been for an old guy who came wandering out of the door we might well just have turned back.

There were no lights on but we could hear voices coming from the back of the club so we stumbled on until we found the bar.

As it turned out we had a very enjoyable pint in the club. There is no denying that the place is fairly run down and past its best. Then again so are we!

There were only four guys in the place and in time-honoured Scottish tradition they were all sitting at separate tables. I got the impression that this would be the set up in there every Saturday. The bar itself was little more than a serving hatch so there was no chance of standing there to knock back our drinks. So we decided to sit with one of the old guys. Gibby Young has been coming to the Violet Club for many years. In fact he is there every Saturday. I toyed with the idea of announcing that Stonehouse Violet had in fact stopped playing football some time ago but kept my mouth shut just in case the old guys didn't see the funny side of that. But I needn't have worried as Gibby was up for a laugh.

Although the club was almost empty while we were there Gibby told us that they still have regular entertainment at weekends, and these nights are well attended by the locals. This was good to hear as it would be a shame to lose this little club. Maybe if the local population could get behind the Royal Albert this supporters club might flourish again.

Pubs and clubs visited;

Larkhall;

The Royal; A good old-man's bar

The Tavern; An even better old-man's bar

Curleys; A good Ranger's supporter's bar

Larkhall Social Club; Excellent bar with good atmosphere

Royal Albert;

The Back Road Bar; A suberb bar, one of the best.

Stonehouse Violet Social Club; clubs like this must be visited, even for the banter. The place may look a bit tired, but it is part of Stonehouse history.

Larkhall-how to get there by bus
X1 or X74; Glasgow to Hamilton Bus Station
Whitehills 254; Hamilton Bus Station to Lakhall

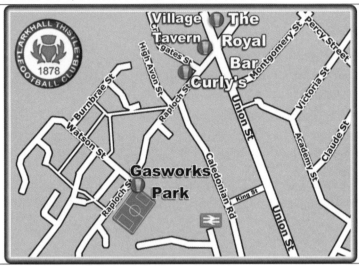

Royal Albert;-how to get there by bus
 X1 or X74; Glasgow to Hamilton Bus Station
Whitehills 254; Hamilton Bus Station to Stonehouse

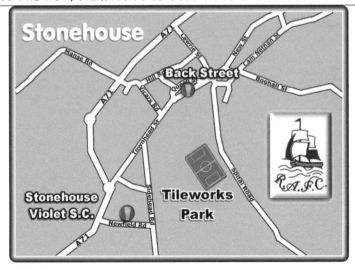

Rutherglen Glencairn V Cambuslang Rangers

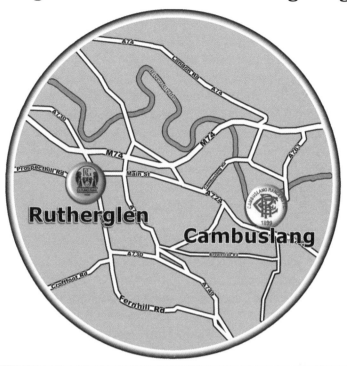

Club Name	Founded
Rutherglen Glencairn	1896
Ground	**Colours**
The Clyde Gateway Stadium	Black and White Hoops
League (2014-15)	**Selection of Honours**
West Super League-1st Div.	Scot. Jun. Cup; 1901-02; 18-19
Club Nickname	1926-27; 38-39
The Glens	

John: Rutherglen and Cambuslang are two wee towns that are very near to EK, so today's trip had almost no travel time. More time for bevy then, you may think. Happy thoughts like that are always dashed when you tell the wife where you are going.

'You'll be home early then'. It's always the same. Sneaking a few extra pints is not easy.

Now Craig is a different kettle of fish. He just tells Irene that 'she'll see him when he's home'. Anyway, that's what he tells me he says. He thinks I came up the Clyde in a Banana Boat!

Talking about coming up the Clyde in a Banana Boat, did you know that the Banana Boat was the SS Shieldhall, the sludge vessel, or shite ship, (that's what we thought SS stood for), which took the stuff from Shieldhall, sailed down the Clyde and dumped it between Garroch Head, at the South end of Bute and the North end of Arran. She was licensed to carry up to 80 passengers and in the summer months used to take mainly pensioners a wee sail down the Clyde. The name Banana Boat came from her yellow funnel.

An interesting coincidence is that the two triple expansion engines she had were the same as the ones in the 'Titanic', only smaller. The pensioners on the 'Shieldhall' were luckier than the ones on the 'Titanic', they were only surrounded by the stuff, not actually 'in it'.

Enough of this Glasgow folklore and back to today's trip, the No. 18 got us down to the end of Main Street in Rutherglen, or Ru'glen to hard men like me.

Craig: I have been through both the towns which we visited today many times. However there should be heavy emphasis on the word through. I don't think that I've ever actually stopped in either of them any longer than it takes traffic lights to change.

Both Rutherglen and Cambuslang are within ten miles of East Kilbride but up until now I have never had any reason to visit either.

Getting to Rutherglen could not be easier since it is actually on the route of our usual bus into Glasgow, the number 18.

Although it was a sunny day it was also very cold. So we were both well wrapped up. John had even brought his bunnet with him. Apparently he has taken to wearing it when he takes his dog for a walk. I said something like; hopefully he has the good

36

sense to wait until it is dark before doing so as it looks like he made the bunnet himself.

This didn't please him at all. In fact he said that when he was in the bunnet shop he noticed that they only came in four sizes, small, medium, large and Ayrshire.

Fortunately I'm not easily offended, and of course it is true that Ayrshire folk do tend to have bigger heads than their Glasgow cousins. There's probably a good reason for that.

John: We got off outside *'Chapmans'*, a pub we had passed many times and always wondered if it was better inside than it looked outside. Well today we were visiting Ru'glen so we had no excuse to avoid going in. Putting on our hard man walk we went in, and got a pleasant surprise. It is a nice old fashioned bar with men of our age sitting around the place on their own, mainly reading their papers and picking horses-a normal Saturday morning. Another surprise was the price of the drink; a pint of lager and a vodka and soda was £4. A good start to the day!

When I spoke to the barman to ask the way to the ground, the old guy next to me told me the game had just been called off. He was a friendly bloke and when we explained what we were doing in Ru'glen, he thought we were daft but wished us all the best. He told us the old ground had gone under compulsory purchase, but we found out it had gone under the new motorway that was opened a couple of years ago. The good news was that the social club was still there.

Craig: John was once again doing the planning for this trip and he had decided that we should get off the bus just outside Chapman's, a pub we have often seen but never entered.

We had always assumed that this pub would be a bit on the grotty side, but were very pleased to be proved wrong. Possibly because of its position the pub doesn't seem to get much natural light, so it's a wee bit dull inside, but I can assure you that it is clean and tidy.

The bar runs the whole length of the place making it seem quiet, even when there are a fair number of customers in there enjoying a tipple.

We didn't get much chance to talk to the barman as he was very busy keeping us all well served. But when he told us how little our drinks cost us I suggested to John that we just stay in Chapman's and not bother with the rest of the places we had planned to visit.

I'm not sure if he knew I was kidding. Actually I'm not sure if I was kidding. Four pounds for a pint of lager and a wee vodie is hard to beat. But professionalism got the better of us and we moved on.

John: Back out on the main street, which is Main Street, we wandered along in the sunshine; honestly, the sun was out for about half an hour. Main Street in Ru'glen is an old fashioned street with a lovely Town Hall which has an iconic steeple that lets you know from a distance where Ru'glen is. There is a café in it and it has a grand hall, so I'm told, but no bar, so it's of no real interest to Craig and me.

As we passed the Town Hall, I asked a wee man who was staggering about just dying to talk to someone where the best pubs near the ground were. 'Ru'glen is a Royal Burgh' he replied, 'and all the pubs are fit for Royalty'. What a great character, and how do you get into that state before twelve o'clock. Ru'glen was off to a flyer.

The main street may have lost a bit of its previous glory, but I'll tell you this: Ru'glen is worth a visit. We should not bypass places like it just to go into Glasgow or some other metropolis. The wee old towns are great. The people were all friendly and Craig and I were encouraged to find a pub as soon as possible before reaching the ground.

The Social is almost right under the motorway and I think it is concentrating on corporate sorts of events. There was nobody in the bar area but the barmaid, who was the Glencairns manager's daughter. She was very friendly and pointed us in the direction of a good bar and a short cut to the ground.

So we left the social club without having had a pint and walked up the few yards and into *'The Sportsman'*. I have passed this bar many times driving into Glasgow and thought I would not fancy going in there. But looks can be deceiving, *'The Sportsman'* is one of the best bars we have ever been in.

Behind the bar, sisters Jacqueline and Helen were brilliant company and we had a great time talking to them and Big Francie, a local worthy who used to run with 'the Wild Team' when he was young. He used to work for a famous Glasgow hardman, even I had heard of him but am feart to mention his name. I think he is still alive!

Jacqueline and Helen

I asked Francie, (we were pals now and I was allowed to miss out the Big bit,) what the new park was like. It's hard to explain exactly what is up with the park, but it was seemingly built on ground that used to be a chemical works, and the surface was actually made of Yellow Jelly. He also told us that most of the men who worked in the plant were dead within a couple of years of the plant closing. Makes you wonder.

We sold a couple of our books in the pub, and would have sold another to a local at the other end of the bar whom the girls called 'The Bigot', but Jacqueline told us not to ask him as there were no colouring-in pages in the book.

This is a really great bar and there's entertainment on every weekend. The décor in the bar is lovely and it would be a nice place to bring the wife for a night out. The owner, John Vicar, and the girls have worked hard to make it one of the best bars we have visited. We have promised to return.

Craig: The idea was to have a look at Rutherglen's park and maybe have a word with their club secretary, Alex Forbes. Unfortunately, there were two stumbling blocks to completing John's proposed itinerary: the game had been called off and we didn't actually know where the park was. But we have had bigger troubles than that on our travels and somehow managed to muddle through.

Building a new motorway right through the middle of a town can fairly change the landscape. It certainly does when they build it right on top of the football ground we were intending to visit.

Rutherglen Glencairn has a new football park and for some reason the powers-that-be failed to inform John of the move.

On our journey of discovery along main roads and under the aforementioned motorway, twice, we found a likely looking pub.

'The Sportsman', on Glasgow Road looked like a good bet for a decent pint and, hopefully, a bit of pub banter. Fortunately that is exactly what we got. We found a couple of barstools and immediately got into conversation with our two barmaids, Jacqueline and Helen.

The Sportsman is a family run pub which has been dispensing good beer and good cheer for 25 years. The girls told us that every bit of decoration, every alteration and all the maintenance in the pub is done by the family.

All the regulars we spoke to were full of praise for the way the pub is run. In fact one guy said that in all the years he had been a regular in the place he had never heard a single complaint, except of course from their resident bigot.

I just had to ask who this guy was and it turned out that he was sitting at the end of the bar, refusing to get involved in the conversation. It seems this gent is something of an equal opportunity bigot: he hates everyone equally.

I like that idea, I might even take it up myself when I'm finished with this book writing lark.

We were talking to Jaqueline about the daft things that can happen in pubs when punters have too much time on their hands. She told us that one afternoon, for no reason she could remember, some of her regular customers took a roll of duct tape which had been left lying around and taped her to a chair. After they had used the entire roll of tape on her they carried her outside and parked her at the side of the road. They then returned to the bar to finish their drinks.

Apparently quite a few cars drove past the poor woman, some even tooting their horns. But not one of them stopped to find out what was going on.

It was a great story but also a good reminder not to get ourselves into any trouble in Rutherglen, because nobody would be coming along to help us.

We were introduced to a gentleman who rejoiced in the name Big Francie. I was going to ask about the whereabouts of Josie but thought better of it when I heard him tell John that he had once belonged to 'The Wild Team'.

For the uninitiated that was not a 'Glens' supporters club but was in fact a group of like-minded young men who got up to some pretty wild things in Glasgow's East End.

Big Francie used to do a bit of work for a rather famous Glasgow character, Arthur Thomson, who was very active in certain areas of Glasgow's alterative economy. According to Francie, Mr Thomson was a great guy to work for and had an interest in a wide variety of businesses. I'm fairly sure that I once read about him doing a bit of consultancy work for The Kray twins. However we thought it was a good idea to agree with everything Francie said.

Anyway, Francie told us that Rutherglen's new park was built on top of the site where White's Chemical Works used to dump waste. When he was a young boy he would often run across this area to sneak into the old football park without paying. Apparently if you kept moving you wouldn't sink too far into the goo of The Jelly Field, as the locals called it.

We had a great time in 'The Sportsman' and would highly recommend it to anyone who likes good company in great surroundings.

John: Saying our fond farewells, we went along the wee lane to the ground hoping to meet the Secretary, Alex Forbes, who I know had been working tirelessly to try and get the game on, but we just missed him. Hope we will catch up later. The park looked in good condition and there was no sign of jelly; possibly it had set in the sunshine.

On the way back up to Main Street, we contemplated going back into 'The Sportsman' for another, but there was a bar just a few yards up from it and as it is our job to advise you of as many alternatives as possible, we felt we had to go into *'The Dubliner'*.

My granny said that if you can't think of anything nice to say about someone or something, don't say anything, so I won't. We had a very quick one and left.

Back up on the main street, we sat in a bus shelter in the sunshine eating our pieces. Cheese and sandwich spread today.

Our bus, the 267, came along and had us in Cambuslang, or Cams'lang if you want, in a couple of minutes.

Craig: We never did find out why the game was called off, although I had my suspicions that it might have had something to do with yellow goo seeping up through the pitch.

Apart from the game being called off things were going really well; too well as it turned out.

We decided, and by that I mean John decided, that we should have a drink in 'The Dubliner', big mistake! This pub is only a few yards away from The Sportsman but is light years away in terms of friendliness and service. Apart from telling us how much our drinks cost the barmaid never spoke another word to us.

From all the memorabilia festooned from the walls I think it would be fair to say that 'The Dubliner' is not one of those fake Irish pubs you see everywhere nowadays. This place has a definite agenda, and could be said to be a bit intimidating to those who don't share it.

There was no sign of any Glens fans so we decided to move on to Cambuslang.

Cambuslang Rangers

Club Name	Founded
Cambuslang Rangers	1899
Ground	Colours
Somervell Park	Royal Blue
League (2014-15)	Selection of Honours
	Scot. Jun. Cup Winners five
West Central League, 2nd Div.	times
Club Nickname	Runner up six times
The Lang	

John: I had checked on Google Earth exactly where the park was and I confidently led Craig down the wrong road. His comments are not worth repeating in a classy book like this. It was only a 10 minute detour and my comment that the walk would do him some good did not go down too well.

We arrived at the ground just as the half time whistle sounded so the social club, which was called '*Sweepers*', was busy

43

as we went in. It was a very nice club and the girl behind the bar, Leslie Reid, was great company and pointed out the Secretary Jim Logan. I had spoken to Jim on the phone and he had kindly invited us into the club at any time.

Before getting too involved with the great company in the bar, we said we had to check out at least one bar near the ground for our readers and would come back around full time for a wee session. Jim said 'The Black Bull' was worth a visit, so we went back up the road and enjoyed a couple of pints. The bar was very busy, but was well run by Wullie and Catherine behind the bar. The only slightly negative thing I could say about it was that there were four big TV's round the place all showing horse racing. Now I have nothing against the gee gees, but a few scores coming through on a Saturday is a given.

Craig: It actually took less time to get there by bus than it did for us to find the football park when we got there. John had printed off a map of the area but to be honest he would have been as well tossing a coin to decide which road to take.

As it was we had ourselves a wee and not very pleasant wander through some undergrowth and along a couple of muddy paths in search of Somervell Park

If it hadn't been for my exceptional hearing we might never have found it. I heard the crowd roaring so we retraced our steps and found our way in just on half-time.

We introduced ourselves, had a pint and arranged to meet the committee after the game. In the meantime we headed up to 'The Black Bull'.

It is a fairly standard old guys' pub. We got a space at the bar just by the door but the noise from the telly was far too much for my sensitive ears and we had to shift.

I've got nothing against people chucking their money away on the ponies but why should I have to watch the dammed things racing round in circles? And why does the volume have to be up full?

As far as I could see there was nobody watching any of the four giant screen tellies anyway. If we really need to watch horses in the pub couldn't at least one screen be showing classic westerns?

The bar was busy but the two bar staff were coping very efficiently.

John: It was full-time when we got back and a no scoring draw against someone or other summed up the game. Not the best this season.

Jim took us up to the boardroom and we were introduced to a smashing group of men and women who help keep the club in business.

John, Caroline, Kevin, Bill, Jim, Glen
Sharon, Audrey, Willie, George, Jim

Among the company were ex-president Billy Miller, committee men George Jamieson and Jim Scoullar, another Jim, whose second name I've forgotten, sorry Jim.

Others with whom we enjoyed an hour or so of good company were Sharon, Audrey, Liz, Caroline, Kevin, John, Glenn and Gordon Hendry, the groundsman. If I have made mistakes with your names, what you do, or if I have missed out anybody, I can only say it is your own fault for getting me so happy!!

We said our goodbyes and walked back up to the main street. I had checked the computer and knew there was a Henderson's number 172 that would take us straight back to EK. I forgot to check when the last one was. To cut a long moan from Craig short, we saw the back of the last bus on its way to EK.

Craig: *Back down at the park we met the Cambuslang committee and were treated to a very nice buffet and a few drinks. It was fantastic.*

Somehow the chat got round to junior teams and their rivals, which gave John the chance to tell the guys that I am originally from Auchinleck. That brought the friendly banter to a screeching halt, but only for a few seconds. Then I had to listen to a catalogue of complaints about my favourite team

Lesley keeps the beer flowing

I managed to hold my own in the animated discussion, but it was all meant in fun, I think. Down in the bar again I got talking to the barmaid, Lesley. She certainly knows how to deal with any awkward customers. Once, when a group of regulars were annoying her, she got out a bottle of baby oil and squirted it down the necks of their shirts. Then she told them to try explaining that to their wives when they got home.

Another time, she launched a full bucket of ice at a couple of drinkers who were holding her back from her work when they couldn't make up their minds whether or not they wanted ice in their drinks. She is a great lassie, just don't wind her up. You have been warned!

By the time we left the club we were both feeling positively happy. That is usually a good indication that something bad is about to happen, and today was no different.

Silverware on Show at Somervell Park

John: We had a pint in a bar called *'Findlays'* to discuss our options to get back to EK. All we could think of was either a bus into Hamilton and an EK bus from there. It never struck us that we could get the 267 back to Ru'glen and the 18 home. It shows just how happy we were.

Somehow we ended up in some other pub and phoned a Kelvin Kab to take us back to 'The Lum'. Why, I hear you ask, have you not had enough? Or was that what Kate said when I foolishly told her?

I have not yet gone on about the clubs' nicknames, so I will. Rutherglen Glencairn have 'The Glens' and Cambuslang Rangers have 'The Lang' or 'The Wee Gers'.

I think 'The Terriers' and 'The Bus Passers' would be more remote nicknames? What do you think?

Although both of today's clubs are supposed to be deadly enemies, the people who work behind the scenes at both clubs are of the same ilk, with the same sense of humour, which is essential to their sanity and the good of Junior Football.

Today, I managed to get legless on very little. If it wasn't for the taxi home, £20 would have covered it. The generosity and hospitality of the people we met today is why I ended up in the state I was. Brilliant!!!!!

Craig: We missed our bus by a good 30 seconds. The only thing for it was to find a pub while we gathered our thoughts on what to do next. What we eventually decided to do was to have a drink, find a taxi and go home. As the saying goes 'two out of three aint bad'.

We didn't go home, well not straight away anyway. Someone, and we don't know who, suggested that we stop off at the 'Lum' in East Kilbride for a nightcap and a quick discussion on how we felt the day had gone.

The upshot of that in-depth analysis was that we agreed that we had had yet another great day out.

Pubs and Clubs visited today;

Ru'glen' –

'Chapmans', a good man's bar, liked it.

The Sportsmans' brilliant bar-one of the best.

'*The Dubliner'* least said the better

Cam'slang;

'*The Black Bull'* and *'Findlays'* were both good pubs.

'*Sweepers*' social club was great.

Rutherglen; how to get there by bus
First Bus no. 267-Glasgow to Hamilton (get off at Rutherglen)

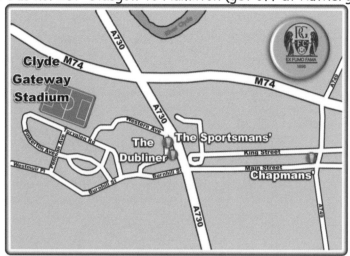

Cambuslang; how to get there by bus
First Bus no 263-Glasgow to Hamilton (get off at Cambuslang)

Benburb V St Anthony's

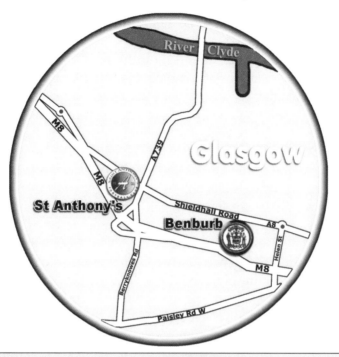

Club Name	Founded
Benburb	1885
Ground	*Colours*
Tinto Park	Royal Blue
League (2014-15)	*Selection of Honours*
	Scot. Jun. Cup-1933-34; 1935-
Central League, 1st Division	36 Runners up three times
Club Nickname	
The Chookie Hens	

John: 'The Bens, or 'The Chookie Hens as I remember them, and The Ants', the two Junior Clubs that were almost next door to me where I grew up. The Bens were the Junior Rangers and played in blue and white, the Ants were the Junior Celtic, playing in the green and white hoops. I remember that almost all their supporters were either Rangers or Celtic fans, and if either of the big two were at home, the support suffered badly, especially the Bens, who, like the Ants, had a park near Ibrox. Needless to say, the Ant's supporters didn't go to Ibrox. Thought I'd mention that in case any Martians are reading this.

I remember as a boy going to Tinto (home of the Bens). Now there was a man outside the ground selling 'Honey Pears'. I had no idea what they were, but thought they were a kind of sweet pear. The funny thing was that he was shouting 'Honey Pears', three for a tanner, four for a bob. For any youngsters reading this there were two tanners in a bob, work it out for yourselves!

I got a trial for the Bens once when I was playing for the great 'Govan High Former Pupils'. I was crap, terrified and lasted till half time. These Juniors are tough guys, especially if you're daft enough to dribble past one of them, I never did it again, but enough of me reminiscing about my youth in Linthouse (the posh end of Govan).

I made my own pieces as Kate was away early into Glasgow for a bit of shopping and a ladies' lunch day. She was also staying overnight in Glasgow so I had nobody to tell me how drunk I was when I got home. That's a worry.

About 10.30am I picked up Craig and we went across the Murray Road and got a 201 along to Hairmyres Station. Craig had told me as we waited that there were new 201s with leather seats and WiFi, and sure enough it was one of them. Craig spent the 10 minute journey trying to get onto it with no success. At least I got a bit of peace except for his cursing about new technology.

The train into Glasgow was packed. Why the train company put a wee two coacher on the EK to Glasgow route on a Saturday morning is anybody's guess. As usual at the barriers in Glasgow Central the new technology means that instead of one guy collecting tickets there are three helping to get you through the barriers. What do these people do when there are no trains arriving?

I have been trying, after each trip, to promise myself that I would drink less on the next trip. So why we should decide, for the first time ever, to have a drink in Glasgow before we left for the first ground is beyond belief, even for me. So we went down the moving stairs next to platform 13, or is it 14 now, and over Hope Street into '*Denholms*'.

Alison and Jamielee

This is our pub of choice in Glasgow now. What is wrong with '*The Horseshoe*', I hear you ask; nothing, I reply, it's just that on a Saturday morning, especially if the Rangers are at home, it's packed. '*Denholms*' is a great wee pub, very reasonable prices and the barmaid sisters Alison and Jamielee are wonderful. Jamielee insisted that she was named after her dad, Jamie. I think her parents must have been Country and Western fans.

Craig: On our quest to find the greatest rivalries in junior football I have had to more or less leave finding the various Glasgow rivals to John. He is, or at least claims to be, our Glasgow expert. Therefore when he came up with these latest two candidates for the role I just had to go along with it. According to John, a man born within the borders of Govan, Benburb and St Anthony's are pretty much mortal enemies. I think he is trying to say that one of them is Celtic and the other one is Rangers. Glasgow can be so predictable can't it?

Anyway the teams are apparently within walking distance of each other. Speaking as someone from the countryside I have to assume they are pretty dammed close to one another as city folk don't seem capable of walking the length of themselves. I have actually seen young, presumably fit, people waiting at the bus stop just to travel a distance of a quarter of a mile or so.

It was a fairly early start for us, given the two teams are only 15 minutes by bus from Glasgow city centre. Unfortunately kick-off time was 2 o'clock which meant we had to be in the city by 12.00pm just to make sure we could catch both teams.

Just for a change we decided to start the day off in our new favourite Glasgow pub, 'Denholm's'. After a quick strategic discussion, and a pint, we set off for Benburb.

I think part of our reasoning for having such an early pint was the belief that there were very few pubs in the area of Glasgow we were planning to visit. Added to that there was the frightening prospect of not finding a social club attached to the football grounds used by Benburb and St Anthony's. It would be a short and not very sweet day out reviewing pubs if we couldn't actually find any.

John: After a quick one in 'Denholms', we walked under the Heilenman's Umbrella into Union Street to catch the McGill's 26 to our first port of call, Benburb. On the way I had the sad sight of passing through my old stomping ground, Govan, and not knowing where I was, and it's not just my memory going, the place has changed out of all recognition. It doesn't look as good as I remember, or maybe it's just me.

After boring Craig to death with stories of my youth in the places we passed, we got off the bus in Shieldhall Road and walked up the few yards into Tinto Park.

Craig: *On the bus out to Govan John decided to lighten his rucksack by scoffing all his pieces. We had been out and about for an hour-and-a-half after all.*

Hurtling along the road we walked up to the front of the bus, intending to get off at the next stop. It is not usually regarded as a complicated procedure but today's driver changed the rules.

54

Personally I didn't think it was either possible or advisable to open the bus doors while it was still clocking 20 miles an hour. I very nearly arrived in Govan a couple of minutes before I should have.

My faith in John's abilities took a major knock when he admitted that, although he had been born and brought up in the area he didn't recognise the place.

After a false start, which found us walking up a cul-de-sac and actively considering cutting through a couple of private gardens, we found the football ground. Tinto Park looked a bit run-down but we soon found out why. Today's game was Benburb's second last home game at their old park. It really didn't make any sense spending good money repairing and maintaining the club structure when within a few weeks, it was destined become a large pile of rubble.

Archie and Frank

John: Tinto is really run down, but the reason is that today was the second last match that will ever be played there. The Ben's are moving to a new park just across the road. Houses are going to be built on the site of the present ground. At least it's not a supermarket. The usual with senior clubs.

We met the Secretary, Archie Wiseman, who took us up to his office overlooking the old iconic ground and he spent a lot of time with us telling stories and giving us some of the history of the club. Archie told us that the last game will be against Johnstone

Burgh, who are managed by the legendary Eddie McKimm, a Ben's hero and top scorer with the club. It will be a sad day for all; I hope they win. Ben's manager Frank Lovering joined us for a while and was great company.

One of the Ben's most famous supporters is Sir Alex Ferguson, another famous Govan High boy. Alex still keeps in touch with the club and helps them out when he can. He has a match-day programme sent to him every home game. What a guy!. Archie was excellent company and before he left us he showed us into the wee bar where some supporters were enjoying a drink.

The barmaid, Ginean Gangel, was good company. She is the manager Frank's sister, a real family club. We enjoyed a pint with Peter McGregor, at 81, one of the Ben's oldest and most loyal supporters. Peter told us that he had worked in almost every yard on the Clyde, I asked him what he did. 'An Electrical Manipulator' was his answer. Now, my dad worked in Stephen's and Fairfield Shipyards and I thought I knew all the trades, but this one was new to me. He saw the vacant look on my face. 'Most people called me a welder', he said. What a character he was. Between him and Archie we heard some great stories that I will let Craig tell you as I have gone on long enough.

We said our fond farewell to everybody at the park and wished them success in their new venue. It was now time to visit the local rivals, The Ants.

Craig and Peter McGregor

Craig: We were invited into the club by Archie Wiseman, the club secretary. He told us all about the move to the new ground next season. In fact he said that the club had asked a well-known former Ben's player to the last game. Although he hadn't replied yet the man fully expects to hear from Sir Alex Ferguson in the next week or so.

While we were chatting I asked the guys if they had any stories to tell us about the rivalry between the Bens and the Ants. It is always a bit difficult to come up with a good story when you're put on the spot like that but Archie rose to the occasion.

He told us that they once had an important home game against their nearest rivals, but had discovered that St Anthony's couldn't field a full team.

The Bens committee was approached about the possibility of calling off the game, but they declined.

Well ... it's still better than jaikets for posts!

On the day of the match the grounds man arrived at the park only to find that someone had stolen a set of goalposts. Rather than let the game be cancelled, and miss out on a really good *chance to stuff their under strength rivals the committee somehow managed to acquire another set of goals. But the referee said it was too late and the game was still called off. A day later they found the missing goalpost lying on the other side of the park's fence. Apparently they now have portable posts; once bitten twice shy it would appear.*

When we were talking about checking out a few nearby pubs Archie said that he had some really bad news for us. It would seem that a good old-fashioned pub just around the corner had been bought over and turned into a church. What the hell is that about? It is supposed to be the other way round, surely?

Anyway, John needed a drink. He gets a bit hyper when he is on a day out and is denied alcohol for more than thirty minutes. In the nick of time I managed to avoid one of his major tantrums when I noticed a nice wee bar in the clubhouse.

Through in that wee bar we met Peter McGregor, one of the club's older supporters. He was a little less than impressed with the club's impending move to the new ground; in fact he said "I'll believe it when I see it".

I had thought Peter would be a great source of reminiscences of past rivalries with St Anthony's. Unfortunately John must have heard me say reminiscence and thought I was talking to him. Neither I nor Peter could get a word in for the next twenty minutes.

If I hear him go on about the time he had a trial for the Bens one more time I will not be responsible for my actions. The way I hear it he was only on the field for half an hour and even then he had to beg the manager to take him off.

Anyway, the bar in the clubhouse was quite comfortable in a run-down sort of way. But since it will very soon be reduced to rubble it is probably not worth reviewing. We enjoyed it and look forward to supping a pint or two in the new one.

Club Name	Founded
Saint Anthony	1902
Ground	**Colours**
McKenna Park	Green and White hoops
League (2014-15)	**Selection of Honours**
Central League, 1st Division	Scot. Jun. Cup Runners-up
Club Nickname	1918-19; 1924-25
The Ants	

John: As we left Tinto and got back onto Shieldhall Road I saw a bus in the distance so we did our impression of someone running for a bus and just managed to get it. This saved us the 10 minute walk to the nearest pub to the ground, *'The Tall Cranes'*. This is a real Celtic bar, everything being green and white. I imagine most of the regulars are Celtic supporters, and if they are, they are doing Celtic proud. What a great bunch of guys they were and didn't give a toss who you supported. There was even a wee guy at the end of the bar watching a Rangers match on a lap top computer the barman had given him.

Lynn, the barmaid, was good company and one of the locals we were talking to, Bernie Ford was a real character and was telling Craig some stories. He bought one of our books. What a guy!

Our plan was to meet the Ants' manager at about 4.00pm so we were watching the clock.

Lynn and Bernie

After another round we said our farewells and wandered along the road and into 'The Fairfield Social Club', or the Tardis as Craig called it. It was 10 times bigger inside than it looked from the outside. It even had a big dance hall, a real old fashioned place-brilliant. When I was young I think it was called a working man's club. Wonder why it changed its name? All the guys we met were great company. While Craig went round the bar getting stories, I spent the time asking all the guys of my age if they knew me; nobody did, or if they did, they weren't admitting it.

There were no Bens or Ants supporters, but the barmaid, Honor, was doing her best to get them to come here after the matches. I wish her all the best; she'll need it.

I felt like Dr. Who as I walked out the door. They should change the name to the Tardis as time goes quickly inside.

Craig: We had seen 'The Tall Cranes' from the bus so we were reasonably sure that it was open for business. The funny thing was I had noticed that the pub was painted a fairly bright shade of green. Given we were a stone's throw from Ibrox Park I found that a bit odd.

Now, if I found the outside of the place to be unusual the inside of the pub was mind-blowing. It actually looked like a pub you might find in one of the better areas of Dublin. Copies of the Irish Times are available on the bar.

A trio of Fairfield regulars

For some reason John was a bit reluctant to start talking about football rivalries, but after a couple of refreshments he eventually felt brave enough to talk to a chap up at the bar. Bernie Ford told us that interest in junior football in the area had declined in recent years. As far as rivalry was concerned, he said that many local football players had played their football with Benburb and St Anthony's. He wondered why both teams just didn't merge to create a bigger and better team, hopefully one that would attract a decent level of support.

I was amazed when John actually found his way to Fairfield Social Club with only a minimal amount of dithering about. It is a massive place with a main hall which I would guess can hold a couple of hundred customers.

Honor , Eddie and customer

In the lounge I got chatting to a few older guys about junior football but found supporters a bit thin on the ground. Its changed days someone must have said. My own personal theory is that since the advent of satellite television and all day licensing the junior game in this area has flat-lined.

Up at the bar John was having a bit of an identity crisis. He was telling anyone who would listen to him that he was really a

61

local boy made good, but nobody remembered him. I'm not a hundred per cent certain that we were in the area he thought we were. He has been having navigational lapses recently.

Not to be denied his wee bit of recognition he started on about his 30 minutes of fame back in the dark ages when he had his football trial. Even the very patient bar staff, Honor and Eddie, couldn't be bothered pretending to be interested.

To make up for bending my ear with his tales of failure on the football field John thought he would brighten up my day by taking me to the local Bowling Green for a drink. For once he had no trouble finding the place, but when we got there we discovered that it was shut. I only hope it's not going to become another church, we don't want that sort of thing catching on.

John: We wished the crowd in the social club all the best and wandered along Langlands Road. I had planned for a quick one in the Linthouse Bowling Club, but it was shut. Not to worry, there was a bus coming and it was approaching at full speed. But we managed to catch it for the two stops, passing my old house on the way, and got off at the Moss Road roundabout.

By the way, that new hospital inside the Southern General grounds is some size. From a distance it looks like a giant Vegas Hotel. Hope the punters that end up in there have more luck than the ones that go into the Vegas Hotels. They come out skint!

So over to the Ants' park we went, just in time to see them equalize from the penalty spot. I cheered like a real supporter, and there weren't many of them, I counted less than 100. Govan locals could do a lot worse on a Saturday than go and watch the Ants or the Bens.

After the final whistle, we met the manager James McKenna, and what a character he is. I don't think I've met a nicer or funnier bloke. He must be a great manager. He took us into the wee bar where we met a great crowd of the backroom people who really keep Junior clubs afloat. The drink was free. What a club. Bet there's no free bar in Auchinleck!

F Bardows, J Doyle, T Allen, F Barnes A.McKenna, M McKenna
A Livingston, J Cusack, D Doyle, J McKenna, R Gillespie, J McKenna

The stories just kept coming, some of them about the rivalry between them and the Bens. Again, I'm going to leave it to Craig to tell you the stories we heard, no point in both of us telling the same ones.

We had great hospitality and the people we met were all very friendly and funny, I think you have to have a good sense of humour to follow the Juniors.

Eventually we said our farewells and promised to return some day. James said he was going to mail us some other stories. I think he could write a book himself. It would be much better than the stuff we write, certainly funnier.

Our bus stop was just across the road and the same McGills number 26 took us back into Glasgow, and into '*Denholm's*'.

Our girls, Kate and Irene, were having lunch in Glasgow today with Irene's friend Nancy. As her husband David was at a loose end, we had invited him to join us in Glasgow after our trip. The problem was that he couldn't make it until later, so to cut a long story short, we waited for him. This resulted in a lot more drink being consumed. What else could we do?

God knows how I got home but I woke up this morning in my own bed. Thank goodness Kate was away for the night. I know she'll not find out by reading the book, she never does.

So ended a fantastic day; thank goodness I took notes.

It was an expensive one, but we sold at least two, maybe three books. I know this cos I had money left at the end of the night and no books.

Craig: We arrived at McKenna Park just before the final whistle. There is no bar as such in the clubhouse but we were invited into the committee room for what John insists on calling a 'wee swally'. He turns into Rab C whenever he gets within a couple of miles of Govan!

While scoffing the aforementioned 'swally' we were regaled with a few Ants stories by team manager James McKenna. He told us that a while back, when they were still playing at their old ground, they had a serious problem with rats. One match day the team were getting changed when they heard someone in the toilet screaming. Some players forced their way in only to find the referee sitting on the loo with his pants down around his ankles, surrounded by scuttling rats.

On another occasion one of the Ant's players was in the middle of a loud rant at his team mates, accusing them of stealing his sandwiches. Apparently he had found his pieces scattered around the dressing room floor. He stopped mid rant when a huge black rat scurried past him still carrying a bread crust in its mouth.

That should have put us off our food, but it didn't. That was because the buffet set out on the table looked and tasted delicious. Isa McKenna has been in charge of all things kitchen-related for more years than anyone can remember. And at 83 she shows no sign of hanging up her pinny any time soon.

Everyone was in a really good mood by this time so I thought I would bring up the subject of missing goalposts.

James denied categorically that it was Ant's supporters who stole the posts round at Tinto Park. He suggested that it was an inside job, though he did admit that there had been a goalpost related incident which had caused a game to be cancelled when his dad had been manager.

His father had asked for a postponement of a game because his daughter was getting married down in England, and of course he wanted to be there. The football authorities didn't agree to his request so he decided to take matters into his own hands, quite literally. He took a saw to the park and cut down the crossbar: game over.

More than once it was said to me that St Anthony's was a real family club. It was only later on when I was checking the names of everyone in the group picture I took that it dawned on me just how true that statement was. There are quite a few McKennas involved out there at McKenna Park

Just before we left the ground one of the committee men, possibly a McKenna, told us about a record still held by the Ant's. During season 1918-19 St Anthony's won four cups in four days. That is a record which is unlikely ever to be matched never mind broken.

With that we made our way out of the park and, unfortunately, onto a couple more pubs, and a bout of chemically induced amnesia. Great day!

Pubs and Clubs visited today;
Benburb
Fairfield Social Club; old fashioned, but great for a drink.

The Ants
The Tall Cranes
A real Celtic and Ants bar-but anybody welcome, no matter who you support.
Both teams hospitality was great, as was the characters we met.
Denholm's in Glasgow is a great wee bar.

Benburb; **How to get there-free with the Bus pass**
McGill No. 26 Glasgow to Paisley Nethercraigs
(get off 1st stop after Craigton Road in Shieldhall Road)
(same map for both clubs)

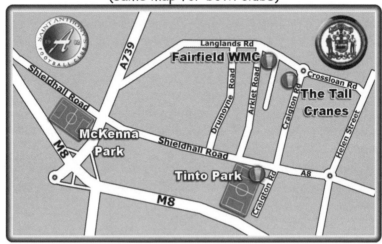

St. Anthony's; **How to get there-free with Bus pass**
McGills No. 26 Glasgow to Paisley Nethercraigs)
(get off at Moss Road Roundabout)

Bonnyrigg Rose V Newtongrange Star

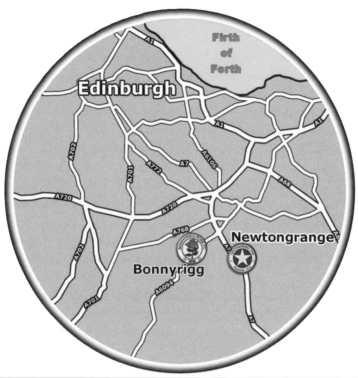

Club Name	Founded
Bonnyrigg Rose	1890
Ground	*Colours*
New Dundas Park	Red with White Hoop
League (2014-15)	*Selection of Honours*
East Region Super League	Scot. Jun. Cup 1965-66 77-78;
Club Nickname	
The Rose	

John: Today was our first trip of this book to the East Region of the Juniors, and we were visiting two very famous clubs, and rivals. 'The Rose' and 'The Star' are official nicknames of the two clubs. Initially I had thought that this was very boring and came up with 'The Thorns' and 'The Twinklers'. Are they not bumpers? Mind you, it didn't take us long to find out that all the clubs and people in this area have nicknames. A selection that I can remember is 'The Germans', or 'Huns' for the people from the local town of Gorebridge. When I asked why, 'It's because they all have square heids', just like the German helmets! The real nickname for the people born in Newtongrange is 'Nitten Bulls', and this is what they call themselves, and proud they are. I hope I'll remember more as the story goes on.

Edinburgh is always a nightmare to get to, and today was worse. Not only were we having to get to Edinburgh, but once there, we were having to catch another bus out of the place to where we were going. My planning was immense; I hoped Craig would appreciate it. He didn't.

I had planned to pick up Craig at 9.00am, so I was up at the screek o' farts to get ready, the pieces made and out the door.

At nine sharp I was at Craig's house ready for our safari to the East. I had managed to contact both clubs officials last night and they had said they would be delighted to meet us. I was starting to change my image of people from the East already and we hadn't left yet!

Our journey on the No. 18 into Glasgow and the big trip on the No. 900 to Edinburgh went without a hitch. I was starting to get my confidence back in my ability to plan bus journeys. As we got off the motorway and passed Edinburgh Airport, I was looking forward to seeing a tram actually moving. I had read they were testing them, but the only place I saw any were in the tram garage, and there's a wheen of them. Hope they need them all. As we were getting closer to the centre of Edinburgh we saw big signs attached to the tram stops telling people that the trams will stop there. I would have thought the tracks were a bit of a giveaway. Mind you, the tracks have been down for so long that people will not associate them with trams.

We got off the bus in George Street and walked down into Princes Street. I had planned to get on our next bus, the No. 31, at North Bridge, but as it passed along Princes Street, I took the executive decision to get on it earlier and save us a wee walk, and I'm glad we did.

As I was pointing out North Bridge, or what I thought was North Bridge to Craig, the bus went right past the corner that I thought took you on to North Bridge and turned up the real North Bridge. Planners need a bit of luck!

Successful authors like us are requested by the Scottish National Library to give them five of their books so they can send them to the five main libraries in the UK and Ireland. I wonder what they would make of this stuff if they ever opened one. They would never find out where North Bridge is anyway, but never mind. The No. 31 passed close by it on its way to Bonnyrigg, so I had said to Craig we would jump off the bus, wander round the corner, deliver the books, wander back and get the next no. 31 ten minutes later. Amazingly, this is what happened, no problems. I was amazed, Craig was speechless.

Our bus dropped us off in the main street in Bonnyrigg. It was cold and windy, but the sun was out, so we couldn't complain as it was one of the few dry days we have had since the last one!

We recced out the ground, which I noticed straight away had quite a big slope going across the pitch. I mentioned this to an old guy who was standing just looking over the scene. 'Worth a goal of a start' he said. But it was a nice park and the place looked well set up.

Because of my brilliant planning and a bit of luck, we had arrived earlier than planned, so had time to visit a local pub before we met the secretary. This was great so we wandered back up to a pub we had seen on the corner of the lane leading to the ground.

Craig: Bonnyrigg Rose and Newtongrange Star, are two teams which are only spitting distance apart, not that I'm suggesting there is ever spitting involved in their relationship with each other, but there is a definite sense of rivalry between them. We didn't know quite what to expect on our visit to the respective grounds but were fairly sure there would be a few tales to be told.

During my extensive research into the clubs I had come across a very strange story doing the rounds on the Internet. It concerned an article which appeared in a fanzine, which really upset a section of the Bonnyrigg support. Without going into too much detail it would seem that, after beating their closest rivals, some Newtongrange supporters wrote a supposedly funny article for their fanzine in which they described Bonnyrigg Rose as a rugby team. There were other references to individual players which, of course, I will not reprint but it apparently annoyed some Rose fans. After a complaint was made to the Scottish Junior Football Association, Newtongrange were fined a couple of hundred pounds. There was also talk about legal action but thankfully nothing came of that.

My problem was just how to bring the subject up in conversation when we reached Bonnyrigg. Obviously I could not just ignore it because I knew if I didn't say something about it my friend, Mister Subtlety himself, John, would blurt it out.

John: '*The Calderwood*' was the name of the bar and in we went for the start of today's adventure. This is a real man's bar and the locals, mostly guys of our age were great company and filled us in with tales of the club and the people who used to play for them. As usual, I'll let Craig tell most of the stories as he has a better memory than me. I do remember them telling us that among the great and famous players that played for the club were John White and Sean Connery (007), who played about five games. John White was a fabulous player who ended up starring with Spurs. He was killed on the golf course by a strike of lightning. You never know the minute!

By coincidence, we found out later that Dave Mackay, one of Scotland's greatest, and toughest ever players, used to play for Newtongrange Star, our next club today. Can you imagine if Scotland had these players today. We wouldn't be shitting ourselves at the thought of meeting Germany, or anybody else for that matter. And if it looked that we might be getting beaten, we could always call on 007 to sort the opposition out.

Anyway, we were enjoying the company; barmaids Christine and Tracy were good fun and the first drink of the day was going down well. Always a bad sign.

Tracy and Christine

Craig: *Anyway we arrived in Bonnyrigg bang on time. That sounds better than it really was since John didn't actually know we had arrived. If it hadn't been for the satnav on my wonder phone we would have been starting our day in a different town entirely. Once we were sure that we had indeed arrived at our objective we immediately switched to pub-finding mode. Like a couple of experienced trackers we soon found some likely candidates for a visit.*

The Calderwood is actually next to the football ground so we decided it would be our first stop of the day. But, first things first, we had to be professional, for a few moments at least, and check out the park. We found an open gate and wandered in. Our usual tactic when having to do this sort of thing is to play dumb. If questioned too severely I have to pretend to be John's care worker and tell whoever is shouting the odds that it is better to humour him than risk a full-blown confrontation. So far we have never actually had to use this ploy but I am convinced that we could carry it off.

New Dundas Park is as nice a junior ground as I've seen. You can tell that a lot of work has gone into the preparation of the ground. It was too early to meet any of the committee but some fans were already gathering.

Just to kill a bit of time before kick-off we decided to visit the Calderwood. Although it is a fairly old building the interior is quite modern, but in a likeable way. After a thirst-quenching couple of sips of our drinks we got talking to the barmaid and some customers. I am always amazed how a few words can change the character of a place. As usual that was down to John who finds it impossible not to chat to people. The trick is getting him to stop. Or should I say getting him to stop before the fourth or fifth pint. That is when he enters the twilight zone of pub life; talking politics or football. These are not his specialist subjects, and he really should steer clear of them. He reads the Daily Mail after all!

Jock and Pat

I wandered over to a table where two older guys were analysing, loudly and critically, an English league football match which was on the telly. After we explained to Jock and Pat what we were doing in the town Jock told me a story about a local man who had played for several junior teams of yesteryear.

Joker O'Neil had moved to Bonnyrigg to work in the pits but played his football in the Western league. He had once been transferred from Blantyre Celtic to Bonnyrigg and the agreed transfer fee had been 24 sheet of corrugated iron. It seems that Blantyre had a problem with the fence around the park and had decided that the iron work was more valuable to the team than his services.

During the laughter which followed we speculated on just how much corrugated iron would be required in a similar situation

72

if Manchester United ever thought of getting rid of Wayne Rooney. Now that would take some shifting!

Incidentally, Jock's pal Pat had been a player for the Rose back in the 1950s. He has been a life-long fan of the team and still manages to get along to the home games.

John: Before we went into the ground, we thought we would give the social club a try, and why not, it sells drink.

The barman, Robin Cairns, was great company and introduced us to Tam Milligan, who, in the past, had been the chairman for 25 years. Now that's dedication.

Robin and Laura

Tam told us stories from the past. I'll tell you one story and let Craig tell you the rest. Years ago, Newtongrange (the rivals) had just moved into their new ground and had won the league that season. At the committee meeting following the triumph, the decision was made to put up a flag pole to fly the league flag. The committee member tasked with getting the pole was told to make it the biggest one he could get so these B******s in Bonnyrigg could see it every day.

Craig: Our next stop was the supporters club which is just behind the pub and across from the park-very handy indeed. Initially I was a bit confused as there didn't appear to be a sign telling anyone that it was in fact a club. I even checked to see if

73

there were any empty kegs outside. When we eventually found our way into the club we found it to be a traditional supporters club. The main hall is a fair size with the bar at one end. It was very clean and tidy and, as we soon found out it was very well run.

John: Time was getting on so we said our goodbyes and walked over the few yards into New Dundas Park and met up with the Secretary Robert Dickson and the Chairman Charlie Kirkwood.

They were brilliant guys and gave us a lot of their time as well as our choice of refreshment. We took them up on their offer as by then 'we had the taste'. These guys, like their opposite numbers in all Junior Clubs, work endless hours keeping their clubs going. They both had a great sense of humour and gave us all the information we needed about the clubs, and more importantly, the local bars.

All too soon kick-off time approached and the lads had a lot to do, so we wished them all the best and wandered back up to the main street. We had been told by the locals in *'The Calderwood'* that the bus to Newtongrange left just outside the pub at ten minutes to the hour. We had about half an hour to kill, but instead of going back in to the bar, we put our job first and found another bar to report on.

I wish we hadn't bothered. '*The Anvil*' was the bar we found. Now it's a very nice bar and very well finished, and the barmaid Hannah was ok once she pretended to warm to us. The bar is more suited to couples and not old guys who make places like this untidy. The only good thing was that they did big measures.

Craig: We had a good laugh with the guys at the bar and before leaving to go over to the park wished them well with their game.

Once over at New Dundas Park, we were shown to the supporters bar down at the bottom end of the park. I think it is a converted trailer or possibly two and it is a great wee bar.

Although there is no draught beer I think it would be a good place to have a drink before the game. If I were a supporter I would definitely spend a good part of my pre-match build-up making sure this place keeps on going. This opinion is in no way coloured by the fact that the club secretary insisted we accept a complimentary drink. Although, for future reference, it disnae do any harm either.

Charlie and Robert

Robert Dixon, the secretary, told us that in his day job he drives the bin lorry. I have to admit I was expecting a story from that and he didn't disappoint. After seeing his team gain a well-

deserved victory over their local rivals Robert was driving his lorry through Newtongrange when a local resident decided to express his disapproval of the Rose. The lad, kindly described as ' no the full shilling ', chased after Robert's wagon throwing rubbish at it. There just has to be some irony in throwing rubbish at a bin lorry.

We had another beer with the guys, and they told us that the men in Newtongrange like to be called ' Nitten Bulls'. I made a mental note to completely disregard this advice as I was pretty sure it was a wind-up and would probably get me a good hard slap if I ever uttered it. Wrong again!

Having at least 15 minutes before our next bus we made our way along to a pub called The Anvil. Let me just say it did not strike me as a great place for a brew before the game. Although it could be fun to have a really heavy drinking session in this pub just so that you could say that you got really hammered in The Anvil.

Newtongrange Star

Club Name	**Founded**
Newtongrange Star	1890
Ground	**Colours**
New Victoria Park	Royal Blue
League (2014-15)	**Selection of Honours**
East Reg. Super League	Scot. Jun. Cup; 1929-30
Club Nickname	
The Star	

John: The sun was still shining and we ate our pieces as we waited for the number 39 to take us to Newtongrange. I was back to my traditional pieces with Corned Beef and English Mustard. It was a new jar of mustard, and it always tastes stronger when opened for the first time.

Good planning meant that we had time to visit a bar before going to the ground at full time. Craig had been on Google Earth Street View and had found a pub called '*The Dean Tavern*'. We found it right away and in we went.

It was a huge bar with a very high ceiling. It was like being in a Cathedral. I believe I was told that it was owned by the village and had been built by the mining community. Miners must have loved to drink somewhere with a high roof after the hell holes and rabbit warrens they worked in every day. The pub is one of only two in existence that are 'Gothenburg' style bars. Write to me if you have ever heard of this fact, but not if you're a Nitten Bull!

I was a bit worried when we walked in that such a large bar would lack a bit of atmosphere. A bar this big would need big characters to fill it, and it had plenty of them. Some of the people and their stories were beyond belief, but they were all true, or so Jas Pride, one of the greatest, and most modest players ever to live told us. Craig will fill you in with his tales.

Keran, Billy and Marion

The barmaids, Marion and Keran, were brilliant company and spent the time calling over more and more crazy people to meet us. It was fantastic.

Jas introduced us to his cousin Norrie (all Nitten Bulls are cousins). Norrie is a past Commonwealth Gold Medal-winning Bowler. It went on like this for over an hour. There are no ordinary Nitten Bulls!

Norrie and Jas Pride

Craig: Our arrival in Newtongrange was almost as unexpected as that in Bonnyrigg. We shot past the park, thinking the advertising board was just telling us that the town had a football team and was not actually pointing the way to the ground.

However we made a good recovery by finding the Dean Tavern. To be honest I thought the place looked like an English village pub and restaurant. We couldn't even find our way into it at first. It was only when a bloke came out holding a pint in each hand that we were sure it was a pub and were fairly sure we had found the entrance.

Inside it was nothing short of spectacular; I've never seen anything like it. There was easily enough space to have an upstairs to the place but it was all open beams, making it very airy. It has to be the highest ceiling I've seen in a purpose-built pub. We have all seen those converted banks, churches and warehouses which have suddenly become trendy pubs, but this is an original.

My verdict on the Dean Tavern is a very positive one. We were served quickly and efficiently by friendly bar staff. Keran, Billy and Marion were up for a laugh and pointed out a few of the customers who they thought would provide us with some interesting stories.

I would urge all public house aficionados to visit the Dean Tavern. You will not be disappointed. The punter patter was also top notch. It is not often that any of us meets a living legend but if you're to believe Jas Pride that's exactly what you will have done when you meet him. He is not short on ego by the way; to quote John "whit a man".

To illustrate his claim to legendary status he told us about his early career in football. Apparently as a kid he played for his county team and his primary school team. One particular day he had just finished leading his county team to a famous victory and had quickly made his way to another game for his school. It seems that for some reason the rest of this team hadn't turned up by kick-off time. According to Jas he decided to take on the opposition on his own. The only thing he was worried about was the coin toss. "If I'd been made to take the kick-off I'd have had no bugger to kick the ball to", he explained. As it was, he intercepted the ball just after the other team kicked off and, with skill rarely seen in one so young, Jas dribbled up the length of the field and scored a most memorable goal. At least that's the gist of what he told us. Anyway, using skill and determination Jas managed to keep the score at one nil until the rest of his team eventually arrived. Things then went downhill and his school ended up being beaten 3-1, the implication being they were cramping his style.

In later life Jas not only played for Newtongrange Star, or the Nitten as he called them, but rose to be captain of the team. Sport is very much a part of the Pride family. His cousin, Norrie, is a Commonwealth medal winner in bowling. Apparently, Norrie shares some similar characteristics with Jas, the main one being

79

that he too is no slouch in the storytelling department. We were well entertained by the pair of them but we had to drag ourselves away to visit 'The Nitten'.

John: Eventually we managed to escape from this fantastic bar and its inmates and headed round the corner and up to New Victoria Park, home of the *'Nitten',* just as the final whistle had gone. I won't mention the score as it's not important to our story. The committee and supporters are a different matter.

Gordon and Stan

The Secretary Gordon Stannars and the President Stan Adams made us very welcome and although today's result was not what they wanted, they did not let it show and gave us all the information we needed. Equally nice was that they took us through to the bar and bought us a drink. What a fine couple of hard working guys they are.

Behind the bar were Megan and Steven. Steven has been on the committee for 35 years and supported the team since he was five. We were in good company and they looked after us well.

Both clubs we visited today are maybe, on the surface, bitter rivals, but both have very similar dedicated men and women who give almost all of their time for the love of their clubs. We had a great day.

We left Newtongrange, just missed the bus I had planned to get, first failure today, but got a local one which wandered through lovely wee towns on its way to North Bridge in Edinburgh. The short walk to the Bus Station was only marred by Craig complaining that he had to walk on a cobbled street for about two yards. What a man!

The journey to Glasgow passed in a flash as we both slept the whole way. Amazingly, we got the train directly to EK and went straight up the road. This is the most sober state we have ever been in when we got home. Are we changing? No chance!

Today, the £20 we each put in the kitty was enough to get us a taxi back up to our houses from EK Station. I've got to say we did do a bit more bevying than the money spent may suggest. The hospitality at Bonnyrigg was considerable, and at Newtongrange it was similar, so you'll be glad to know we have not signed the pledge completely.

Craig: New Victoria Park is probably the most modern ground we have visited so far on our tour of junior grounds. A lot of money has been spent on the ground and its facilities. In fact it looks almost brand new.

Steven and Megan

In the clubhouse we met and chatted to Gordon Stannars and Stan Adams, secretary and president respectively. Despite getting a slight gubbing in that day's game, the guys were still upbeat. Their team will no doubt bounce back from this defeat. According to Gordon and Stan, Newtongrange have a strategy in place which will see the club grow and be in contention for the sports major trophies in the future.

The social club is really bright and modern with a well-stocked bar. Gordon introduced us to Steven and Megan, the bar staff, and asked them to pour us a drink. It was a pleasant way to end our day out. Except of course it didn't end there. We enjoyed the atmosphere in the lounge so much we decided to have another drink and a bit of a chat with Steven and Megan.

The journey back home was also very enjoyable in that we missed most of it. Asleep is a great way to travel.

Pubs and clubs visited today;

Bonnyrigg;

The Calderwood is a brilliant man's bar.

The Club's Social Club was also great.

The Anvil is an ok place if you have the wife or partner (could be anybody of any sex)-the modern John strikes.

The Hospitality Bar in the ground is worth visiting to show your backing for your local club.

Newtongrange;

The Dean Tavern was the only pub visited, but worth two of any other bar, if only for the patter and outrageous stories.

The Club's Social Club, like Bonnyriggs, was great.

Bonnyrigg; How to get there-free with Bus pass
City Link No. 900 to Edinburgh
No. 31 North Bridge Edinburgh to Bonnybrigg

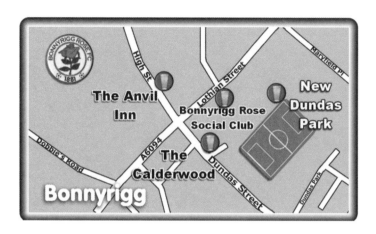

Newtongrange; How to get there-free with Bus pass
City Link No. 900 to Edinburgh
No. X95 North Bridge to Newtongrange

Lochee United V Tayport

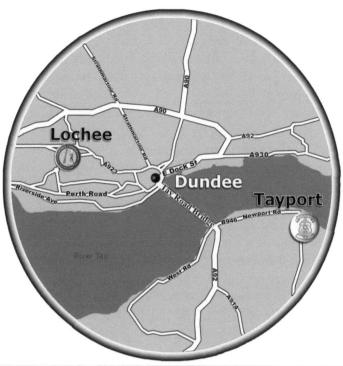

Lochee United	1892
Ground	*Colours*
Thomson Park	Blue and White
League (2014-15)	*Selection of Honours*
East Reg. Super League	East Reg. Super League
Club Nickname	Winners 2005-06; 07-08
The Bluebells	

John: The two teams we are visiting today have been rivals for many, many years, mainly because they are the two most successful Junior clubs in the Dundee area, by which I mean Dundee. Tayport have had the most national success, getting to the Scottish Junior Cup final about six times and winning it about half the time. Lochee United are no slouches either, winning about every honour possible except, sadly, the big one, The Scottish Junior Cup.

So it was two of the fairly big boys of Junior Football that we were paying a visit to today. But we don't care how good, or bad, the clubs are. It is all about the hospitality, the quality and service we receive in the ground and the hostelries in the area around the ground.

I know I've mentioned nicknames before, in fact in every chapter, I make no excuses for this or any of the other crap I write, although I do believe I am an expert at nicknames, so it is well worth noting what I come up with. Lochee United are nicknamed 'The Bluebells'. They play in Blue, granted, but 'The Bluebells'; 'It's not great, is it? Mind you, compared to Tayport's attempt, 'The Port', Lochee win hands down.

As usual, it's up to me to come up with new and better nicknames for the clubs, and ones that are not so obvious. I may be mentally unbalanced, but it's me who is writing this, so there! Lets take the really crap one first, 'The Port'. Now Tayport is a lovely wee place on the shores of the river and has seen hard times. Before Tayport moved to the present ground, I believe the land used to be owned by the Army and was used for exercises so how about 'The Gun Ports'? You've got Guns for the Army and Port for the Tayport. Some may say this is not very good, and they may be right.

Lochee, 'The Bluebells', it's a bit, how can I say it in today's politically correct shithouse we live in, unmanly. Even this may be incorrect. I'll ask the wife. You can't shout 'come on the Bluebells' at a match, not in Govan or Auchinleck anyway.

Talking to the locals at the ground, I discovered that Lochee's Park is on the site of a quarry, into which, so the story goes, a horse and cart disappeared before the attempt was made to fill it in and lay the park. Now this story is obviously true, so the nickname should reflect that occasion. So 'The Carters' would fit the bill. No one would laugh at that, or anything else they read in this book for that matter. Not to worry, on with the day out in Dundee.

I've always wondered who decides what is politically correct. Is there a committee, and if there is, how do you get on it. I would like to start up a committee that decides nicknames for anything and everything in Scotland. I would be the chairman, although I would have to think up a nickname for the committee. Where am I?

Dundee, that's where, famous for Desperate Dan, Oor Wullie, The Broons and Jute. There are many other very famous people, and things that Dundee is famous for, but today it is the football we are interested in. Also, I've no idea what the other things are.

Another very early start was needed, early for retired people that is. I went online and booked two seats on the 10.40am Dundee bus, that's a pound I'll never see again, and fifty pence of that is for Craig! Working backwards, which I'm famous for, I reckoned we would have to get a No. 18 from Craig's house about 9.20am, so I would have to be up at about 8.30am. Not that early really.

I had looked into the Travel Web page and found that there was a number six and an 18 at roughly the same time. Now they both pass on the Murray Road next to Craig's house, but they go in different directions. Because the six was due a few minutes earlier than the 18 we crossed the road. Sod's law was working and the 18 appeared first, so we had to rush back over to the side we had been on already. You'd have thought I'd asked Craig to cross the Sahara in his bare feet.

Safely on the bus and with Craig's breath back, we enjoyed the trip into Glasgow. During the journey we discussed ideas for our next book and actually decided on an idea I claim to have came up with. We also decided on a title. 'Is there no end to this?' I hear you say.

In no time at all we were in Buchanan Street Bus Station to be met with a big queue for our M9 to Dundee. We joined the waiting throngs in time to be told by a wee man with a safety jacket that the bus was going to be 15 minutes late. He seemed quite pleased, but there was no reason for him to be smiling.

The coach, when it arrived, was a big double decker that looked as if it had seen better times. Written on the front of the bus was the legend McLeans Executive Coach, thank goodness it was the Executive version. We were one of the last ones to get on and had to go upstairs and got a seat in the back row.

The run up to Dundee was ok. I had bought a bag of chocolate things that they sell dead cheap at the tills. I wish they'd stop doing that, I'm trying to diet. The wee woman sitting in the corner seat beside had a small bottle of wine that she was downing on the quiet; I think she was enjoying her trip.

At Craig's insistence, I had phoned the Waterstones Store in Dundee yesterday to see if they wanted any books. They ordered 11. This was a result as we could deliver them when we got off the bus and the money would cover the day's bevy. It doesn't get any better than this!

The late arrival of our M9 meant that by the time we delivered the books we had missed our planned No. 203 bus. Now we have found in the past that the bus drivers in the East are very friendly and helpful, so holding on to that memory, I stuck my head in the door of the bus that was sitting at our stop and asked if he knew how we could get to the ground. He didn't let us down. Not only did he tell me which bus to get, he gave me a full set of instructions on how to get to the ground. By the time I had finished thanking him, I had forgotten half of the information he gave me.

The easy bit was the next bus. It was a number 28 which was due in two minutes. This driver was just as helpful and even gave us a shout when we were at our stop.

Craig: We set off on our journey to Dundee at about 9.30am. I say about because I'm not sure if the first bit of our journey actually counts. John for some reason decided we should get a different bus down to Glasgow. I have to admit that I wasn't really listening to his explanation of the need to change our tried and trusted routine.

Apparently, had his master plan worked, we would have knocked a good two and a half minutes off our usual time. If he is on any medication I think it's high time that the strength of it is drastically reduced. After wandering back and forth across the very busy road, because someone kept seeing buses which turned out to be the wrong ones, we ended up getting the same bus we usually get.

The bus up to Dundee was more of a cattle truck than a luxury coach. It must have been about 30 years old. We were so late getting on to it that the only seats we could find were upstairs at the very back of the bus. As we were getting settled I noticed that John was trying to find his seatbelt. I told him that, given the age and state of the bus, he was damn lucky to have padded seating never mind seatbelts. Actually I could see quite a lot of the padding as many of the seats were burst.

John has become a bit safety conscious in recent times, I put that down to his advancing years. Just to set his mind at ease I told him that we didn't really need seatbelts since the seats were so close together that we would be snugly trapped in the wreckage should the bus crash. This seemed to do the trick as he kept quiet for the rest of the trip.

John: We got off at the back of the ground and right away we noticed a wee run down looking pub on the other side of the road called '*The Whip*'. It was the sort of pub we love, and Craig was delighted by its name. He does the captions for the pictures he takes on the trip and right away he came up with 'John gets into the lash in the Whip', or words to that effect. He was delighted anyway. I like to keep it that way, so I agreed it was brilliant.

The entrance was on the other side of the ground, so we wandered round there. The first thing we noticed was that this was one of the biggest grounds we had been to. There were cones all down the road stopping people parking and when we went into the gate a wee man appeared out of nowhere and said we had to pay to get in. He was a great bloke called Joe who said that he appears out of the woodwork to make sure no one gets in for nothing. I told him why we were here and he gave us instructions on how to get to the bar in the ground.

On the way over to the stand that held the facilities, we had a look over the park. It is a good set up but the park itself certainly has its ups and downs, and then some more. As I think I said earlier, the park was built on top of a disused quarry and a lot of settling has taken place. I'm not saying it goes up and down a lot, but I reckon some parts of the park will have their own climate. We were told later by the locals that some opposition players, who don't know about the dips have actually fallen over in the bottom of them if they're trying to run too fast. I'd pay good money to see that. It was a great set up.

Actually it's no a performance graph, it's a contour map o' the pitch.

Joe, the suddenly appearing gateman, had said that he'd let the Secretary, Larry Duncan, know when he arrived that we were at the bar.

Amazingly, to me anyway, we had only taken our first sip of the day when a gentleman came up and introduced himself to us. The first thing he said was, 'I hear you are here researching the history of Clydebank Juniors'. We had no idea what he was talking about. When we asked him what he was on about he told us that Joe (the appearing gateman) had given him this information. That guy Joe is some comic.

This guy's name was James Thomson, who is a Junior Football Historian, a very nice guy who was a great help to us. Not so much in the historical part of our travels, but in telling us about the various rivalries that exist all over the country. That information was very useful and will save me a lot of time researching. He told me to contact him if he could be of any further help. People from the East are very helpful.

One thing I did find out from James, I think, is the reason that a lot of the teams in the East have links to flowers in their nicknames. There are two Bluebells that I can think of. The reason is the love of flowers by miners. There were lots of mines in the past and the smell of flowers must have been great for men stuck down a mine shaft all day. A nice story.

Larry and Ian

The Secretary Larry (the Legend) Duncan arrived and introduced us to Stewart Wilson, an ex-president of the club and Gordon Daly, an ex-player and coach. These guys, along with the barman Ian Anderson, gave us a lot of their time and told us some interesting stories about the club and its history. We really appreciate the time these officials give us, especially before or after a game when they have a lot to be getting on with.

I don't think I have mentioned that Craig now has a recorder that he uses to get all the stories from the people we talk to, so I rely on him to recall most of them to you. If he buys any more gadgets I'm going to call him 'Inspector'.

One of the stories I do remember was the time Lochee were playing Bo'ness in a cup match. Bo'ness was a great team at the time and hot favourites. Now the park was almost waterlogged, but because Bo'ness had come a long way the referee decided to let the game go ahead. Lochee won. I think the score was 3-1. Anyway, their bonus was £5 which each player received in 10 pence pieces. The coins came from the money taken at the gate. Great days.

Kick off time was approaching so we thanked all the people who had given us their time and headed out of the ground. At the gate, Joe appeared and wished us success with our history of Clydebank!

Craig: We had arranged to meet Larry Duncan in the clubhouse at Thomson Park. To kill some time while we waited for Larry, John suggested we have a little drink. The hospitality lounge is only open on match days so is a bit limited in the range of drinks it can offer. In other words there is no draught lager. I made do with a perfectly acceptable can instead.

Our barman Ian, told me about a very unusual game they played back in 2005. It was a Scottish cup quarter-final game against Arthurlie and things were not looking good for The Bluebells. In fact they were down 4-1 and reduced to ten men with only 10 minutes to go. The majority of the Lochee crowd were doing their best to beat a hasty retreat from the park. Ian said that it if it hadn't been for the mobile phone most fans would have missed one of the club's greatest victories. Within a few minutes the score had changed to 4-4. The game then went to penalties and Lochee scraped through 2-1. The shine must have been taken off this great victory a little when their biggest rivals, Tayport, beat them in the final.

Larry, the club secretary, came in to see us and I asked him if he had any favourite stories to tell us about his team. After a second or two he told us about the time there was a bit of a mix up at the funeral of a much loved-club official, Dave Mitchell.

92

He had been on the committee of the club for 62 years and his wife had asked if some music associated with the club could be played during the service. The choice was obvious, since the nickname of the club is The Bluebells, 'The Bluebells of Scotland', a traditional Sottish ballad, would have fitted the bill perfectly.

Dave's grandson announced from the lectern that they would now play one of his grandfather's favourite Lochee United songs. However someone got it wrong. The assembled mourners were instead treated to a rousing rendition, by Jimmy Shand, of the Bluebell Polka. As Larry said, nobody knew where to look.

After another quick drink we decided it was time to move on.

John: We went back round the ground, crossed the road and into *'The Whip'* where we received a warm welcome from the barmaid Gemma. There were two guys sitting at the bar, so I asked them if they were going across the road to the game. The man nearest to us was Paul Ireland, who, like a lot of people we met in Lochee, came from Tayport. He told us he was going to see Lochee Harp because his son Conor was playing for them after five weeks off recovering from a broken nose. When we told him about us going round the country to Junior Football clubs he warned us not touch the pies if we are ever in Brechin. Now I don't know why, but I thought you got great pies in places like Brechin, but no, the pies there have a thin layer of mince in the bottom of them, (good mince mind you), but the top of the pie is removed and the top half of it is filled with Skirly. Now I had no idea what Skirly was, but he filled me in, just like the pie. Skirly is a lump of breadcrumbs, which he assured us was terrible. It stuck to your top lip, and had to be avoided at all cost.

Now the man sitting next to Paul, John Watt, disagreed. He said he had a mixed grill once which had Skirly as a main ingredient and he said it was lovely. An argument started about the Skirly which only stopped when Paul had to leave to see his son, with the fixed nose, play for Lochee Harp. Now I know that we are not here to talk about Lochee Harp, or Brechin pies for that matter, but that's what happens when you visit pubs and meet interesting people.

An interesting fact about '*The Whip*' is that it used to be a Coaching Inn and in fact was the last one in use on the famous Dundee to Perth route.

Time was flying past so we said our farewells to '*The Whip*' and vowed never to eat a Brechin Pie, although I quite fancied the recipe.

Paul, John and Gemma

Craig: We had noticed a wee pub just outside the ground. However, when I mentioned the pub's name to the guys in the club they all had a good laugh before telling us that we might need crash helmets if we were going to pay it a visit. That was all the encouragement we needed, besides who could resist a pub called the 'Whip Inn'. I could already see the chapter heading: 'John out on the lash in The Whip Inn'. It made me laugh but, surprise surprise, John didn't get it. Or at least he said he didn't. He was probably just jealous because he didn't think of it first.

I must admit I was a bit disappointed by the Whip Inn, at first. After all the daft talk in the club about crash helmets, I had expected something akin to a Wild West saloon, but the Whip turned out to be a cracking wee pub. It is well laid out, tidy and comfortable. And, best of all, the beer was reasonably priced and above-average in taste.

I got talking to the barmaid while John got involved in a heated argument about pies with two other guys who obviously had far too much time on their hands. Gemma told me that before and after the game her pub can get really busy. I thought about asking her if it was mainly motorcycle gangs who drank in there as I was still trying to work out the crash helmet thing. However I decided she would probably think I was some kind of nut so I settled for ordering another pint.

Tayport FC

Club Name	Founded
Tayport United	1968
Ground	**Colours**
The Canniepairt	red, Black and White
League (2014-15)	**Selection of Honours**
East Region Prem. League	Jun. Cup 1995-96; 2002-03;
Club Nickname	2004-05; Run. Up three times
The Port	

John: The bus stop was just across the road and we had only a couple of minutes to wait for our no. 28 to pick us up and take us into the centre of Dundee. A short walk to the bus station and the no. 42 was waiting to take us on the 15 minute or so journey to Tayport. The journey also took us over the famous Tay Road Bridge. The name Tay Bridge will always be associated with the rail disaster, and if you look over to the new rail bridge you can see the foundations of the original bridge, as a reminder of that fateful night. Back to happier times.

Craig had checked 'street view' on Google to find pubs near the ground and knew which one we were heading for. Unfortunately the bus shot past the pub and we had to walk back, I never complained that it was his fault.

The pub, *'The Tayport Arms'* looked from the outside like an old-fashioned English Country Pub, all whitewash and black beams, and it was the same inside. Craig asked me if I liked the Tudor look. I thought he was talking about Tudor Crisps and asked for cheese and onion. The man has no sense of humour. It was a nice bar and the barmaid Gillian was friendly and good company. She introduced us to a guy called Ally Doctor (I'm sure that was his name), his usual name being Ally Docky. Ally was great fun and had been a goalkeeper in the old days. He told us a great story about him and a referee, I'll let Craig tell you that one.

We had a couple of pints and a fine time with the locals before leaving to make our way along to the Tayport ground.

Gillian and Ally

Craig: *Once again my smart phone came to John's rescue. As usual he had produced a multitude of maps of the area to be visited. Why he does this I do not know. I'm not saying he is forever trying to read them upside down, but they never seem to help us very much. They are more of a historical curiosity than a navigational tool. By that I mean eventually they will show me where we should have been rather then where we are going.*

My satnav-equipped phone, on the other hand, is very useful. Recently I have even found an application which shows you where all the nearest pubs are, an invaluable tool for the thirsty traveller. Or it would be if John believed in it. He doesn't really trust gadgets. His mobile phone was built last century and if it wasn't for the sticky tape wrapped around it the poor thing would have given up the ghost years ago.

Anyway, we found the pub we were looking for. The pub appeared slightly out of place in a Scottish coastal town. The mock Tudor design needed a bit of an explanation, but since we were a bit short of time we didn't ask for one.

Inside, we ordered a drink and introduced ourselves to the barmaid, Gemma. She told us that the Tayport Arms used to be a favourite pub for football supporters but in recent years that has changed. However she did manage to find one supporter for us to talk to.

Ally Doc came over to talk to us. It turns out that Ally was once the Tayport goalkeeper and he had a story to tell us about his exploits between the sticks.

In my limited experience, goalkeepers are rarely controversial figures but, as they say there are exceptions to every rule. Ally told us that he had once been sent off and banned for three months. Since we were talking about junior football I asked him who he had killed to warrant such harsh treatment. He claimed it was for not agreeing with a refereeing decision. Apparently, Ally had been put in charge of the money to be paid to the ref to cover his expenses. Unfortunately, the referee had had a bit of an off-day, according to the Tayport committee, and they decided to withhold his fee. Ally had to break the bad news to him and, as it turned out, he also had to shoulder all the blame as well. Bravely, the committee decided to let him.

John suggested that, given the severity of the punishment, Ally would have been better off just nutting the ref instead, but that was possibly just the drink talking.

John: Tayport is another junior club with a good set-up. The only boring thing is that the park is flat, and no way as interesting a park as Lochee.

The secretary Albert Oswald introduced us to Graeme Irons, the assistant manager, David Bain, the manager; and Derek Carr, the coach. They all told us stories about the history of the club, some of them very funny. I hope Craig's tape was working.

These guys never stop and all too soon they had to leave as they take both teams to a local bar for a drink and a bite to eat.

Graeme, Albert, David and Derek

Craig: Once again we had timed things to perfection as the final whistle was blowing just as we arrived at the park. Upstairs in the trophy room we met some of the club officials.

Our earnest conversation about club rivalries and such quickly descended into a comedy routine with each of the guys sending up the others. Unfortunately, much of the friendly banter is not suitable to print. But David Baine, the manager, told me about one of his team talks which got away from him.

As manager of a losing side, he felt that his team needed a few words of encouragement. In the dressing room after the game he gave them the benefit of his tactical experience. The team had played well below its potential and David was in full flow, pointing out their shortcomings. As he did so he started getting changed. Every time he wanted to make a point he would slam an article of clothing on to the floor. Before he knew it he was striding up and down the dressing room, still ranting but stark naked. I think the impact of his team talk may have been lost on his players who by this time didn't know where to look.

On another occasion, David was having a major seethe and was once again striding up and down the dressing room, at one point lashing out at a pair of discarded underpants, kicking them into the far corner of the room. Unfortunately that was where the physio was giving one of his players are much-needed massage. The airborne pants landed on the physio's head but to his credit, and the amusement of the rest of the team, he carried on with the task in hand. That must surely be above and beyond the call of duty.

I think the stories could have continued all afternoon but we had to leave the guys to get on with their work.

John: Craig and I made our way down the road, with the smell of the sea in our nostrils, and after asking a couple of locals, found the last bar in our quest, '*Cobbies Inn*'. I don't know if Cobbie was in, but it is a suberb bar and Donny, the very reserved barmaid was great company. We met up with a couple of locals, the Scottish Nationalist fanatic John Connor, and the more sensible Lynn, who was born in England but has lived here for over 30 years. Lynn seemed to have the more balanced and realistic views on the up-and-coming Independence referendum, but they were both excellent company.

John and Lynn

Craig: *Since we had a little time in hand I suggested to John that we should perhaps visit another nearby pub which I had found on my phone. He fancied the idea of the pub but didn't trust my ability to find it.*

Instead he chased after an unsuspecting local, demanding to know the way to the pub. I'm quite used to this kind of behaviour but God knows what strangers think when they are approached by a drink-crazed Glaswegian demanding to know where he could go to get even more annoying.

Using the poor bloke's directions we arrived at the pub a good five minutes later than we would have if my technophobic friend had just listened to me in the first place.

I really liked the pub and not just because they serve a good pint, although that never hurts does it? No this was a nice pub and had everything I like in a good boozer: good beer, barstools and friendly people who enjoy talking to newcomers.

As it turned out it was also where the Tayport players and officials retire to after the game. There was a buffet through in the lounge and it was apparently open to everyone who fancied a quick sausage roll and or a piece.

We chatted to a guy who was about our age and tried to steer the conversation towards football, but he was having none of that. Politics was first choice of topics and we could not persuade him otherwise. I've said it before probably several thousand times, and I will say it again, politics and religion are not fit topics for a public bar.

To cut a very long and loud story short we agreed to disagree and settled for just having a laugh. I have the vague feeling that all the laughing was somewhat enhanced by quite a few beers, as the journey home seemed to pass in a flash. One minute we were getting on to yet another potential death trap of a bus in Dundee, the next we were turning into the stance at Buchanan Bus Station in Glasgow.

John: I had booked us on the 6.05pm and the 7.05pm bus back to Glasgow, (that's yet another £1 I'll never see again). Thank goodness I did. By the time we left '*Cobbies*' and waited for the no. 42 to take us back over the Tay Bridge into Dundee, we had to rush to buy a couple of Fritter Rolls and a bag of chips to eat on the bus. Talk about fancy dining.

Thank goodness the bus, a big double decker again, was almost empty. We had a seat downstairs with a table between us and drove the man across the aisle mad with the smell of our chips.

Craig, to his credit, offered to give him one of his Rolls, the guy accepted. You could have knocked Craig down with a feather. Thank god he was sitting down. It was very good of him. I was starving and offered nothing.

By the time we were out of Dundee the rolls were finished and we both slept all the way to Glasgow. The best way to travel!

We had planned to go straight home, honest, but we just missed the EK train by two minutes and as we had almost half an hour to kill. It was over to '*Denholm's*' at the bottom of Hope Street for a swift one. There was Karaoke on and I've got to tell you, Glasgow has some great singers, but also some who should stay in the house.

We left the singers and went back up into Central Station and on to the EK train. As we sat there preparing to sleep, one of my son Alasdair's pals passed us and stopped to talk, 'give me a minute', he said. Away he went and came back a moment later with two cans of Stella. What are today's young people like? Great!!!

As far as money spent goes, it was a pretty average day and I was sober-ish when I got home. That's two weeks in a row. Just over £20 covered the day. Then again, a round in the Lochee Bar was just over £3.00. I'm not complaining.

Pubs and Clubs visited today;

Lochee United;
Lochee Uniteds hospitality bar is brilliant.
'The Whip', a great bar.
Tayport F.C.
Tayports wee bar upstairs looked great, no time to drink;
Tayport Arms is a good wee bar, worth a visit
Cobbies is another good wee bar, also worth a visit
No apologies for saying all the bars are great, they just are.

Lochee; **How to get there-free with the Bus pass**

M9; Glasgow to Dundee

Wee walk then No. 28 to the ground

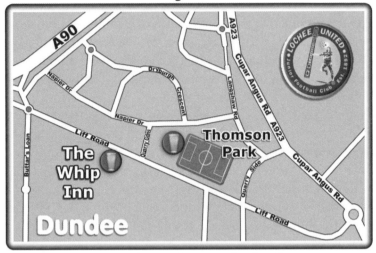

Tayport; **How to get there-free with the Bus pass**

M9; Glasgow to Dundee

No. 42 to the ground

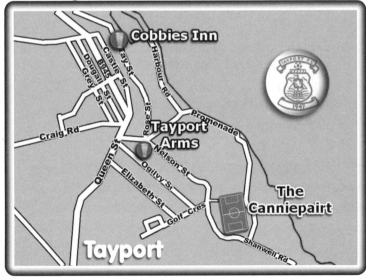

Dundonald Bluebell V Lochgelly Albert

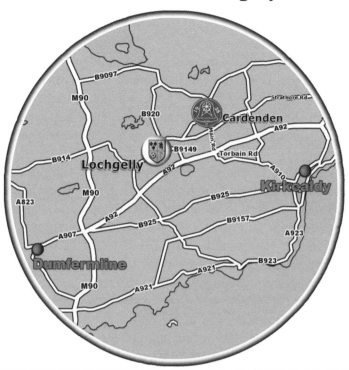

Club Name	Founded
Dundonald Bluebell	1938
Ground	**Colours**
Moorside Park	Royal Blue and Dark Blue
League (2014-15)	**Selection of Honours**
East Reg. Prem. League	East Reg. Cen. Div.
Club Nickname	Winners 2006-07
The Bluebells	

John: Today's adventure was to take us to the East of Scotland, between Dunfermline and Kirkcaldy. This is not an area where visitors from abroad, or Scotland for that matter flock, but it is one of my favourite places. As I always say, it is the people who make the place; I say that and a lot of other things not worth remembering, but I do like this part of Scotland.

Some of you will say this book is about pubs and Junior teams. It is, but I like to tell you all about the places we pass through. Who knows? We may never pass this way again. Makes you want to burst into song, or kill yourself, doesn't it?

Dunfermline and Kirkcaldy both have Waterstones stores so a quick phone call brought the good news that they wanted books, one five copies, the other ten. Not many, but it will cover today's bevy.

This meant that the planning of the buses was more complicated, and I'm the one that does it. However, with the help of the Traveline web site, and a few mistakes, I managed to complete the task. Kate told me that in the time I was on the computer doing the planning, we could have walked it. Didn't want to come back to her about women's map reading abilities, it's just not worth it, and you always lose, even though you're right.

Craig also put in his fetishes about not wanting to change buses out in the middle of nowhere. He also wanted us to split up in Dunfermline where he would deliver the books and I would continue on to deliver in Kirkcaldy, meeting up with him at the first ground, Dundonald. I was pretty sure this meant a lot more travel for me and more bevy time for him, but I agreed. Anything for a quiet life. It's like having another wife!

Another very early start today was called for. Thank goodness my 15 year old mobile phone alarm went off at the right time. Kate had set up her new all singing and dancing Apple thing. Cost a fortune. After she set the time it even told her it was set up and would go off no bother. It never told her not to switch the thing off! Early morning abuse is not worth the effort, anyway, I had to get up, shower, have breakfast and make my pieces, yes, corned beef and English mustard.

All that accomplished, I was out and knocking on Craig's door just before eight. I wanted to get the number six into town for a wee change. It's depressing getting the same no. 18 every Saturday morning and passing through the Commonwealth games sites and seeing the continuing camouflage attempts Glasgow Council are making to ensure the place look like an area you would want to visit. I'm sure it will be ok on the day.

So I talked Craig into the outlandish idea of crossing the Murray Road to try and get the six into Glasgow, remembering if an 18 turned up first we would have to dash (that's a laugh) back across the road. Craig and I definitely live on the edge.

Amazingly, the No. 6 arrived straight away and fairly shot into Glasgow in no time at all, or 50 minutes to be exact.

The only worrying moment on the bus was when a wee guy came on in Pollokshaws Road with an accordion and sat opposite us. Craig hates accordion music and once, in the past, was trapped by one for ages listening to Jimmy Shand. It has changed him. Luckily the wee guy was just on his way to his work in Buchanan Street entertaining the passing accordion music lovers.

We nipped into one of the many 'Local Sainsbury' stores to get a paper and a wee snack. The one we went into was at the bus station, but there are hundreds of them all over the city. It's funny how supermarkets managed to close all the corner shops by opening huge stores on the outskirts of towns and now that the wee shops are away the big supermarkets are opening up their own wee shops on the same sites. I wonder if it was all planned!

Our X24 Glasgow to St. Andrews bus left at 9.25 sharp and we had a nice run up to Dunfermline, passing Cumbernauld, and other nice places and lovely countryside before crossing the old Kincardine Bridge and 10 minutes or so later arriving at Dunfermline Bus Station.

Craig had decided to stay with me and not bugger off for extra bevy-I think he's getting old. So we went into the indoor shopping mall and found the Waterstones Store no problem. Apart from the girl trying to steal my pen, everything went smoothly and we were soon out and onto our next bus, the X26 which would drop us off at Kirkcaldy.

There was a wee man sitting behind the driver who talked non-stop to him. He told the driver and half the bus his life story, how he never smoked or drank but was still wee, but his grandfather drank like a fish and was seven feet two. It went on like this until, sadly, he got off in Auchtertool or some wee town with a great name. If that wasn't enough excitement for one trip, five minutes later, out in the country, the bus came to a sudden stop, the driver got up and announced that he had just knocked down a pheasant. I thought he said a peasant. Mind you, he probably wouldn't have stopped for a peasant.

He got off and looked under the bus. 'I'm afraid it's dead' he said. He was quite upset. 'Who gives a toss?', Craig said, 'we've books to deliver'. I don't think Craig meant the driver to hear him, but he did. It's not PC to slag off dead birds nowadays. As we got off the bus in Kirkcaldy, we thanked the driver. Craig stopped me from asking him if he wanted us to put a hat round for the pheasant.

Books delivered, we had about 25 minutes to kill before our next bus, so we decided it was enough time for our first quick one of the day. Dash me if we couldn't find a pub on our way back to the bus station. It was pub-type streets, so we were a bit surprised. Probably it was no bad thing for us to stay dry for a bit longer.

We were still early for our next bus, the 33, when we arrived at the bus station, but there was a 34 at the next stance, and, after I had checked the bus information board at the stance, I found that we could get this bus. That was five minutes wasted as the driver then decided the bus was broken. Not to worry, the 33 arrived and after a detour for roadworks, dropped us off just outside the ground in a wee town called Cardenden.

Craig: When John first proposed a visit to Dundonald I thought he had lost what little is left of his mind. What I didn't realise was there is more than one Dundonald in Scotland. The only one I had ever heard of was in Ayrshire. It's a nice place to visit, and even has its own castle. The one thing it doesn't have is a junior football team. Given that this is what we are supposed to be writing about you can see why I thought he had finally cracked under the pressure. Once he explained that we would actually be going to the village of Cardenden in Fife, although still confused, I agreed to join him on the journey. As it turned out, we needed to deliver books to Dumfermline and Kirkcaldy anyway, so we could combine both tasks.

We did manage to get ourselves into a right fankle trying to arrange buses to all the places we had to visit. By the time John had finished printing out the various timetables he couldn't make head nor tail of them at all. In the end we chose the simplest option and headed for Dunfermline. All the buses worked for us up until we were about to leave Kirkcaldy. As he waited in the queue a fellow passenger told us that there were road-works en-route and the bus would have to follow diversions. Since we only had a vague idea where Cardenden was, this was not welcome news.

Just to check our progress I kept an eye on the satnav on my phone. That seemed like a good idea but to be honest it only confused me. We shot past the cut-off to Cardenden and headed for Lochgelly before turning away towards the wide open spaces.

John: It was just about 12.30pm, so we had plenty of time before meeting the Secretary at the ground. As luck would have it, there was a pub across the road from the stop, '*The Village Inn*'. Craig had seen it on his Google Street View, and here it was, so in we went.

Gordon Cuthbert, Gordon Quin, Brian Shields and Willie Webster

Right away we knew it was a great pub. An old-fashioned bar, oxter height, with old-fashioned customers, about half a dozen

107

of them who were obviously Dundonald Bluebell supporters. The barmaid, the lovely Maureen Milne, or Mo, introduced us to the bevy merchants. They took us into their company right away, and what a crazy bunch of guys they were. I think you must be crazy to be a Junior fan. They introduced themselves. If I remember rightly they were Gordon Cuthbert, Gordon Quinn, Brian Shields, Willie Webster and Eddie Tinney.

I think it was Willie, nicknamed the Splinter, because he gets under your skin, who filled us in on the geography of the village. Although it's a fairly small place, it has four distinct areas. I can't remember the other three, but we were in Auchdendern, the best one. These areas have their own clubs and the boys are members of the Auchdendern Rambling Society, or Ars's, as they're called. I think there's more going on here than in the West End of London.

The owner Roy Haxden came in and introduced himself. His daughter and his granddaughter came in as well so he was on his best behaviour.

Roy Haxden and Maureen Milne

Craig: eventually we arrived in the place. It's not a big town so we got our bearings quickly and headed to the Village Inn. As soon as we got into the bar I knew that we had found another good pub. You would never call it fancy but we felt right at home in there.

The bar itself reminded me of what pubs looked like when I was just a boy starting out on my pint-drinking career. The bar was oxter-high and just right for leaning on. The addition of a foot-rail would have made it just perfect. Almost immediately we got into conversation with a group of supporters. Gordon Cuthbert told me that the Village Inn used to be a Gothenberg pub. Up until very recently I would have made an arse of myself by asking how come some Swedish brewery was opening pubs in Scotland. Fortunately I had found out that these pubs were built to benefit the mining community. They were non-profit making businesses run by the miners. It was a very good system that regulated the consumption of alcohol.

That is to say everybody knew what their neighbour was getting up to down the boozer. Apparently there were three such pubs in the town at one time. All of them have since become private concerns. The lads told us that each area in the town, (he named them but I have since forgotten) had a very separate identity.

It seems that people who lived only a few streets apart would be considered outsiders depending on territorial lines. Times have changed, but apparently there is still an element of this rivalry going on.

One of the boys told us his nickname was Splinter and, when we asked him why he said it was because he gets under every one's skin. The conversation got round to a very thorny subject which is of great concern to us all: pub closures.

On our travels we have seen far too many pubs boarded up with 'for sale' signs posted over the bar name. The very thought of it sends a shiver down my spine. When I asked how the Village Inn was managing, Splinter told me that things are a lot quieter than they used to be. But between them the guys are trying their best to help. Being fans of the Bluebells they also feel obliged to keep the social club down at the park going. So they divide their time between them both. These guys are selfless!

John: All the guys were going over to the park for a refreshment before the game, so we said our temporary goodbyes and went on the two minute walk to the park. Once inside the bar, we met up with Andrew (Mr. Bluebell) Davidson and Allan Halliday, the two secretaries of the club. They were great guys and filled us in on details of the club, told some stories and introduced us to the locals.

Andrew and Allan

I could spend all day talking about the people and the stories they told, but I will let you off with one. I was introduced to The Bluebell's oldest supporter John (Jock) Bradford who, at 79, can still recall stories from the time that, at six years old he was the mascot for the club.

I was telling him about some of the slopes and dips we had seen at some of the previous clubs we had visited caused by old mine workings and the like. 'Slopes', said Jock, 'there was a club called Steelend Vics, who closed down a couple of seasons back who had such a fierce slope on the park that if you were at one end of the park you could just see the players at the other end from the waist up'. What a great bloke and a loyal supporter. His friend told me that Jock had just donated £100 to the club to help with the improvement of the playing surface next season.

Another interesting fact I discovered is that Snuff, or 'Cardenden Coke' as it is called, is seemingly still popular in ex mining communities and Willie, the Splinter, insisted I try some. It looked like ground up brown stuff, but I gave it a try. I'll tell you this, it clears out your nostrils better than a wet hankie. So the splinter not only gets under your skin, but up your nose as well.

As normally happens, we were having a grand time, but had to move on to the next club, so we said our farewells, promising to return, which I hope we will.

Dundonald is a great club, so I'm not going to slag off its nickname, 'The Bluebells', although the 'Den Dens' might be worth a shout.

Craig: Down at the social club we met up with Splinter again. He had moved down there 10 minutes before us. It is a very nice club with a fairly large lounge and a quiet bar area. I was very impressed.

Through in a bar someone gave us a quick history of the club. Apparently the local council had given the football team an old caravan to use at the park. Eventually, some enterprising lads started selling booze out of the back of the caravan. This proved so popular that the committee decided to expand the venture. Unfortunately they didn't have much money to spend on building a brand new bar, so it was decided that it would be done in instalments.

When I said we need to think bigger this is not what I meant!

To start with they put up four walls around the caravan. After that it took a while before they could get enough money together to put a roof over it. Eventually that was accomplished and all that was left to do was to dismantle the caravan, which was still inside. I just wished they had taken a few pictures of that operation.

That was a few years back and the club is well established now and serves a really decent pint of beer. So much so we stayed around for two or three. Just to be sociable you understand.

While we were chatting away to some of the supporters I mentioned that we would be visiting Lochgelly later that day. This really got them going.

After a fair bit of sniggering one of them said that we really had to visit The Old Ship Inn as soon as we got off the bus. This idea seemed to be a very popular one as everybody at the bar started roaring their approval. Call me paranoid if you like, but this seemed a wee bit suspicious to me. So I asked what in particular we should be looking out for in this pub. After even more laughter they said we should check out the toilets of The Ship as they are uniquely manky, possibly the worst in the developed world. We took this as a challenge as believe you me, on our travels we have seen some stoaters.

We managed to miss the bus to Lochgelly but, as ever, John had a Plan B. We sauntered back into the Village Inn for a pint and a chat to the barmaid, Maureen Milne. Eventually the beer was finished and the bus was stopped and we were on our way to see Lochgelly Albert.

Lochgelly Albert

Club Name	Founded
Lochgelly Albert	1926
Ground	*Colours*
Gardiners Park	Black and Gold
League (2014-15)	*Selection of Honours*
East Region South Div.	Fife Cup 1934-35
Club Nickname	
The Berts	

John: After a 10 minute wait, our next bus, the 33 arrived. We asked the driver where we would get off to get to Lochgelly's Park. 'Just get off when I get off' he said. We assumed this was the terminus and it was next to the park. Ten minutes later we were off the bus and lost. How you can get lost in Lochgelly? I have no idea.

After wandering about for a few minutes we asked a local where the park was and five minutes later we were outside the nearest pub to the ground. It was called *'The Old Ship Inn'*, and we had been told by the Dundonald supporters it was worth a visit, if only to see the toilets.

I'll let Craig describe the toilet, but the bar itself was great and the barman Rab Robertson and a couple of regulars, Roger Murphy and Don Robertson (no relation), were good company. This was another 'man's' bar and is popular with locals and visiting support alike, if only for their toilet.

Leaving *'The Old Ship'* behind, we floated up the road and into Gardiners Park, home of Lochgelly Albert, nicknamed 'The Berts'. I like it.

Craig: *Our friendly bus driver told us that he would ending his shift when we got to Lochgelly, and that we should get off the bus along with him as the football park was close to the bus stop. That sounded good to me as John's homemade maps looked a wee bit ropey.*

Unfortunately something must have been lost in translation. As soon we got off the bus the driver disappeared, leaving us with far too many directions to choose from. It will surprise no one to learn that we chose the wrong one. After about twenty minutes wandering around the streets we stumbled into The Old Ship Inn.

Rab, Roger and Don

I had been expecting the worst. After all the patter we had been given by the boys up in Cardenden, I had assumed that we would be stepping into a right midden, But I was wrong. It is really quite a nice place, with everything the drinking man needs to enjoy the perfect day out. Namely, cold beer and a friendly barman.

That being said, I couldn't wait to have a look at the famous toilets. Actually after all the socialising we had been doing so far that day I needed a visit to the facilities no matter their condition.

You could say that what I saw fair took my breath away. It's just a pity that my sense of smell hadn't been taken as well.

Once the word gets out about this place they will be laying on bus trips just to see it. Words cannot describe the atmosphere in there; they certainly cannot convey the stench. To be honest it looks like the set from one of those old Hammer House of Horror films, one of the really low-budget ones. It looked to me as if the urinal area had been carved out of solid rock by someone using a blunt spoon.

The toilet door had obviously been rescued from a skip. While it did fit across the door frame it was about a foot and a half short. One thing is for sure, nobody will be hanging around the toilets instead of standing in the bar spending money. The length of your visit will be governed by how long you can hold your breath.

I had never been to Lochgelly. In fact I'm not entirely sure that I had ever heard of the place before. But like many men of my age Lochgelly had left its mark on me. When I was a young schoolboy there was the odd occasion when some particularly evil teacher would decide that I needed a little encouragement to behave. The standard technique back then was to thrash obedience into children using a large leather belt. At no time on those occasions when I was being legally assaulted did I ever stop to wonder where the instrument of my torture was made.

According to Don, our barman, school belts, or the tawse, are still manufactured in Lochgelly to this day. Though none of us could imagine where the market for these horrible things would be anymore.

A customer, who shall remain nameless to avoid being barred, told us one of his favourite stories about The Old Ship Inn. Apparently a large articulated lorry lost control at the top of the hill and smashed into the pub causing about 50p worth of damage.

We enjoyed our visit to The Ship, especially the patter of the guys in the bar. The beer was good and reasonably priced. In fact there were only two things which stopped us from having another couple of beers. For one thing we had made arrangements to meet Lochgelly Albert's club secretary, James Brown, round at Gardiners Park.

The other reason we felt we really had to move on was neither of us fancied a return visit to The Ship's cludgie.

John: The final whistle had just gone, and the 'Grand National' race had just started, so all the players were in the bar in their strips watching the race-no idea who won. The place soon settled down and we met the Secretary James Brown, what a great name, and Jock Kinnell, the Chairman.

James, Graeme, Alex and Jock

Like all people in their position, they spend their lives working tirelessly for the club. They are also excellent company and gave us all the information we needed about their club. The chairman insisted on buying us a round and inviting us down to the pub they frequent after the game for more drink and a bite to eat from the buffet. The owner lays it on for supporters after the game, free of charge. So after a chat with the supporters it was down to the main street and into '*The Minto Bar*'. This is a lovely bar, Mel and Raymond were great hosts and as well as being treated to drink, soup and food were laid out for you to help yourselves. We were having a fantastic time and my memory of the details are not as clear as they should be. It's my age. But we had a great time and all too soon we were saying goodbye to the company and getting on the number 19 bus to take us to Dunfermline Bus Station.

Craig: It was full-time when we got to the ground, so we made our way straight to the small club there. The committee men we met inside were in good form and definitely up for a laugh.

James suggested that we might like to meet up with the rest of the committee and players round at The Minto Bar where there would a post-match tea laid on. The only drawback to this plan was of course our inability to follow directions. After yet again wandering around Lochgelly for what seemed like ages we found

116

the pub. God knows what the good folk of the town must think of us. Two old guys shuffling round the town all day arguing, pointing, usually in opposite directions, and pestering the general public.

In the pub there was soup, sandwiches and sausage rolls on offer. John was in heaven. Mel and Raymond Wilson serve up the food after every away game and have done so for years. We took it upon ourselves to make sure that there was no food left to go to waste and knocked back a few pints, just to be sociable.

As we were about to leave, James insisted on buying us yet another drink. John saw this as a challenge and even more booze was consumed.

A few months after our visit to The Old Ship Inn, we received an e-mail from Jane Paxton, the daughter of the pub's owner.

Apparently our presence on the premises had been noticed. It appears that the gent's toilet has now been given a total make-over and is no longer the midden it once was.

Personally that news made me a bit sad and ever so slightly nostalgic. I suppose now I'll have to cancel my plans for guided bus tours of infamous Scottish cludgies.

Mel and Raymond Wilson

John: A quick visit to the facilities and we were sound asleep on the bus back to Glasgow. Our new sensible attitude to excessive drinking, a bit late today I hear you say, meant we went straight back to Glasgow Central, passing *'The Horseshoe'*, (no mean feat,) and getting the first train back to EK.

At the ticket office in the Central Station there was a huge queue of people waiting for a ticket and only one girl serving, and as you cannot get through the new barriers without one, you have to get a ticket. I had to wait for ages and ended up running up to the platform, passing about ten employees who help you through the barriers which don't work. There is a better way, but it is too obvious to insult our readers with. Irene picked us up at EK, amazed at our sober state. Hope she doesn't think this will be the norm. It won't!

So ended a great day out, the kitty of £20 each almost covered the day, but again the drink we bought was very reasonable, and a lot was free. What a day!

I would advise all readers, especially the ones with a bus pass, to follow our routes and bars. You will have a great day out and it won't cost you a penny, unless you drink, which you don't need to!

Pubs and clubs visited today;

Dundonald Bluebell
'The Village Inn'
The Bar at the Ground

Lochgelly Albert
'The Old Ship Inn'
'Minto Bar'
The Bar at the Ground
All the above hostelries are great and worth a visit.

Dundonald; How to get there-free with bus Pass
X24 Glasgow to Dunfermline
No. 33 Dunfermline to Cardenden

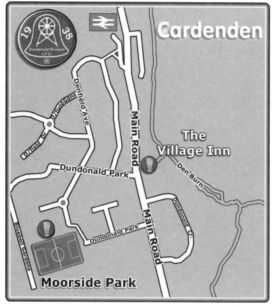

Lochgelly; How to get there-free with Bus pass
X24 Glasgow to Dunfermline
No. 19 Dunfermline to Lochgelly

Kilsyth Rangers V Kirkintilloch Rob Roy

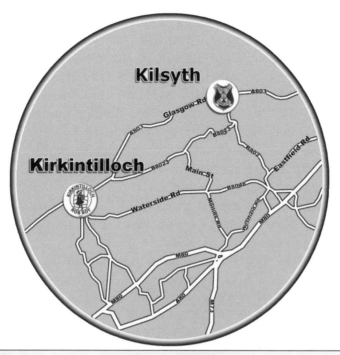

Club Name	Founded
Kilsyth Rangers	1913
Ground	*Colours*
Duncansfield Park	Royal Blue
League (2014-15)	*Selection of Honours*
	Scot. Jun. Cup; 1954-55; 1996-
West Super League-!st Div.	97
Club Nickname	Runners-up once
The Wee Rangers	

John: Today we are off to the North of Glasgow. The two clubs we are visiting are close rivals, both grounds being linked by Glasgow Road. Although the two teams are in different leagues this season, rivalries go deeper than just what division you are in.

We hoped to get some stories to highlight the rivalry during today's visit.

After a couple of weeks of very early starts visiting teams in the East, today's trip was a dawdle. I worked out that I would not have to collect Craig till about 10.30am. So it was then that I knocked his door. As usual he was ready and fully pieced-up with chocolate biscuits on the side.

The old No. 18 took us the familiar journey through Rutherglen, then past the work going on to get Glasgow ready for the Commonwealth games this summer, past the Barras, where we noticed that although it was now after eleven, 'Danny's' Do-Nuts was still closed. Danny's would make a fortune if they put about four do-nuts in bags and got someone to get on the passing buses for one stop to sell them to the passengers. They would have sold a couple of bags on our bus right away!

Anyway, that idea will have to be put on the back burner for another time, although I believe there is a 'hole in the market' for increased Do-Nut sales.

In no time at all we were off the bus and walking up Buchanan Street to the Bus Station. I knew there were a couple of buses that went regularly to Kilsyth, our first port of call, and sure enough, we only had to wait about ten minutes for our No. 89.

The bus was one of these low single deckers where the seats have absolutely no padding. Not only that, but there seems to be a metal spar right across the seat where your backbone rests. I hope that's the correct medical jargon.

The sun was out as we made our way up past Springburn, Bishopbriggs and Torrance before passing today's second port of call, Kirkintilloch. As I've said before, get the longest journey out of the way while the bladder is empty. Lenzie was only another ten minutes and, as we alighted from (got off) our bus. The sun was shining, although it was blowing a gale, and freezing.

Craig: As the weeks go on I have noticed that John is producing more and more paperwork for our day trips. Once upon a time we just hopped aboard the first bus to come along and that was us off on another adventure. Not anymore. He really should have a briefcase to carry all his official looking documents around with him instead of his old rucksack. The day he tries to get me to sign a health and safety form will be the day we start flying solo. As it is he spends most of his time on the bus going over those precious home-made maps and timetables. I shouldn't really complain though, when you consider that without this essential work I will be reduced to talking to him.

On the bus up to Kilsyth he was once again furiously searching through his collection of maps when I noticed that the bus we were travelling on had one of those digital display units up near the front. I was fairly sure John hadn't seen it so I thought I might as well have a bit of fun.

Every time the display changed after stopping to let someone off I would look out the window then tell John where I reckoned we were. I would announce that I thought such and such a street was just around the next corner and he would start shuffling through his maps faster and faster trying to check if I was right. Before he did himself any permanent mental damage I admitted what I was up to.

John: We had time to visit one pub before heading for the ground, but the one Craig had seen on 'Street View', wiz'nae there. After wandering about for five minutes, we found 'The Coachman' and in we went. We had no idea what this place was set up for, but it wasn't for blokes like us just in for a pint. It looked as if there was a wedding party at one table. There was a bar and a couple of people behind it, but they ignored us so we just turned round and left. They didn't look like the sort of people who will read this book, so they will never know what they missed.

Outside, we saw that next door, but attached to 'The Coachman' was a pub called 'The Campsie'. Craig and I don't hold grudges, well I don't, so in we went. To be fair, this was more like a pub, so we had a quick one. Nobody seemed interested in talking to us so we drank up and left. I can only imagine that somewhere in Kilsyth there is the sort of pub we like, but time was marching on and we didn't have the time to find one.

Craig: *We didn't have a lot of time to spare in Kilsyth so I'm afraid our search for a decent boozer was a bit half-hearted. When we couldn't find a particular pub I had seen on my computer, The Scarecrow, we gave up and headed for The Coachman instead. And what a total waste of time that was.*

It was a very modern building inside and out and suggested to me that it had been designed with an English clientele in mind. So, as you can imagine, we thought it was crap.

That about sums up the service in this place as well. We counted four staff behind the bar and none of them seemed to be doing anything pub-related. Our entrance didn't increase their work load one little bit as they remained standing exactly where they were, even though they had clearly seen us.

I suppose you could say that things turned out well for all of us. They didn't have to do a hands turn and we didn't have to give the lazy buggers any of our cash.

As we marched out of the Coachman, in a state of justified annoyance, we noticed that there was actually a pub attached to the side of the building. The Campsie Bar looked a bit more like a pub, but only marginally.

I didn't really enjoy my pint very much; maybe it was just an off day but I thought I could taste something other than Tennent's Lager in my glass. On the upside at least we know they use good quality washing up liquid in the pub dishwasher.

As ever, we were keen to talk to fans of the local team, therefore we asked our young barman for directions to the park but he said he didn't know where it was. Quick as a flash John concluded that the boy probably wasn't a fan.

John: Following the map I had printed out we were soon at the ground of Kilsyth Rangers, the 'the Wee Gers'. I might as well get today's rant out of the way right now. 'The Wee Gers', and for that matter, Kirkintilloch Rob Roy's 'The Rabs' or 'The Roy' are both examples of just not trying. For two of Scotland's most famous junior clubs, they deserve better.

Kilsyth's 'The Wee Rangers', I don't think so. How about 'The Sythers', this not only has part of the team name, but it describes the tackles put in by at least one of their former great players. I won't mention names, but Johnny Glover, you know who I'm talking about. He actually told me about a famous 'Syth' he made which flattened a linesman who made a questionable decision against him. But I'll keep that to myself.

'The Rabs' or 'The Roy' are equally as bad. 'The Red Roys' has a better ring to it. If you can come up with a better one, write your suggestions on the back of a fiver.

Kilsyth's ground is a really nice set up and we soon found the wee hospitality house where the Secretary, Russell McKay, warmly welcomed us and introduced us to the men who help keep the club to the fore. To give you an idea of the years of service Russell has put in at Kilsyth, he used to be a ball boy. I managed to tell him that I was a ball boy for Partick Thistle before Craig shut me up. He's fed up listening to that story.

Stewart Dunbar, John Nelson, Johnny Glover, Russell McKay, Walter Hamilton, John Fergusson.

Stewart Dunbar, John Nelson, Johnny Glover, ex. star player and syther, Walter Hamilton (a past president) and John Ferguson, who has written a great book about the history of Kilsyth Rangers, were just some of the guys I remember talking to.

Another unsung hero they told me about was their groundsman, Bill Fletcher, who at over 70 years is still looking after the excellent playing surface and is at the park at seven in the morning on match days to get everything ready. This is all the more amazing when you realize that the playing surface was built on top of a rubbish bing!

When all these guys are gone, and I hope it's a while yet, I wonder if the next generation will have the same dedication. Unfortunately, I'm pretty sure I know the answer to that one.

As usual, Craig had his tape recorder with him and I know he will regale you with some of the stories the guys told us.

As is normally the case, we were really sorry to have to leave this great company, but the book won't write itself. Mind you, if it could, it would make a better job than the rubbish I write.

Craig: We found the park ourselves, using only John's dodgy maps. I took a few minutes to check out the place. It was a nice looking wee ground and the pitch looked in really good order. While I was casting my professional eye over the playing area John had spotted the small social club.

It is situated opposite the half way line on the right hand side, and that's exactly where we headed next. It's a very compact little bar; but all the better for that. Only open on match days, it is the perfect place to soak up the atmosphere of the junior game. It also helps when you can meet such a variety of characters, all of them dedicated Kilsyth fans. Straight away we were invited into their company.

I had just mentioned that we had been on a visit to McKenna Park to see St Anthony's when one of committee, I think it might have been Walter Hamilton, came up with this story. Many years ago they had been at the Ant's ground with Kilsyth. On that occasion he had brought his daughter along with him. It seems that the young girl was suddenly in need of a visit to the toilet. Naturally Walter asked the main man, Felix McKenna, where he could find one. With a twinkle in his eye Felix pointed in the direction of the nearest toilet. Seconds after entering it she came flying out screaming hysterically. It would seem that the convenience was anything but convenient. It was in fact a hole in the ground over which the user is required to squat.

Russell McKay the Kilsyth secretary told us a story about one of his team's best players, Johnny Glover. It would seem that after a great career on the field Johnny became the team coach. During a game against Hurlford he got a bit upset with his opposite number Ross Findlay.

Johnny shouted at him to get back into his dugout and sit down. There followed a short discussion on each man's footballing credentials, ending with Johnny demanding to know how many Scottish Cup medals Findlay had to his name. Obviously Johnny was rightly proud of the three he had won in his long career.

Unfortunately for Johnny, Ross Findlay was a leading light in Auchinleck Talbot's record breaking-breaking Scottish cup team and answered his question with a single word: five. Johnny decided it was high time that he returned to his own bench and kept quiet for a while.

We were still laughing when Johnny himself came over to talk to us. After a bit of banter he told us about another of his escapades. Back in the days when linesmen were not the neutral professionals we admire so much nowadays Johnny got into a bit of a stramash with one of them.

Every time Johnny got the ball this guy would start shouting, swearing and encouraging his team's players to put the boot in. Having heard as much as he was prepared to take Johnny kicked the ball along the line just past the official. Pretending to go for the ball he 'accidentally' clattered into the man, sending him flying. Making a big show of helping him to his feet he told the offending linesman in a quiet voice that he would be getting the same again or worse if he didn't stop his nonsense.

The drink was flowing and the patter was really great. So much so that nobody had noticed that the game had actually kicked off. We could quite easily have stayed but we had places to go and people to meet and of course the odd beer to knock back.

As we made our way out of the wee club I stopped to shake hands with one of the committee men at the top of the stairs. As a joke I said, "I'll give the lads over at Kirkintilloch your best wishes". He surprised me by saying he would be grateful if I *would. It seems that Kirkintilloch Rob Roy were playing their last ever home game at Adamslie Park and this bloke thought it would be fitting if they could finish up with a win. So much for bitter rivals then!*

Kirkintilloch Rob Roy

Club Name	Founded
Kirkintilloch Rob Roy	1878
Ground	*Colours*
Guys Meadow	Red and Black Hoops
League (2014-15)	*Selection of Honours*
	Scot. Jun. Cup 1920-21; 1942-
West Super League-1st Div.	43
Club Nickname	1961-62 Runner up five times
The Red Roys	

John: Our bus, another No. 89, turned up right away and 15 minutes later we were on the main street in Kirkintilloch. We had the time, and as usual the inclination, to do more research, so we quickly found a bar we had seen on our way through the town to Kilsyth.

'The Buzz Bar' was our first port of call in Kirkintilloch. This was more like the bars Craig and I like, just a down-to-earth bar with no fancies, if you know what I mean. The barman, who I think was the owner, was not a local. He was an Iranian guy. I wanted to find out how he ended up in Kirkintilloch, but the time got away from me and I forgot to ask.

I remember asking the bloke next to me at the bar, Scott McLuckie, if he was a supporter. Right away he whipped out his season ticket. His brother had won two season tickets in a raffle. Scott did say that he went to some matches. Considering today was Kirkintilloch Rob Roy's last ever match at the legendary 'Adamslie Park' and he was standing in *'The Buzz Bar'*, I doubt he was their most loyal fan. He was great company mind you, and we enjoyed our stay.

Craig was in one of his 'we must visit as many bars as possible' moods, so we left and walked up the road and into *'Bar Bliss'*. I thought that this was strange name for a bar, as was *'The Buzz Bar'* for that matter. Maybe Kirkintilloch people go in for weird names. However, the guys we met in the bars were brilliant and the *'Bliss'* was no exception.

We met an old fellow called Roddie McLean (probably younger than me) who told us that he had been a brick layer all his life and had travelled all over Europe laying brick. (grammar note; the plural of brick is brick). He told us he helped re-brick parts of Germany, which he found funny as his old man had been a bomber pilot during the war. You meet great guys in pubs; you just have to talk to them.

John and Roddie

Craig: The Bus trip to Kirkintilloch only takes a few minutes, just long enough to eat two roast beef sandwiches in fact. Before we got off the bus I decided to ask the driver if he could point us in the direction of a pub I had found out about. Actually I had checked it out on my computer and I was just about to find out that sometimes these dammed machines can't be trusted. The driver did

129

a bit of head scratching before announcing that he had never heard of Flannigan's.

Luckily for me one of the passengers had been eavesdropping and had heard of it but said it had changed its name to The Buzz Bar. He gave us clear directions, without even once glancing at a map, and we found it within a couple of minutes. It is on the High Street and it is a fairly big affair. It was also fairly empty.

On hearing that the barman/owner was Iranian we decided not to bother him with too many questions about Kirkintilloch Rob Roy's history. It did sort of explain why the place was no longer pretending to be an Irish pub.

There were two other guys in the bar. They didn't look like junior supporters either, but we had to ask. Sometimes I find that even I can get things wrong and this seemed to be one of those rare times. It turns out that one of the guys was actually a season ticket holder. *I was about to admit that I had got the wrong first impression when the bloke admitted that he had actually won it in a raffle. For me that went a long way towards explaining why he was sitting at a bar instead of making his way along the road to the football park. Or it did until I realised that there wasn't a social club at Adamslie Park.*

With a wee bit time on our hands we decided to cram in one more bar visit before going down to the park. Bar Bliss just does not sound like the kind of place you would expect to find either me or John, well certainly not me anyway.

It was a fairly nice bar as it turned out, in a modern sort of way. The clientele was quite mixed with both older and very young people enjoying a drink. In fact it was so busy we couldn't even get an elbow on to the bar. While I was complaining about this we got into conversation with Roddy McLean who told us a few stories about the trials and tribulations of being a Rab's supporter.

Somehow, however, the conversation got round to foreign travel. Apparently Roddy was a brickie and had plied his trade in Germany for a few years. He found this a bit ironic as his old man had spent a fair amount of time and energy reducing Germany's housing stock to rubble with thousand pound bombs from his Lancaster.

John asked Roddy if he'd told many Germans about his dad's demolition exploits during the war, but he said that it never seemed to come up in conversation.

John: It was still a good wee walk to the ground, so we got another 89 right to it. We were early and there was still about 10 minutes of the game to go, so we sneaked in and watched as tragically, 'The Red Roys' lost a last minute goal to lose their last game at the park. It might also mean they are relegated. Craig and I are 'Jonahs'.

Even in such tragic circumstances, the Secretary Charles O'Brien welcomed us warmly and introduced us to Davy Smith, Gerry Allen and Jim Robertson, men who are used to the highs and, in this case, the lows of running Junior Clubs. I have great admiration for these guys and hope 'the Red Roys' stay up.

We had a nice time, and when we left, they told us to wander round to a wee red portacabin that doubled up as a bar where they said some real characters would be having a wee refreshment and that we would be welcomed and would be treated to a small refreshment. Junior football people are the salt of the earth.

Ian Muir, Danny Livingston, Douglas McNicol, Charlie Letham

In we went and found a motley crew, or men like us, who made us welcome. Ian Muir (on the bar), Danny Livingston, Douglas McNicol and Charlie Letham gave us the history of the club and some of the famous players, like George Young, who played for the club. Craig will tell you the true story of how Rangers signed him. It's worth hearing.

I find it sad that none of the players stick their heads in to talk to these guys after the match. They should. They might learn something. But enough of me going on about the younger generation, it was time to leave as the place was closing for the last time. What a sad day. I felt part of history as I walked, slightly unsteadily, out of Adamslie Park for the last time.

Craig: In the clubhouse we met Chris O'Brien, the secretary, and despite the last-minute defeat he was happy to speak to us. One of the stories we heard concerned a little bit of a transport difficulty.

It seems Rob Roy had an evening game against Lesmahagow. On their way to the match the team bus broke down on the M74. Apparently it was not possible to find another bus in time to make it to the game. That's why the whole team arrived at their destination on the back of a coal lorry. Despite having to spend an hour sitting on top of a couple of tons of nutty slack the Rabs were still fired up enough to win the game 2-1.

Davy Smith, Gerry Allen, Jim Robertson, Chris O'Brien

Through in the committee bar we met up with a gang of Rob Roy stalwarts, or auld yins as they might describe themselves. Among the many stories we heard from them was one about a little bit of financial sleight of hand.

George Young, the famous Rangers player, had been playing for Rob Roy but was still an amateur at the time. Rangers started showing an interest in him but somehow the committee got wind of their intention to sign George and took decisive action. While he was changing for the match, a couple of the committee persuaded George to put his name on some paper work. According to our informant George was 'just a daft boy at the time and didnae have a clue what he was signing'. By nipping in just before Rangers, Rob Roy got a substantial transfer fee for their newly registered player.

There were many more tales told in the wee bar, but unfortunately John was in charge of note-taking and by this time he was getting a bit tired and emotional. Suffice it to say we enjoyed our stay there.

The journey home was uneventful and too short to get any serious sleeping done so we topped up our tanks in Denholm's back in Glasgow before heading for home.

John: Our fourth time on a No. 89 brought us back to Buchanan Street. We were earlier than expected, expected by the wives that is, so we had time for a couple in *'Denholms'*, a great bar at the bottom of Hope Street, before getting the train back to EK. Craig's Irene collected us at the station. I've said it before, but the only reason she does this is so Craig will go home, if not he would be out all night, what a man!

Our kitty of £20 each covered the day. It's not a lot to spend on drink at today's prices. Luckily for us, the hospitality at both clubs was brilliant, and much appreciated.

Pubs and Clubs visited today

Kilsyth
The Coachman-ok for weddings
The Campsie-better, but not great

Kirkintilloch
The Buzz
Bar Bliss
Don't be put off by their weird names, both great bars.

Kilsyth or Kirkintilloch; how to get there-free with the Bus Pass

No. 89 or 27 will fit the bill to both grounds

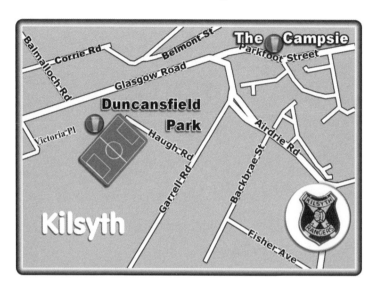

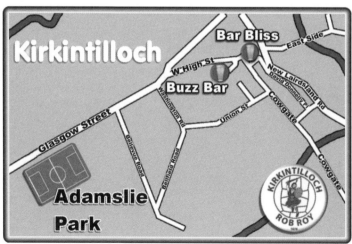

East Kilbride Thistle

Club Name	Founded
East Kilbride Thistls	1968
Ground	*Colours*
The Showpark	Black and White Stripes
League (2014-15)	*Selection of Honours*
Cen. League; 2nd Div.	Scot. Jun. Cup 1982-83
Club Nickname	West of Scot Cup 1973-74
The Jags	

John: Our home club EK Thistle, *'The Jags'*. I'm not going to say anything bad about their nickname. They have enough problems at the moment sitting at the bottom of the lowest league without me slagging off their nickname. I hope by the time you are reading this they have returned to the time of their former glories of the 70s and 80s when, among other honours, they won the Scottish Junior Cup, the trophy that all Junior clubs want to lift, even more so than winning the league.

I don't think East Kilbride is a natural football supporting town. It was Scotland's first 'new town', and was built onto the village, the first schemes appearing around 1947.

For all the bad publicity it gets for its hundreds of roundabouts, it was, and still is, a great place to bring up a family. We still live in the same house we bought in 1972.

Like everywhere else in the UK, the last few years has seen a decline in the money being spent keeping the place ship shape. I think it is a shame that the local council can't employ more people to look after the town. The wages would not be any more than is given out in social security. I imagine there must be a reason, but I don't know what it is.

Anyway, back to today's visit. I had another fear which materialized when I phoned the secretary Martin Sutherland. When I asked him about local rivals, he said that apart from the teams geographically closest to East Kilbride, there are no clubs that really hate, or even don't like East Kilbride a wee bit.

Unlike teams from other places in Scotland where hating your neighbours is a way of life, and Craig, I don't just mean Auchinleck, East Kilbride is more of a 'going shopping on a Saturday with the wife' sort of a place. East Kilbride had 'modern man' long before it became fashionable.

Because nobody hates us, it doesn't mean we should ignore one of Scotland's greatest Junior teams, and our own local club to boot. So we decided it was important to check out the 'Jags'.

For us it was just a walk down the hill, through the town centre and into the village where the Showpark is situated.

But this was not enough for Craig. He wanted to give today's trip a feel of authenticity, so he insisted we get the bus down to the bus station, one stop away! What a man. He's just a lazy B! Any one of at least four buses would fit the bill.

So I collected him at noon and we waited all of two minutes until a bus, the old No. 6, arrived and gave us an uneventful one minute trip to the bus station. When I say an uneventful trip, it was, but the getting on the bus was a laugh, even the driver was knotting himself. As the bus approached the stop, Craig noticed what looked like a black band sort of a thing on the ground, and to my amazement, he bent down, or gave his impersonation of bending down to pick it up. Now as you all know if you have read one of our previous books, Craig suffers from a lot of problems that affect the bending down ability, so by the time I was getting on the bus, Craig was almost on all fours trying to get the band off the ground. The passengers on the bus had almost finished the first chorus of 'why are we waiting' before Craig discovered the band was not the thing he thought it was, whatever that was, and joined the rest of us on the bus. The driver said to me that even if we didn't have a bus pass he wouldn't have charged us. A great start to a sunny day.

It was Easter Saturday and the sun was blazing down on us as we got off the bus and passed 'The Exchange', a Wetherspoons sort of place full of people having coffee and children, if you know what I mean. More surprisingly, we even passed 'Hudsons'. This is a funny sort of pub, but worth a visit. My then to be daughter-in-law Mary was working in the pub years ago when there was an incident with a man brandishing a gun and I think demanding money. I'm not sure of the details, but if I remember, I'll ask Mary, I'll change this bit of the story. Anyway the way I remember it is that Mary gave him a look and he froze. Mary should have got a medal for her bravery, only matched by my boy Alasdair for marrying her-only kidding Mary!

Craig: *For various reasons, all of them to do with John's social life, we decided to pay a visit to our local junior football team, East Kilbride Thistle. The Jags play at the Show Park which is about half a mile from my front door. On average I probably pass the ground a couple of times a week. It is therefore a wee bit embarrassing to have to admit that I have never set foot in the place before never mind seen the team play.*

139

We couldn't have picked a better day for it. Under a clear blue sky we made our way down to the village to sit inside our first pub of the day The Mongomery Arms.

Since this was a legitimate fact finding trip I insisted that we had to travel the short distance down to the pub by bus. It's what we have done in all of our other trips and I saw no reason why this one should be any different. My travelling companion didn't entirely agree. In fact he called me a few hurtful names, suggesting that I was less than fit and unwilling to walk the length of myself.
As it was, we had to wait longer for the bus than it would have taken us to walk, but that wasn't the point.

John: The village in East Kilbride still has the feel of an old village and has three pubs in the vicinity of the ground.

The first, and oldest pub in EK is 'The Montgomery Arms', or 'The Monty' as it's known. The pub is actually attached to the village church and can easily be found by following your nose to the steeple which can be seen from all over the town. We have visited 'The Monty' many times, mainly on our way home from trips when just another drink was needed.

So at about five past twelve, in we went, on the way to the ground. The barman probably didn't recognize us sober.

Robbie and Adam

The 'Monty' is a brilliant bar and the service is always first class. It sponsors 'The Jags', and the team visit the bar after the games for a bit of hospitality laid on by the owner. The barmen Robbie and Adam were excellent and although most of the customers were outside enjoying the sun or a fag, we enjoyed our first pint of the day. Hopefully, an EK sporting success was on the cards today. The guy at the bar next to me, Raymond O'Neil, was going to watch the EK rugby team play. If they won today they would be promoted. Hope they did. Thought I'd mention this as it's a sports story.

The pub across the road, *'Legends'*, was next on today's journey. Although it's in the village, I think I've only been in it once. The bar reminds me of somebody's living room, I don't know why. The bar was busy, but everybody was watching the telly, where Celtic were playing Motherwell. Everybody in the bar was supporting Celtic, so the atmosphere was a bit fraught when Motherwell scored early on. We left without a word being spoken to anyone. There's nothing wrong with the pub though, and seemingly the restaurant upstairs is good. Got to mention the good things about EK pubs-I live there!

Time was getting on, so we decided to visit the third pub *'The Village Inn'* after our visit to the ground. Just before arriving at the Showpark we passed the sad sight of the Supporters Club, closed. A fire finished it off about three years ago. No money was found to open it up again.

Craig: *John suggested that we should sit outside with our drinks and enjoy the sunny weather. I was forced to remind him that we were not there to enjoy ourselves, this was work. Besides I burn very easily.*

Given the number of times we have ended our road trips in the Monty you would think the bar staff would have recognised us when we walked in. Then again John was sober at that time of the day so I can see where they might have been confused.

There were a few supporters in the bar but unfortunately for us they were of the Celtic variety. However, while we were chatting to the bar staff Robbie and Adam about the pub's sponsorship of East Kilbride Thistle, a customer, Raymond o'Neil, came over to announce that he was a supporter. The only problem was, he had misheard us. It turned out that it was the East Kilbride's rugby team he was interested in. He told us that at least his team had won something recently. Apparently they are in line for promotion to a higher division and could actually win a league trophy.

With a bit of effort we tried to steer the conversation back to football again but Raymond was in full flow. He told us a story about winning an all-expenses paid holiday. It was a lottery prize drawn at the end of a Celtic Supporters Club night out. He was quite excited to win the trip to Arran and was really hoping he would be staying in the Auchrannie Spa Resort on the island. Unfortunately he had misheard the announcer and it was a little later in the night that he discovered he had in fact won a short break in Annan. There may have been drink involved in his confusion but I wouldn't like to speculate. Things didn't get any better when his chauffeur-driven limo turned up to whisk him to his hotel down in Annan. It was a campervan.

His travelling companions in the 'limo' turned out to be none other than Bertie Auld and Tommy Gemmell. That at least made up for the disappointment of his holiday destination, though Raymond did complain that Bertie Auld never stopped talking all the way to Annan.

Still hoping to meet an actual East Kilbride fan we moved across the road to our next pub, Legends. The public bar of Legends is a bit of a mixed-up affair. It has lots of armchairs and couches and bare wood tables. The bar itself is fairly modern. We only had one drink in this place as there was no sign of any of the football fans we were searching for. Had we been looking for Celtic supporters we would have been in exactly the right place; it was mobbed with them watching their team making heavy weather of the big game on the large screen telly.

The beer was more than passable and about average price-wise. At the time of our visit there was only one girl serving behind the bar and she was so busy that we didn't even attempt to talk to her. Beyond the, "I'll have a pint of Tennent's and a girly vodka and soda for my strange little friend please" that is.

John: The sun was still blazing down as we went into the ground and found the secretary, Martin Sutherland busy doing the team lines. Secretaries are always busy; I don't think the players have any idea of the work they do behind the scenes.

He was soon finished and we spent almost an hour with Martin and their ex-president and co-founder, 78 year old Alan Cairns being entertained with great stories from 'The Jags' past.

Martin and Alan

Apart from being a fantastic bloke and a great laugh, Alan is an encyclopedia of knowledge about the Junior game as well as being an ex Govan High boy like other famous people including me and Sir Alex Ferguson.

Apart from some brilliant stories that I'll let Craig tell you, we found out that 'The Jags' have been treated badly by some other teams in the past, none more so that Craig's beloved Auchinleck, who stole half the 'The Jags' players after they had won the Scottish Cup. This is just buying success and very unfair to clubs like 'The Jags' who were bringing along a lot of great young players. That shut Craig up for a while as he is always on about other clubs doing that to try and keep up with his 'Bot'.

Craig: *It was time to move round to the Show Park for our meeting with East Kilbride Thistle's club secretary. On the way to*

143

the ground we had to pass the old supporters' club. Unfortunately it has long since closed its doors to the public after a series of break-ins and vandalism.

This was a personal tragedy for the football club and a bit of an inconvenience for us as we like to meet supporters on their home turf, i.e. their social club.

Instead we met Martin Sutherland and Alan Cairns, the club secretary and past president respectively, in the cafe at The Show Park.

We don't normally do cafés, obviously, and as we entered John was looking like a jakey who had just seen his dealer fall under a bus.

When Martin offered us a cup of tea I couldn't look John in the eye as I hate to see grown men cry. Fortunately for me there were no mirrors in the place or I might well have caught sight of another moist eyed sufferer.

When we asked Alan about the Thistle's closest rivals he, like us, was stumped. He said they didn't really have any rivals as such, only geographical ones. However, when certain other teams were mentioned Martin said that most of them at one time or another had stolen some of East Kilbride's best players. It would seem that many successful junior teams and a few senior teams have benefited from raiding the Jags' player pool.

According to Martin, Auchinleck Talbot had made off with a couple of their best players the year before they won the Scottish Cup. At this point John helpfully informed the lads that I was from Auchinleck and should therefore take some of the blame for this. There was some definite eyebrow raising going on but after I assured him that ' it wisnae me' he calmed down again and we all had a good laugh. Just to make sure the subject was well and truly changed I asked Alan if he had any tales to tell us about the teams toughest away games

He told us that East Kilbride once had a game against a team up in Aberdeen. The weather that day was particularly Scottish and, by the time the bus got as far as Perth the drifting snow forced it to stop. Sometime between then and when the decision to turn back was made by the committee, half the team had become separated from the main party. The team officials were a bit concerned about all those young men lost in the freezing temperatures and worsening blizzard but it was felt they had no choice but to leave them behind and make for home. The next morning Alan's phone rang. Fearing the worst he answered, only to find out that the missing players had actually slipped away to a well-known Perth disco in pursuit of some local talent.

Once again we were so busy having a laugh that the match had kicked off without us noticing. Usually we blame the drink for this kind of thing but we were no position to do that on this occasion. It was past two o'clock and John was stone cold soberish. We decided to rectify this by visiting the Village Inn.

It was really quite busy in the bar with a large number of drinkers watching the game on television and imaginatively expressing their views on Celtic's inability to get the ball between the sticks.

We were served quickly despite the crowded bar but it was obvious that we wouldn't be able to talk to any of guys there due to the noise and the fact that nobody in the pub was in the least bit interested in junior football. Or so we thought!

Just off the main bar I noticed a small back room which was also crowded with noisy drinkers. Although they were watching the same match on the telly it was obvious the guys in that particular room were not hoping for a Celtic victory. We hoped this would mean they might not mind taking a few minutes to talk to us.

After a quick couple of drinks, we had been pint-less for more than an hour after all, I managed to have a word with two of our fellow drinkers.

Billy Burke and Jim Ferguson actually did most of the talking. Due to the combined noise of all the Celtic fans cheering on their team, and the old boys in the back room cheering every time Celtic missed a chance to score, it was quite hard to hear what Billy and Jim were on about.

145

I'm fairly sure that Jim claimed to be a former East Kilbride player, but I could be mistaken! The one direct quote I got from Billy had nothing to do with football, but everything to do with his own peculiar outlook on life. He announced, to anyone who was listening, that, "Behind every great man is a greetin' faced woman."

Billy and Jim

Another fan I talked to had an interesting tale to tell. It seems that East Kilbride Thistle was involved in a very tense game. Nerves were at breaking point and fans were trading insults. Suddenly it all got too much for one Thistle supporter. He stormed out of the crowd and onto the park where he grabbed a corner-flag, pulled it up and charged over to a bunch of opposition fans. Once there, and no doubt to a rousing cheer from the East Kilbride faithful, he laid out one of his tormentors with it.

Mission accomplished, he dived back into the safety of the home stand, where he remained anonymous while the police searched for the culprit.

What makes this story different from the run-of-the-mill story of football hooliganism is the fact that the post wielding fan was, and possibly still is, a local councillor.

It seems to me that the whole incident was a rather extreme and misguided attempt to capture a few extra votes come election time. But since most politicians would sell their own granny for a handful of votes I suppose it was understandable.

I did ask my informant for the name of this well connected football hooligan, but he was unwilling to tell me. Actually he wouldn't even give me his own name, possibly figuring that his 'Cooncil tax' might suddenly double if he did.

John: The game had started by the time we left and walked back along the road into *'The Village Inn'*. The name makes it sound like a village inn, which it's not. It's a bar full of bears and old guys like me. It's a great pub. When we went in the main bar area was full of mainly youngish Celtic Supporters watching their heroes. By this time there was only a few minutes to go and the 'Tic were winning 3-2, so everybody was happy. Well almost everybody!

We noticed a wee sort of snug bar through the back with about a dozen or so guys of about my age, or older, who were definitely not Celtic supporters. You could tell by looking at them, if you know what I mean. So in we went. In no time we had joined in the company and had a great time with them. It's amazing, but unlike women, men just talk the same load of shit that they have done since they were young It's what makes us more fun than women!

Among the guys we met were Billy Burke, Jim Ferguson, Jackie McNab and his brother Billy. That's all the names I can remember. By this time it was a miracle I could stand. I do remember they were all delighted when Motherwell equalized in the last minute. In typical Old Firm fashion, a young Celtic fan stuck his head in the room and told us all to 'get it up you', brilliant! This is a great place for an older guy to spend an hour or so on a Saturday being abused by like-minded old nut cases.

I had promised Kate that I would be home by three as we were going to a birthday party for our neighbours Richard and Jackie's wee girl. This is always a great party as you don't see any kids and just eat, drink and get quietly drunk. What a great end to a day, pissed twice.

Just having visited one club, albeit one of the greatest, I had change out of my £20 kitty, although not as much as I should have had. Never mind, I'll be deid soon.

Pubs we visited;

The Monty-great traditional old pub

Legends-a younger man's traditional pub

The Village Inn-A more modern old pub-try the back room

All the pubs are worth a visit.

East Kilbride; **How to get there-free with the Bus pass**

No. 6, 18, 21 from various places in Glasgow will do the business (park is in village)

The map at the start of the chapter lets you see how to get to the ground.

Linlithgow Rose V Camelon FC

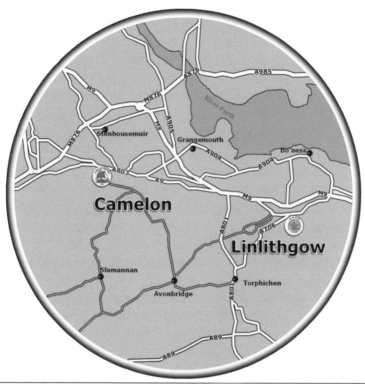

Club Name	Founded
Linlithgow Rose	1889
Ground	*Colours*
Prestonfield Park	Maroon
League (2014-15)	*Selection of Honours*
East Reg. Super League	Jun. Cup; 1964-65; 2001-02
Club Nickname	06-07; 09-10 Run Up 3 times
The Gallant	

John: Today we were visiting what I always think of as the industrial East. This part of the country, flanked by Grangemouth, Falkirk and Bathgate was a traditional industrial area of Scotland, the sort of places where Junior Football is at its best. Nowadays, I doubt very much whether there is as much industry about. I know Grangemouth has a lot of oil based companies, but I don't know how well the other areas are faring; maybe I would find out today.

Both clubs are among the big boys of Junior Football, with Linlithgow having won the Scottish Junior Cup four times and Camelon once, also reaching the semi-final this season.

Although Linlithgow will claim to be the bigger and better supported club of the two, they do not have the best nickname. Camelon's 'The Mariners' is a good nickname, although I've got to admit that Linlithgow's 'The Gallant' is not that bad, although it sounds a wee bit 'Englishy'.

Craig told me a story once, that back in the days when he actually followed his club Auchinleck, they were playing an important cup match against Linlithgow, and their large support were shouting 'come away the Gallant Rosey Posey'. Even I had to admit it's a bit un-Junior sounding. Mind you, shouting about anyone's nickname when yours is 'The Bot' is a bit of a cheek. I'm sure 'The Bot' is the butt of a lot of other supporter's jokes.

An interesting bit of information I have for you is that both of today's clubs, as well as Kirkintilloch Rob Roy and Kilsyth Rangers have their grounds within spitting distance of the same road, the A803. How about that? Is there another road somewhere in Scotland with more than four grounds. I would give good money if anyone could come up with one.

As usual, I was arranging the journey. Now, a potential problem was arising. I went into the 'Traveline' web site, and being the sort of guy who believes what the computer tells him, printed out the details. It was a two bus journey to the grounds. We were also changing buses outwith bus stations. Always a worry, especially if the bus companies alter the place you have to change buses. So it was complicated!

The day before our trip, Craig had asked to see the bus plan as he was having a night out with Irene on the Saturday night and he wanted to know when we would be back. As a wee aside, how Craig could do anything on a Saturday night after the state he is usually in is beyond me. Never mind, I gave him the paperwork.

I got Craig at 9.30am on the Saturday morning and we got the usual No. 18 to take us into Glasgow. I casually mentioned that I hoped he had remembered the bus information. You can guess the reply. The most complicated bus journey to date and he had left what he claimed I had told him were copies in his house.

He was not concerned, and spent a while on his web phone trying to get the information. A load of crap was produced. Eventually he took my advice and phoned Irene. A word of warning here to oldies like us whose hearing may not be as good as it used to be, don't phone on a bus. Anyway, after much shouting and bawling from Craig, we had the information from Irene. Mind you, everyone on the bus 'knew our business'. One guy even asked if he could join us for the day!

When we got off the bus we walked up to the bus station and found our first bus, the X27, no bother, and had a nice, but nervous run over to the East where Traveline, via Craig's call to Irene, told us that we would get off the bus in the centre of the town of Larbert. As we reached the outskirts, we went into a huge hospital, to allow people to visit sick friends I suppose. When the bus left the hospital, instead of heading into the centre of Larbert, it turned left and headed back the way it had come. I panicked!

To be fair to Craig, and his magic phone, which showed him where we were all the time, he was out of his seat in his impersonation of a flash, and we got off the bus at the stop just outside the hospital. If he had tried to move any faster, I think he would have ended up in the hospital.

Amazingly, our next bus, the X38, stopped across the road from where we got off, not only that, we only had a few minutes to wait. Craig was rightly proud of himself and his new technology which I slag off all the time. I was quiet for a few minutes.

We had done our normal thing and had picked the furthest away club to visit first, for obvious reasons. Because the famous A803 was the road both clubs were close to, we were able to check out from the comfort of the bus, where to get off on our way back to visit the second club, Camelon, before getting to our first port of call, Linlithgow Rose.

Craig: *There are days when you just know that things are not going to work out as planned, and today was one of those days. I should have realised something was going wrong when I discovered that, unbelievably, I was ready and waiting for John a good 10 minutes before his ETA (estimated time of arrival). Incidentally that is the kind of patter he uses at our planning sessions. He fair loves his acronyms.*

The only problem is that we tend to hold our planning sessions at the pub, and after a couple of pints of inspiration we sound as if we're just shouting random letters of the alphabet at each other. Anyway, perhaps it was my unusual state of readiness that caused John to make his first mistake of the day. He had forgotten to bring his bus timetables with him. The first thing he did when he found this out was to look around for someone else to blame. As usual it was me in his cross-hairs.

Although he tried to blame me it was obvious that he had completely arsed things up all by himself. Not that I feel the need to justify myself, but I feel that I should point out that I had asked for a copy of the itinerary, not the original print-out. I wouldn't dare bring my copy just in case he thought I was checking up on him. Fortunately I managed to save the day by phoning Irene and getting her to read out the bus timings.

We often make jokes at the expense of the bus drivers we meet on our travels, but it is meant in jest, usually. However the driver on X 27 from Glasgow takes the proverbial biscuit. After getting his ticket John asked this bloke if he could let us know when we arrived in Larbert, but the driver just shrugged his shoulders and said that he had no idea where that was. Where the hell are they getting these guys? There is surely a requirement of bus drivers to have at least a reasonable idea where their buses are going or in this case supposed to be going.

A less well-adjusted pair of travellers may just have given up at this point but we are made of sterner stuff. As it turns out Larbert is where the X27 turns back on itself after visiting the hospital. So the next time you are rushed in to Forth Valley Royal Hospital you will know where you are.

As we raced through Camelon on our way to Linlithgow I managed to spy out the pub nearest the ground. Spotting the nearest bus stop could help save us a bit of time later.

John: Our earlier, Craig based screw up with the bus information was behind us and all was going well. Our bus dropped us off right outside the pub Craig saw on his phone. The pub was called *'The Black Bitch',* without doubt, the best named pub we have ever been in.

After introducing ourselves to the barmaid, Barbara, who was brilliant, and a couple of very funny and knowledgeable locals, I asked what the story was behind the pub's name.

Barbara

Many years ago, I was told, a local boy was charged and found guilty of stealing a sheep, or it might have been a loaf. He was put on the island in the middle of Linlithgow Loch to die. Now the boy had a dog called Black Bitch, I'm not one hundred percent certain if the dog was called 'Black Bitch' or if it was just a Black Bitch. The locals would give the dog food, or she might have stolen it, and then would swim out to the island with the food. What a dog and what a great story! I wish I had remembered to ask if there was a happy ending. I'm sure there was.

The locals in Linlithgow are called 'Black Bitches', but you have to be born within the town boundaries to become one. I wonder if any women leave town to have their babies so they won't be 'Black Bitches'. We found out later from another local that to be a proper 'Black Bitch', you must be born in the house, not a hospital. I'm guessing that the person who started that part of the story was one of the Politically Correct weirdos who want to stop the words Black or Bitch being used. Could be!

These are the stories that make travelling such a great way to pass a Saturday, that and a few drinks. Another less interesting fact about Linlithgow is that Mary Queen of Scots was born there in 1542.

'*The Black Bitches*' would be a brilliant nickname for Linlithgow; think of the fun the opposition would have chanting abuse at them.

Talking about abusing the opposition, when Barbara found out that Craig was from Auchinleck (and I didn't tell her), she told a story of the day she went on the Linlithgow supporter's bus for a match against 'The Bot'. Auchinleck, as normal, Craig would tell you, won the match, but it didn't stop some of their supporters throwing a couple of half bricks at their bus as a friendly reminder to get out of town.

The time fairly shot in and we said our goodbyes to all the '*Black Bitches*' in the '*Black Bitch*'. Our return bus stop was just across the road so we checked out the times for our next bus before wandering up the road to Prestonfield, which is one of the best, if not **the** best set-ups I have seen to date on our journeys.

Craig: Linlithgow is only a few miles from Camelon so as soon as we left it John started to worry. He was less than kind about me being able to get us straight to the first pub I had been telling him about. What he didn't know was that we were not in fact heading to the Old Port for our first pint of the day. There was no way I could tell him the name of the pub we were actually going to. It was called the Black Bitch. He would have been uncontrollable. As it was he got so excited that he managed to

154

bring the pub name up in every conversation for most of the day and at random intervals ever since.

It was a nice old-fashioned pub and we found it very comfortable. There were only three customers in the bar but they were having a heated discussion about local politics. The consensus of opinion seemed to be that all politicians are inveterate liars, so we felt really at home. Once the lads had settled down a bit we asked the question John had been dying to ask since we first clapped eyes on the place.

Including the barmaid, Barbara Park, the four people in the bar came up with four different explanations of the name. Even John came up with one and, as you might expect, it is far too unsavoury and non PC to print here. But just buy him a couple of drinks and you will very definitely hear it.

Ah just asked her if she was a Black Bitch ...an she thumped me!

The Black Bitch explanations ran from calling the pub after a very loyal big dog which swam out to the island on Linlithgow Loch, taking food to a young boy who had been exiled there, to the dubious personal hygiene of Mary Queen of Scots. My own personal favourite was the one from the guy who thought the name

155

came from a story about a dog which had been exiled on to the island for biting Mary Queen of Scots.

Barbara settled the argument by nipping through to the lounge to read the plaque describing the source of the name. Incidentally it was the first one.

I asked if there were any Linlithgow supporters in the bar. Only one man was prepared to admit that he was. Old George - hopefully he won't mind me calling him that - has supported the 'Rosey Posey' since he moved to the town many years ago. He declined the chance to have his picture taken or even give his second name, as he thought he could be in trouble if his former hometown friends ever found out that he had changed allegiances. He was originally from Bo'ness. Junior fitba can be a hard game, even for the fans.

John: We wandered round the ground and met up with the Secretary James Harkins in the excellent facilities under the grandstand. James introduced us to Les Donaldson, the clubs president, and David Roy, who is the assistant secretary and had been secretary for 50 years. That's loyalty for you.

James, Les and David

These three gentlemen entertained us for a long time with their stories and facts about their beloved Linlithgow. Craig had his recorder with him and collected many of these. One story I do remember was about the time James, then a player with the club, was ordered off for hitting an opposition player with a snowball. The player he hit was Geordie Fairley who was playing for Whitburn at the time. Goerdie later in life became Linlithgow's manager. Just think of the state the park must have been in to be able to have snowball fights during a game, and I bet they weren't wearing gloves either.

Kick off time was approaching and we were sorry to leave our hosts, but the good news was that they directed us over to the Social Club to meet the fans.

The club is huge and very impressive, as was the number of fans that were filling both the bars. As we settled into our seats, some of the fans were starting to leave to watch the match, but there were still plenty of people to talk to and we were lucky with the family of fans we sat beside.

Colin, Harry and Ryan

Three generations were enjoying a day out at the match. Harry Piehl, the oldest generation, Colin Batchelor, second generation, and his son Ryan were great company and we chatted so much that by the time we left, they had missed most of the first half. It was great to meet them all and Ryan, who is signed up with Raith Rovers, was a credit to his parents.

Colin even bought one of our books, so not only were they great people; they had good taste as well.

There's no doubt Linlithgow are one of the best set up and supported Junior Clubs in Scotland, but as I've said before, that's not what we're about, it's the people that run the clubs, their supporters, and their local clubs and pubs. To be fair, Linlithgow Rose are in the top few in Scotland on all three counts.

We left the ground and retraced our steps to the bus stop, only to see our X38 going away from the stop. This tragedy meant a 20 minute wait, or a pint in the 'BB' (the politically correct Craig wants me to stop saying Black Bitch, or at least to stop enjoying saying it). So another drink was enjoyed before we said our goodbyes to Linlithgow, a very nice town full of Black Bitches and a great team.

Craig: We left the pub and walked down to the football park. Even just a quick look at Prestonfield is enough to remind you that Linlithgow is one of the biggest clubs in Scottish Junior football. We noticed that the stand and the surrounding area were well maintained and the pitch looked to be in perfect condition as we headed round to meet the committee men in the clubhouse.

One of them told us about a Linlithgow supporter who underwent a major character change when he attended matches. He was apparently a very quiet gentlemanly chap in his day-to-day life, but a bit like Dr Jekyll after drinking a potion when he passed through the turnstiles at any ground where his beloved Linlithgow was playing he changed drastically.

On one occasion when the Rosey was playing a Scottish Cup match at East Kilbride his enthusiasm got the better of him. He had been on his best behaviour all through the match, appearing calm and collected in his rather expensive-looking camelhair coat.

But when the final whistle went, with Linlithgow ahead, he charged on to the park and celebrated by doing a forward roll. East Kilbride is quite possibly the wettest place in Scotland so you can imagine the state of him and his coat after this acrobatic display.

Round at the social club we were surprised to find such a big bright place. The lounge would not be out of place in a three or four star hotel. Grudgingly I admitted to John that it was at least as good as the Auchinleck Talbot's. Right enough I didn't say it very loudly so he may have missed it.

The big lounge was so busy we had to move through to what I assume is the main hall. It's not quite as fancy but is still among the best I have seen. Eventually we got talking to a small group of supporters at the next table.

There were three of them Harry Piehl, the elder statesman of the group, Colin Batchelor his son-in-law and Ryan Batchelor his grandson. Young Ryan has just signed for Raith Rovers and his grandad was like a dog with two tails as he told us this.

Whether he was just feeling sorry for two well-travelled old guys, or was genuinely interested in our writings Colin bought a copy of our latest book 'Inn Aff the Bar'. I just wished we had said a few more nice things about Raith Rovers in it.

Camelon

Club Name	Founded
Camelon	1920
Ground	**Colours**
Carmuirs Park	Red
League (2014-15)	**Selection of Honours**
East Reg. Super league	Jun. Cup 1994-95
Club Nickname	Runners up twice
The Mariners	

John: Our X38 took us the 30 minute or so journey back to Camelon, which is part of Falkirk. We had been given directions by the 'Bitches' on how to get to the ground and the pubs around it, so it only took us a couple of minutes to find *'The Union Inn'* which is situated on the side of the Forth and Clyde, or is it The Union Canal; I'm not sure but it doesn't matter. I think the canal is fully open now and it must be lovely to sail your boat up the canal, tie up and visit the local bars. A word of warning for you boat owners, there may be one or two places on the canal where the locals would have the *wheels* off your boat while you were enjoying a pint. Not in the Falkirk area of course, but beware anyway.

As we tried to get into the *'The Union Inn'*, a customer was being shown the door, head first. He looked like he had been dragged out of the canal. *'The Union'* is an old fashioned bar with old fashioned people like Craig and I enjoying a quiet pint. It would be lovely in the summer, whatever day it falls on, to enjoy a pint while watching the wheels coming off the boats. This is a bar worth visiting if only for its position on the side of the canal.

Full-time at the Camelon game on the other side of the canal was approaching, so we left, crossed the bridge and found the ground in no time.

Craig: *Following closely to John's carefully worked-out timetable, that will be the one he forgot to bring with him, we missed our bus and had to take refuge back in John's newly found favourite pub, the Black Bitch. I thought he would have run out of steam with his alleged jokes about bitches, black or otherwise but I was wrong.*

It was suggested that we should visit the Union Inn when we got to Camelon as, in the opinion of some of the guys in the bar, we would be more likely to find some Camelon supporters in there than in any other place. This sort of buggered up my carefully laid plans but I'm nothing if not adaptable. It simply meant getting off our bus one stop earlier than I had planned and walking down to the canal.

160

The Union is a really substantial building set on its own, right beside a lock on the Forth and Clyde Canal. I can only assume that it was formerly the lock keepers house back when the canal was used to shift cargo around Scotland.

I would have asked someone about that but nobody seemed in the mood for a chat in the pub.

Inside the Union we found a reasonably good pub with plenty of space to sit and take in the atmosphere. It was very quiet during our visit if you don't count the Jakey who was being invited to leave the premises and never bother coming back, just as we arrived.

I would imagine that during summer this pub will see a lot of trade from the boating crowd. We only had time for a single drink before we had to make our way over to the park. Against his better nature, John allowed me to lead him round to Carmuirs Park using my phone to guide us. In no time at all we were standing outside Camelon Social Club. The only problem was we couldn't be sure how we were supposed to get into it. A wee bit more advertising might work wonders for the club's cash register.

John and Robert

John: We went into the social club at the ground and although it is nothing like Linlithgow's, the supporters were a great bunch and we enjoyed their company. The Secretary, Robert McTaggart, one of the youngest we have met, was rushed off his feet trying to do god knows how many jobs at once. The set-up here seems a bit less organized and I think Robert needs a bit of help. Having said all that, he came over to join us and was good company. His dedication to the club is remarkable and, like others in his situation, he deserves great credit for the hours he puts in to help keep the club running.

Back down on the main street, we checked our bus times and found that we had a while before our bus. *'The Roman Bar'* filled the time nicely. This is a nice, very old-fashioned bar, and the barmaid Carol was great fun and an excellent barmaid.

Craig: This club is quite a bit older than its rival along the road though it is just as friendly, but it really is in need of a bit of money being spent on it. I don't know if it has anything to do with the success or otherwise of the respective teams but something needs to be done.

John had as usual been in contact with the club secretary, in this case Robert McTaggart, but as it turned out he was extremely busy. One minute he was behind the bar talking to the barman the next he was running through to the back office to sort out some club business. Eventually he had a couple of spare minutes and sat down with us.

Even then he was answering questions from other supporters. I suggested that he should maybe think about getting himself an assistant. Without missing a beat he asked if I was applying for the job. I'm pretty sure he's not quite that desperate, not yet anyway.

He was a bit disappointed that his team had lost the match but, there was still a lot to be done. Before we could chat any more he was called away to solve some problems behind the bar.

When we first came into the club we found out that Camelon had just been beaten by Tayport. That sort of explained why there were so few customers in the lounge. I was therefore a bit surprised to see about half a dozen players come into the place laughing and joking.

John then had to listen to me ranting on about the lack of responsibility and respect young players sometimes show towards their fans until he could take no more. Less than tactfully he pointed out that these players were in fact from Tayport and entitled to be in a good mood.

Luckily for me I spotted a couple of Tayport committee men we had talked to a few weeks back. This allowed me to quickly change the subject and to enjoy a couple of rounds of drinks and a lot of banter.

Somehow the subject of football sponsorship came up and one of the Tayport men told us about an odd deal one of their players had recently been offered. We thought he was just having a laugh but he produced an email which proved what he was saying was spot on.

A restaurant which shall remain nameless sent the following message to the player,
'...... all the best for the remaining games. Connaire, you will get £10 for every goal you score from now to the end of the season plus a large portion of breaded haddock'.

I don't know about Connaire but the breaded haddock would be enough to get me into a goal scoring frame of mind.

After a few more laughs and the odd sip of beer we decided to head back up to our bus stop. Strangely, we found that we had just enough time for a quick drink in the Roman Bar up on the main street before our bus was due.

There were no supporters in the bar but our barmaid, Carol, kept us well entertained. The pub is well worth a visit. It is huge and very traditional and I would imagine very busy before Camelon home games.

Carol

Once we had finished our drinks there was only one thing left for me to do and that was of course to enjoy John's panic about his timetable gaffs. It may not be fair but it made me laugh for a while.

John: Our confidence in our bus information was restored-a good bucketful will do that-and we went back out to the main road, and sure enough, the X38 turned up on time for the short run back to the big hospital where we got off in time to nick into the shop for a packet of crisps. I wanted a coffee, but a minor screw-up in translating my own writing meant we had to rush out of the hospital to get our bus, the X27 back to Glasgow.

We wandered down to the Central Station to get our tickets for the train back to EK. After pocketing the tickets, we headed out and down Hope Street and into *'Denholms'* for our usual nightcap. As normal at this time on a Saturday night, there was Karaoke on, and as usual, some of the performers should have been in the jail for murdering some superb songs. We had a great time there, as always. By the way, Glasgow is still a great place for a wander about reasonably early on a Saturday night; you see some sights!

After the train back to EK, we got a taxi home, as Irene was at a night out, as was Kate, and walking was out of the question.

So ended a fine day out in the East, both clubs have devoted people at the helm and we enjoyed their company and the stories we heard. I hope Craig can remember more than me. He has his recorder after all.

About £30 was my spend for the day, and that included a 'Black Bitch' buying us a round, so a lot was consumed. Another great thing about today was that I was allowed to say 'Black Bitch' and not be politically incorrect, I hope!

Pubs and Clubs visited today;

Linlithgow;
'The Black Bitch', a brilliant bar.
'Linlithgow Social Club' also brilliant place

Camelon;
'Union Inn', nice old bar, handy for sailors
'Roman Bar'. great old fashioned bar
'Camelon Social Club', bit tired looking but ideal for supporters.

165

Linlithgow; How to get there-free with the Bus Pass
X27 Glasgow to Leven (get off at Larbert Hospital)
X38 Stirling to Edinburgh (get off at 'Black Bitch)

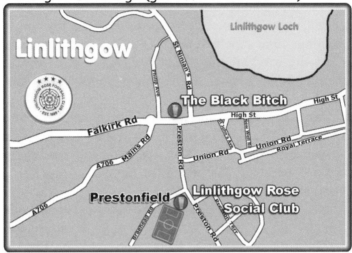

Camelon; How to get there-free with the Bus Pass
X27 Glasgow to Leven (get off at Larbert Hospital)
X38 Stirling to Edinburgh (get off in Camelon)

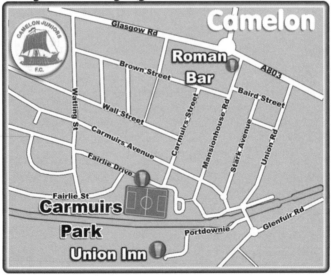

Pollok V Arthurlie

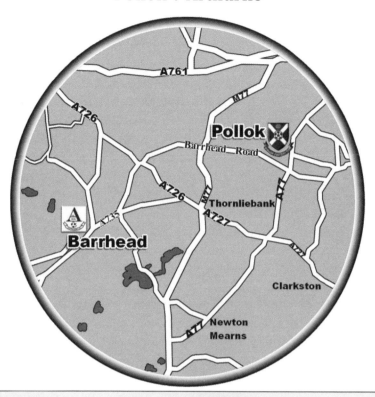

Club Name	Founded
Pollok Football Club	1908
Ground	**Colours**
Newlandsfield Park	Black & White stripes
League (2014-15)	**Main Honours**
West Super League 1st Division	Scot. Jun. Cup Winners
Club Nickname	1980-81/1984-85/1996-97
The Lok	

John: Pollok and Arthurlie are two of Glasgow's bigger Junior clubs. It is one of the easiest trips in the book as both clubs are not far from East Kilbride, or Buchanan Street Bus Station where our bus directions are from, this for the readers who are not lucky enough to come from 'the windy city'.

Our plan is always to try and visit both rivals on the same day, one before kick-off and the other after, but as it was getting to the end of the season and there were few games on, we decided that as both teams were not at home, we would visit the rivals on different days. Today it would be Pollok's chance to be honoured by a visit from two old fogies.

Pollok's nickname, 'The Lok', lacks any imagination. An ideal one would be 'The Shaws'; this could be after the area in Glasgow where the club is near to and it could also be rhyming slang, if you know what I mean. An example would be, 'the ball hit him in the 'Pollokshaws'.

There was no need for me to check timetables or 'Google Earth' the park. I know the area reasonably well and it is one of the many, many places where Craig has lived, always for a short time, if you know what I mean.

We got the No. 6 bus from the Murray Road outside Craig's house just after 10.30am and got off at the old Victoria Infirmary. I was worried that Craig would not want to walk over the hill to Shawlands, but what a trouper he is. He led the way up the steep hill to the Langside Monument.

My ignorance of these famous places is beyond belief, but the monument and the church, which is now a pub at the top of the hill, were looking great in the sunshine. At the other corner of the top of the hill is a garage that does repairs and other things to cars. Now this is fine, but why they have make the place look so out of character with the rest of the buildings is beyond belief.

Not to worry, we were enjoying our walk past Queen's Park in glorious sunshine. It was about eleven-thirty when we got to Shawland's Cross, one of Glasgow's nicest places to live.

As we got to the corner in Shawlands, across from Queen's Park, there is a Wetherspoon's pub and a nightclub above it. But years ago when I was young, it was, as most Glaswegians will know, the impressive building that housed 'The Marlborough'. It was there that Kate and I had our wedding reception.

The wedding itself was in a church in Craigbank, not far from Kate's house. What I remember most about the wedding was the young minister, who arrived at the Church on his bike about two minutes after the ceremony should have started. After getting himself sorted out, but forgetting to take off his bicycle clips, he started the service by welcoming everybody, then saying 'the first hymn (pause) will be the first hymn' it was magic, he didn't have a card with what we were all meant to sing. He was coming to the reception and I could just imagine him cycling from the church to 'The Marlborough' with his black robes flying out behind him.

He made it all right because by the time we arrived after all the photos were taken, he was enjoying a pint at the bar. It was a great reception and near the end one of the waiters asked 'Whose carry-out is this?'-'Mine' said the minister. I could see him cycling up the hill to the monument looking like E.T. I was reminiscing to Kate about this a while ago and I asked her if there was any chance we were not actually married. 'That's my second wish after the Lottery', was her instant retort! What a cheek.

I think I am going on too much about the past, so back to today's trip.

Craig: Pollok JFC is a big name in junior football. Since 1980 they have won the Scottish Junior Cup three times. Their keenest rival we are told, is Athurlie JFC. Usually we try to visit both sets of rivals on the same day, but unfortunately that isn't always possible. Today was one of those days.

Due to circumstances beyond our control we could only manage a single visit this time and Pollok, just down the road from us in the Shawlands area of Glasgow, was our chosen team.

I actually lived quite close to our target area for a couple of years and thought John would benefit from my local knowledge. Strangely, he didn't seem too keen to listen to my carefully thought-out running commentary on what it was like living on the south side of Glasgow. But I persevered.

After walking from Battlefield up to Pollokshaws Road we stopped outside The Corona. It is now a Wetherspoons pub but when I first moved to the area it was a fantastic traditional bar.

Inside it was all oak beams and well rubbed antique brass. It really was a pleasure to sit in of an evening. Another great thing about it was the fact that it was only a five minute walk from my flat. More importantly it wasn't The Mullberry Bush which was only a two minute walk away but was a no go area as far as I was concerned due to it being a bit of a cesspit.

Anyway, I had many a good night in the old Corona. As you can imagine I was gutted to find out that the pub had been sold. Worse still, the new owners decided to gut the pub's interior. All of those authentic oak beams and hundred-year-old brasses were ripped out and replaced with a mass produced and shoddy version of what passes for a 'traditional British pub'. Somebody probably made a fortune selling off the original fixtures and fittings to an Irish pub-building company.

By the time I had finished my rantings John point blank refused to go into the place for our first pint of the day. So it was mission accomplished then.

Instead we headed along the street to The Georgic, another old favourite of mine. I have to admit that after going on so much about good pubs being ruined I was more than a bit worried about what we would find inside. What if The Georgic had also been 'modernised'? A lot of pubs on the south side of the city have been gentrified in recent years. Generally this simply means they have been tarted up to suit weans who have a large disposable income and very little between the ears.

John: Craig knew all the bars in the area and first of all wanted us to visit the 'Georgic', as he said it was one of the best bars in Shawlands, if not Glasgow. Craig's favourite bars are usually closed, but this one was open, and what a great bar it is.

It is a man's pub, the decoration and paintwork making it look like a bar that has been inhabited by people who have smoked all their lives, but it is just an illusion.

It was a great bar and the barmaid, the lovely Barbara, filled us in with the history of the bar. If you are in Shawlands, this is the place to visit.

Craig was on form, his first pub had been a success. His second bar was 'Findlays'. This is a bar that people of my age know from the old days. Nothing wrong with the place, but too much white, or light coloured paintwork to make the place anything other than a couples pub. (that's a nice way of saying it).

Barbara McGinlay

Craig: The Georgic had for the most part resisted the trend towards modernisation. It looked almost untouched since the last time I had visited. The bar did seem a bit brighter than I remembered, but I put this down to the smoking ban. Once they stopped the punters from smoking in the pub the owners obviously thought it was time to chip off the inches thick layer of tar which had built up on the walls from many decades of exposure to Capstan full strength and Senior Service.

There was one rather drastic change to the place though. There was a woman serving behind the bar. There will be generations of old Georgians turning in their graves. I was only ever in the lounge of the Georgic once, and that was by accident. There were some women in there but like the pub itself they were a bit scary.

Despite the changes to the pub I was pleased to discover that one very important thing remained the same. The service was as good as ever; we were served as soon as we got to the bar.

Barbara, our barmaid, was soon chatting away to us. She told us that the Georgic would soon be celebrating 70 years in business. When we asked about Pollok fans using the pub on match days and she said that they did get the occasional fan stopping off for a drink on the way to the game, but not very often.

One of John's greatest concerns when we are out and about is the proximity of licensed premises. With that in mind I asked Barbara if she knew whether or not Pollok had a social club at the ground. I was fairly sure that a club the size of Pollok would have one but I was a little concerned that non-members might not be allowed in. There would be no controlling John if that happened.

It was fortunate then that he had a strong drink to hand when she said that there had been a social club but it was now closed. That was bad enough but she also told us that there was a rumour going about which suggested that it was to re-open soon, but as a Bistro.

What is going on with the world?

I persuaded John to visit another pub just along the road. That could never be claimed to be much of an achievement, but this time I was soon wishing that I hadn't bothered.

Findlay's on Kilmarnock Road is a wee bit upmarket for your typical football supporter's pub. There's far too much carpeting and leather-effect bench seating in the place for my liking.

The service was a bit on the slow side, bordering on grudging if you ask me, and there was a severe lack of friendly banter from the bar staff. Perhaps we didn't quite fit their preferred customer profile.

I base this notion on the fact that the special offer in Findlay's that day was a choice of exotically flavoured Martinis. While there is no doubt that it was competitively priced we decided to pass on the chance to experience the delights of Mango flavoured Martini.

In fact, by mutual agreement we decided to finish our drinks and get out of there as quickly as possible just on the off chance that somebody might see us.

There is a big Wetherspoons pub just across the road from Findlay's and we reckoned that if there were any Pollok fans around they would probably be found in there. But we were not about to find out. We only had enough time to visit one more pub before meeting the club secretary round at Newlandsfield Park

John: Things started to heat up with Craig's third bar, 'The Quaich' This was a bar I had not been in for years, and it was a well known Shawland's institution in the old days.

Today it is a fine bar that on match days has a few loyal supporters coming in before the game to enjoy a few pints, and the good thing is they are not old guys like Craig and me.

We got into company with a crowd of Pollok supporters who filled us in with stories of dressing up as Pandas for Hallowe'en and other crazy things they did, mainly on away games.

Greg Downs, John Chessar, Brian Mallon, Mark Rush, David Young

Craig: I had found The Quaich while searching for local pubs on my computer. To be honest it didn't look like a football fan's pub. If you could ignore the surroundings, tenements, railway bridges and half a million people wandering around The Quaich looks like a perfect example of a country pub.

Inside we found a really decent pub. The beer was good and the bar was comfortable. Almost as soon as we were served we got talking to our first genuine Pollok supporter.

David Young follows his team religiously. In fact he has had to arrange overnight accommodation when Pollok have been away up north on Scottish Cup business. I was about to ask why he couldn't have just come home after the games when the penny dropped. A good night of celebration would be required after travelling the length of the country to see your team thump some minnows of the junior game.

The pub had been very quiet up to this point, but the noise level fairly jumped when the rest of David's pals arrived. They had formed their own supporter's club and arrange all their own transport to the away games. Since there were only about half a dozen of them, I asked why they didn't just travel with one of the bigger supporter's clubs. One of the guys simply said "We are not welcome on any of the other buses". That seemed a bit harsh to me. Anyway I asked the lads if they would mind if I took their picture. Immediately they unfurled the biggest banner I've ever seen and began pinning it to the wall of the pub. The club colours and team logo were perfectly understandable but the picture of Bob Marley had me scratching my head. It was explained when one of the guys told me that they all liked a wee smoke now and then. Mystery solved. I didn't like to ask about the skull and cross bones.

With only about 30 minutes to go before kick-off we decided to make our way round to Newlandsfield Park.

We had arranged to meet Frany McNeil, the club secretary, and although we had been told that he was recovering from surgery, I wasn't quite ready for what I saw. I had assumed that since he was back looking after his club he would be on the mend, but the poor bloke was still hobbling around on crutches. That's what I call dedication.

John: We had to leave the boys to their drinks in 'The Quaich' to get to the ground in time to meet the Secretary, Francis (Franny) McNeill, who, although he had two sticks to help him get about after a hip replacement operation, still gave us his time and introduced us to many of the members of the committee who have worked for the club for years. I hope we have not missed out any of them in the photo of the Pollok Worthies. These people are the salt of the Junior Game.

We eventually had to say our goodbyes to Franny and wish him all the best in his recovery from his hip operation.

Back outside in the sunshine we were like two schoolboys, because we were only visiting one club and it was only about two o'clock, so we were free for a couple of hours. Not only that, but both our better halves were in Glasgow having lunch using one of these 'Groupon' deals where the meal is dead cheap, but if you have as much as a glass of water, it costs a fortune.

Craig: Despite his troubles Frany insisted on taking us up and down stairs to introduce us to his fellow committee men. We felt quite guilty about this but there was no stopping him. It was good to meet so many of the people who keep the club running and interesting to note the age range of the committee. Along with the older guys who have been with the club through thick and thin for many years we were introduced to some of the younger people.

Hugh Blair and Frany McNeil

As an organisation Pollok Juniors have a lot going for them but I have to say they are severely lacking in one of the most important areas in junior football: a decent social club. I didn't

175

want to bring up the subject of the alleged Bistro, just in case it was a wind-up, but they should definitely open a wee bar in the clubhouse, even if it was only for senior committee men and visiting authors.

John Fife, Gib Fyff, Gordon Ritchie, John Shaw

John: Talking about Groupon deals, which I was, Kate and I had lunch with friends recently and the deal was £12 for two. There were four of us, so instead of the bill being £24, it was £140! You cannae beat a good bevy on a sunny Glasgow day out, but back to our end to the day. We got the No. 38 back into Hope Street, wandered into our favourite bar '*Denholms*', and had a couple, or more.

It's funny, even at our age, when you're enjoying a wee drink on a Saturday afternoon and the barmaid says, 'a double is only a pound extra', what do you do! To say no means you are a nancy or a tight-arsed bastard, so you have a double, it's great, so you have another.

Thank god the girls were in Glasgow with a later start than us. We got the train back to EK and had recovered enough to have a drink in 'The Monty' before going home. It was funny, we were home before the wives. We could have stayed out longer, they would not have minded, but we were all drunk out. Getting old is a terrible thing.

Although it was only a one club day, my spends were more than most two club days. All the bars in Shawlands were expensive, and there was no free bevy, so about £30 was spent. Who cares? The wife (Kate) probably spent more. Anyway, we're getting on a bit and running out of time, not money.

Arthurlie

Club Name	Founded
Arthurlie Football Club	1874
Ground	**Colours**
Dunterlie Park	Light Blue & White strips
League (2014-15)	**Main Honours**
West Super League	Scot. Jun. Cup Winners
Premier Division One	1937/1995/1998
Club Nickname	
The Lees	

John: It was in August, at the start of the season when we managed to close this chapter by visiting Pollok's rivals Arthurlie. We still had the light nights so it was an evening game with a 18.45pm kick off.

The McGill's No. 3 bus from Glasgow to Neilston dropped us off on Main Street, Barrhead, just a short walk from the ground, or that was what I thought. Halfway along Main Street the bus turned left, away from the ground and we fairly shot up from our seats. For anyone who has met us, shooting up from anything is not easy. The short walk was now a long walk, well long for Craig, whose feet are killing him. Every step is a challenge. Thankfully, he's up to the challenge or we wouldn't get anywhere.

Craig: After a gap of a couple of months we at last set out to complete our Pollok v Arthurlie rivalry investigation. The weird thing was Arthurlie was actually playing Pollok on the night we decided to visit. It sounds like we chose this encounter intentionally but it was just a coincidence. We are not that good at planning.

Although Barrhead is only about ten miles away from East Kilbride, as the crow flies, it took us about an hour and three quarters to get there. That journey included two buses, a long walk along some back streets in Glasgow and fifteen minutes hanging about at a bus stop arguing about who may or may not have misread the timetable.

John: After a slow stroll down to the ground, we spotted 'The Brigg Inn' just across the road from the ground and as we had plenty of time in hand we crossed the road. Well Craig did, I nicked into the train station which was right next to the ground. I suddenly realized that we would be able to get a train from here to Pollokshaws West, and from there we could get the EK train. Now this is not in the spirit of the book as we travel everywhere using the 'Bus Pass', but with Craig's feet and the fact that we were within the £0.90p cost area for oldies on trains, I am sure you could forgive us for planning to go home on the train.

'The Brigg Inn' is a very atmospheric pub. The walls are completely covered with pictures of old Arthurlie teams and action shots from the glory days, and there are also pictures from heroes of every other sport. It's a real man's pub.

The bar staff, Eileen Kierney, who was just finishing her shift, and her replacement Archie McIntyre were both great company, even if Archie kept taking the piss out of me. When we asked about the rivalry with Pollok, they both said that the Pollok supporters where fairly even-tempered people, unlike the teams in the West of Scotland where hatred is the norm. To highlight their claim, they related the story of the time Arthurlie beat Pollok 4-1 in the Junior Cup Final. That evening in the pub as they were celebrating, about a dozen or so Pollok supporters came into the pub. The locals anticipated trouble, but the Pollok supporters were just in to join the party as it was so depressing in the bars down in the Pollok area.

We had a great time in the pub, but as we were planning to leave, I looked over to a quiet corner of the pub and there was a lone Pollok supporter with the strip on. I was sure I recognized him and asked Craig. He said he felt the same and got out his high-tec camera. Sure enough, he found a photograph of the guy that had been taken in a pub the day we visited Pollock. What are the chances? We went over and he recognized us right away. It was mad Davy, who goes to every Pollok match, home and away, and has done for years. So I suppose the chances of meeting him tonight were fairly good.

Craig: Being totally professional we went straight up to the park to check it out. That took about 30 seconds. Then we moved on to the real business of the day finding the nearest pub. As it turned out we failed, initially at least. The Brigg Inn is about 500 yards past the park and looks like a traditional Scottish pub and it didn't disappoint. Inside the Brigg gets my vote as a typical football supporter's pub. There is hardly an inch of space on the pub walls that isn't covered by photos of sportsmen. John declared that the pictures must all be former Arthurlie players. I wasn't convinced. To my knowledge Muhammad Ali has never set foot in Barrhead, never mind played for the Lee.

John: After a chat with Davy, and wishing his team well in tonight's game, well to finish in the top two anyway, we wandered over to ground, which is Dunterlie Park. Needless to say, the club's nickname is 'The Lee', don't suppose they could use the exact last three letters of the grounds name. I would imagine the opposition fans call them 'The Dunderheids', I would anyway.

Arthurlie's Secretary, Andrew Pollock, not to be mixed up with their rivals, and tonight's opposition Pollok, met us in his office and answered all our questions about his team. Like many Junior teams, money is very tight. Andrew told us that the club's Social Club up on the Main Street used to contribute around £50,000 in a year. Today it is lucky to break even. He said that the club are hoping to become a Community Club in the future. Other clubs, such as Jeanfield Swifts, have gone down this road with great success.

Andrew and Steven

Andrew introduced us to Steven Connolly, the clubs groundsman. Steven is the youngest groundsman, by a long way, that we have met. It is great to see a young guy interested in doing something that benefits his club. The guys then took us over to the wee social club in the ground, which is like a big hut. It was very nice and cosy inside, and once we adjusted our stance to allow for the slope on the floor, we had a great time. The barmaid Sarah Coubrough was great company and told us some funny stories. One of them about a misplaced shot at goal hitting the club was hysterical. I'll let Craig fill you in with the details as he was using one of his gadgets to tape the stories we were being told. Hope the thing worked, I've no faith in new technology. By that I mean I have no idea how it works.

A guy called Robert Burns came into the wee bar, Robert writes reports on the games and is writing a history of Arthurlie FC. It was good to talk to a real writer!!

The ground had a good crowd in by then, but nobody came into the wee club. A can of lager and a vodka and soda was £2.50, the cheapest price we have ever encountered, and you could sit and watch the match if you wanted. If everyone at the ground came in and bought a couple of drinks, even soft ones, at every home match, I think the money raised would make a difference to the club's finances, even at the prices they charge. Come on 'The Lees', help the club.

Talking about the park, which I wasn't, the more you looked at it, especially after a couple of vodkas, the more you wonder what way the slopes on the park are going, and they are going somewhere. Having said that, we loved the slopes and the set-up of the ground in general, and the park looked in great condition, so well done Steven, and forget about the spirit level.

Craig: We had a couple of drinks in the Brigg but to be honest I don't know what the first one tasted like, I do know it went down very smoothly, all that walking and hanging about, waiting for buses, can be thirsty work. The second pint was great and I decided to savour it as I wasn't sure there was a social club round at the park. On our way round there we were stopped by a very talkative man who asked us who was playing. He seemed really pleased to have someone to talk to and after a moment or two we found out why. It seems he is a part-time referee and was on his way to another game. John, no doubt remembering his early footballing days felt obliged to swear at the poor man. I can only assume the bloke is used to that sort of behaviour as he didn't seem to mind.

In the clubhouse at Dunterlie Park we were taken to meet Andrew Pollock, the club secretary. It was nice to chat to him about his team and the club setup, Of course John had to stick his oar in and 'accidentally' let it slip that I am from Auchinleck. Instead of the usual good-natured abuse I have received so often before Andrew seemed quite impressed. He said that the Talbot is a great example of what a junior team should be like, both in the playing side and the organisation of the club. That didn't half take the stupid grin off John's face!

Steven Connolly, the young grounds man, came in while we were talking and we complimented him on his good work on the playing surface. I think he was fair chuffed and possibly a wee bit embarrassed by this so I decided not to mention the slope. There must be a ten foot drop from one side of the park to the other. I had been about to suggest that Dunterlie Park must be one of the best drained grounds in the country. Taking a corner from the Calibar Road side of the park must be a doddle. In fact you could just sit the ball down on the line and it would take the corner itself.

Just as I was thinking that our chances of a refreshment where a bit slim Andrew told us that the was a small bar next to the main clubhouse. It is in what I assume is a Portakabin. We were the first customers of the day. There is no draft beer to be had, but with the prices being charged for a can of lager I wasn't complaining.

Sarah and John

Standing in the bar looking out at the park I thought something was different about the ground but I couldn't put my finger on what it was. Sarah, our barmaid, solved the riddle.

It seems that the wee bar was doing a roaring trade one match night when a bit of a disaster happened. During the game one of the players made a long range attempt on goal. It was a ferocious shot but none too accurate, missing the goals and striking one of the stanchions of the wee bar. The support collapsed and the whole cabin tipped over at an angle.

Aw naw I've hit the bar again

According to Sarah, glasses, people and a mini tidal wave of alcohol came sliding down the floor towards the bar.

This all happened a while ago but for some unknown reason the cabin has been left sitting at this unnatural angle. The funny thing is, the angle of the cabin almost matches the slope of the pitch. So when I looked out of the windows the ground looked almost level. Or maybe the beer was beginning to have an effect.

The bar was starting to fill up a bit just before kick-off, and one of the customers came over to speak to us. Robert Burns is a lifelong Arthurlie supporter and is at present writing the complete history of the club. With a name like his you would feel obliged to put pen to paper, although, I don't fancy his chances of getting too many words to rhyme with Arthurlie.

John and Robert Burns

After very little encouragement Robert told us a story about another writer he knew. For reasons of cowardice and self-protection I will not name the writer in question but the story itself is too good not to use.

It seems that a local reporter, who has since gone on to much greater things, was sometimes led astray by a liking for the odd refreshment. Some might say that taking a good bucket and being a reporter tends to go hand in hand, but getting the basic facts right is still expected of them.

On one occasion the reporter in question had once again taken a little more alcohol than is advisable for clear thinking and dedication to the task of accurate reporting. Instead of covering the Arthurlie game the reporter stayed in the bar and after the match simply asked some of the players how the game had gone. That's the reason why one of the Arthurlie strikers was credited with scoring all four goals in his team's victory that day, when in fact they had been beaten 1-0. The moral of that story is of course, never believe anything you read in the newspapers.

Since the game was now under way it was time for us to drain our glasses and move on.

That's when we discovered that we had not in fact visited the nearest pub to the football ground, well not yet.

John: The game was about to start, so we said our thanks and goodbyes to Arthurlie, turned right at the gates and walked up and into 'The Fereneze Inn', which is only about a hundred yards or so from the ground. The owners Christine and Paul Deehan, made us very welcome and are working very hard to make the pub a success in very trying times.

Another worthy at the bar was Allan Urquart, who played 14 years with Neilston, another local club. He also managed the club for one year. I didn't like to ask the obvious question about the longevity of his managerial experience. Some questions are better unasked, especially if you don't want a sore face.

Craig: *The Fereneze Inn is only a matter of yards away from the entrance to the park. We had been concentrating so much on finding Dunterlie Park that we failed to notice the place on the right on Carlibar Road.*

Christine and Paul

We were very impressed with The Fereneze. It was clean, tidy and very roomy. Since the game had already started we didn't expect to find any football fans in there. But we did manage to chat to the owners of the pub, Christine and Paul

185

They run a very good pub and despite the downturn all pubs are experiencing nowadays, The Fereneze Inn is doing well. There is a simple recipe for this, good beer, at a reasonable price, and pleasant surroundings. Throw in good service and you are onto a winner.

The only problem I found with our journey home was the planning of it. John had decided we should catch the train back. There is no direct journey from Barrhead to East Kilbride so he had to check through the timetables for a connection. My problem was, he did it too well. Everything worked out perfectly. He will be insufferable from now on.

John: It was getting on, so we wished the owners all the best for the future and walked the short distance to the train station. We were home in no time and Kate was surprised that I arrived home an hour earlier than I had planned. That is a first for me.

It was one of our cheapest visits ever. The fact that we were only visiting one club, linked to the prices in Arthurlie's wee club on a slope meant I had change from a twenty. Now that's a first.

Pubs and Clubs visited on our two trips;

Pollok
'*The Georgic*' great old-fashioned bar
'*Findlay's*' nice bar but more for couples
'The Quaich' good bar, Pollok's supporter's bar
Visited '*Denholms*' and '*The Monty*' on way home (mistake)

Arthurlie
'The Brigg Inn' and 'The Fereneze Inn'
Both great bars with good atmosphere and worth a visit.

Pollok; How to get there-free with Bus pass
No. 38 Glagow to Eastwood (off at Newlandsfield Road)

Arthurlie; How to get there-free with Bus Pass
No. 3 Glasgow to Barrhead (off at Main Street)

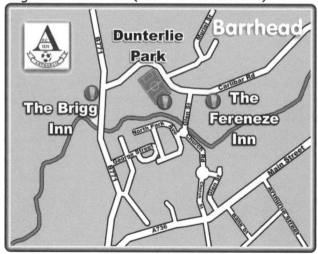

Cummnock V Auchinleck V Irvine Meadow

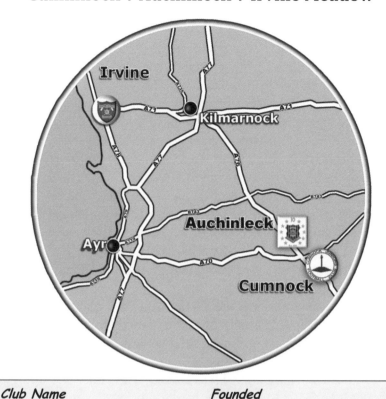

Club Name	Founded
Cumnock	1912
Ground	*Colours*
Townhead Park	Black and White
League (2014-15)	*Selection of Honours*
	Scot. Jun. Cup; 1978-79; 98-
West Super League-Premier Div.	99
Club Nickname	Runners-up twice
The Green Gingers	

John: The sharp people reading this will have noticed that there are three teams in this chapter. The truth of the matter is that there could have been dozens.

189

Picking the rival teams we would visit in the West Region was easy to sort out, or so we thought. Craig comes from Auchinleck and he knew that although his beloved Auchinleck had a few rivals, Cumnock were one of their oldest and fiercest. It was only when we spoke to other teams' Secretaries that we realized that half the teams in Scotland, and all the ones in Ayrshire, considered Auchinleck their main rivals. To be fair though, this is mainly because of the success they have had in the last 20 or so years, but more of that later and earlier, in the book.

Being the oldest and fiercest rivals we decided that Cumnock should be the first visit to Ayrshire.

The weather at this time of the year, early February I think, had been terrible. It had rained non stop for months and most of the Junior games had been postponed because of the waterlogged pitches, so finding a match on was a real problem.

The two teams we had planned to visit today had their games cancelled on the Friday, so Craig and I had an emergency meeting. The outcome was that as the Cumnock match was on we would go there. It meant only one club visited but if we wanted to get this book off the ground, we would have to take all the opportunities that came our way.

Late on Friday night I was on the 'Traveline' site trying to work out how to get to Cumnock by the shortest bus route.

It turned out to be no problem, on paper. The old X16 from the EK Bus Station to Kilmarnock then the X76 from there to Cumnock was the route.

After an uneventful two stops run down to the EK bus station, I had time to get my 'Daily Mail' before our first bus, the X16 arrived to take us to Kilmarnock. We were lucky to get on as the bus was packed and we got the last two seats. As we were sitting apart, I had time to absorb the Mail's sensible approach to crime, punishment and The Scottish Parliament, all good stuff. I would fill Craig in later, or more likely he would fill me in if I mentioned the content of his most hated paper.

At Kilmarnock Bus Station Craig managed to stop me getting on the wrong Cumnock bus, the one going to Glasgow.

190

These new buses with the names of all the places they are going to painted all over the side of them are very easy to misunderstand. It's hard to work out if they're coming or going, a bit like myself. Never mind, we got the right bus and endured a journey which took about an hour as it detoured through almost every village in Ayrshire. If that was not bad enough, Craig gave a running commentary about every street, pub, school and swingpark we passed. I was a bit worried about his knowledge of swingparks, but let it pass. He is from Auchinleck after all.

Craig had made me promise not to tell anyone that he came from Auchinleck. He was terrified. I could only assume he thought that he would be beaten up by the Cumnock people if they knew he came from Auchinleck.

How wrong could he be? Every person and supporter we met were gentlemen, some louder than others, but gentlemen never the less. Mind you, they never did find out where Craig came from.

Craig: The towns of Auchinleck and Cumnock are only a mile apart but they could never be described as good neighbours. The rivalry between their respective football teams is legendary. I don't think that there is anyone involved in Junior football in Scotland who hasn't heard of the not so friendly rivalry between these two East Ayrshire teams. That fact gave me a bit of a problem as far as visiting Cumnock Juniors was concerned.

I thought it was very unlikely that I would be able to do my usual 100% totally impartial pub report if anyone suspected that my allegiances lay with a certain 10-times Scottish Junior Cup winning club situated just along the road. It would be useless if I had to spend all my time listening to people question my parentage instead of getting on with some really good pub banter.

I therefore decided to hide my true identity. But, as I should have suspected, John found it quite hilarious to threaten to spill the beans.

The day started like any other of our trips, with me panicking about getting on to the bus. Down at the bus station John in his wisdom decided that we should check out the timetables in the travel office. John likes a good timetable; can't make head nor tail of them but he does like them.

His other reason was that it would be a lot warmer in the office than hanging around at the stance. He was right of course, but we could so easily have missed our bus because of his nonsense.

When we eventually got to the stance we found that quite a few other oldies, who were obviously made of sterner stuff than John, were in front of us in the queue. It was touch and go whether we would get a seat on the bus. Fortunately some people in front of us decided they didn't fancy their chances either and moved away.

I had exactly 38 minutes of perfect peace on the journey down to Kilmarnock as John had to sit at the front of the bus while I sat in the middle: the calm before the storm.

Once in Kilmarnock he had made up for lost time and started talking the ears off me. Strangely enough his first pronouncement was along the lines of finding a pub for a quick apres bus drink. Although we only had 15 minutes he seemed to think that it was sufficient time for us to have a 'wee swally'

I did point out that the only pub within striking distance was one we had rubbished in a previous book. Perhaps not the wisest choice! Anyway I managed to dissuade him from getting our arses severely kicked and we just waited for our next bus. When I say our bus I mean the bus to Cumnock and not the one going to god knows where that John thought we should be getting. I still find it hard to believe that John finds his way home at the end of every day.

The high point of the day for me was that I was able to point out many places of interest to John as we moved through East Ayrshire on the X 76. I think he really appreciated the insight I provided into the past and present of that great county. To be honest though, most of it concerned the past bit. Everything has changed since I used to travel around the area by bus all those years ago. I will have to admit that almost every sentence I came out with began with the phrase, 'that used to be'.

As we passed through Auchinleck other memories flooded back to me. I remembered the time Cumnock won the Scottish Cup. I didn't remember it fondly. It sent a shock wave through my old home town. But, in the spirit of sportsmanship the good people of Auchinleck applauded the returning victorious Cumnock team as they passed through the village on their open topped bus. Well they did at the top end of the town. By the time the bus got down to the far end of the Main Street I'm sorry to say that the waiting masses didn't confine themselves to hurling insults, though some of those insults were quite choice, inventive even! No, I'm afraid some of the fixtures and fittings of The Cross Keys and The Eagle Inn were lobbed at the bus. Now that's what I call rivalry!

John: When we got off the bus, our first port of call was Cumnock's ground, where we found the Secretary George Morton. George showed us around and gave us the background to the club. He was really helpful, a great guy and showed us over to the social club to let us meet some of the loyal fans.

Tom and Ashley

Barstaff Tom and Ashley were good company and got on with everyone, even though Tom came from New Cumnock!

The bar was packed and the first thing I noticed was that one half of the bar was filled with young supporters who were quiet and well behaved. The other half was filled with mainly old guys, people about our age, and the noise coming from them was deafening. It was only when we joined them that we realized that some of them had been miners and were a bit hard of hearing, so everyone was shouting at each other. It was great, and what a brilliant crowd of supporters they were. In amongst them were Willie, Jim, George, Ross, Archie and John, and the patter was non stop. One of them kept asking Craig if he had been to Cumnock before, Craig was lying through his teeth. It was magic.

John talking about his ball boy career.

The rivalry with Auchinleck is still very strong. When the boys in the bar heard that a man in Auchinleck had hanged himself, Willie said 'I didn't know we were playing that well'.

Another true story came from John Barns. John was running the line one day in the derby match when he got into a slight altercation with the opposition winger who booted him in the 'Pollokshaws', his words not mine. Anyway, reporting this to the referee is not the Cumnock way, so John just got a hold of the corner flag pole and battered the winger over the head with it. 'The bastard was offside anyway', said John.

An old guy was wandering about shouting and bawling. When I asked who he was, George told me he was John Flynn, a mad old guy who knew everything about Junior Football. I thought it would be a good idea to ask him why Cumnock have the great nickname 'The Green Gingers'-they play in Black and White strips. I think he told me why but I couldn't understand a word he said, so I'm none the wiser. It's a good nickname anyway.

About ten minutes before kick-off time we said our goodbyes loudly to the supporters and went over to the ground and into the bar reserved for players and other people, mainly mature people like us.

We enjoyed a drink bought for us by George Leishman before leaving to visit a local bar for research. We said that as we were only visiting one team today we would come back at half time to return the favour and have more chat. We were really starting to enjoy ourselves, even if some people were looking at Craig in a 'do I know you' sort of way.

Craig: By the time we got to Cumnock John had a lot more knowledge about the first 40 years of my life. We made our way straight to Townhead Park. Actually that is not entirely true; we did get to the park but I'm afraid the route was anything but straight. So much had changed since my last visit to Townhead Park that I didn't recognise the area.

But because of the absolute faith John has in my path-finding abilities I had to pretend that I knew exactly where we were. It was quite hard to be convincing when we found ourselves walking across some wasteland, but I think I managed to carry it off. We slipped in a side entrance to the park and a bloke standing there showed us into the clubhouse then found us the man we were supposed to be meeting.

George Morton, the club secretary, welcomed us warmly then showed us around the clubhouse. While doing so we got talking about club characters and George immediately mentioned one of Cumnock's greatest players Bobby McCulloch. He reckoned Bobby was a great inspiration to his team and scared the life out of many opposition defenders. Never mind defenders he said, sometimes he scared the life out of me.

After our tour George suggested that we visit the social club to meet more Cumnock fans. I had been in the social club before so I told John just to follow me. The only problem with that was that I had forgotten how long ago it was since my last visit. We almost ended up back on the waste ground again. If a couple of guys hadn't decided to leave the club just at that moment we could well have found ourselves back down at the bus station.

Inside we found a very nice lounge with quite a few supporters getting into the mood for the game. It was good to see that some opposition supporters were visiting the club as some times you find that fans don't tend to mix.

Up at the bar we found Tom and Ashley serving a constant flow of fans. Between customers I managed to talk to Tom about Cumnock's forthcoming Scottish cup quarter-final game. I was surprised at his response.

He said that it would be a very busy day but that he wasn't particularly looking forward to it. Apparently he comes from New Cumnock, next week's opposition, and he sees the whole thing as a bit of a lose-lose situation.

As per usual I took a photo of the bar staff. This led to a great deal of joking from the older fans sitting to the right of the bar. The main thrust of the banter concerned suspicions that I was an undercover DSS Inspector. John could hardly contain himself at the undercover reference as he could see how uncomfortable it made me.

As promised, George Morton came into the club to introduce us to some of the fans. He told a noisy group of older guys next to us what we were doing at the club and as soon as he mentioned the rivalry aspect of our visit the whole top corner of the club got considerably noisier. Most of the generated noise it has to be said was caused by the repeated use of four letter words attached to the name of Auchinleck. I surprised myself by remaining calm.

I got talking to a fan and he told me about one of the guys sitting in the crowd, who is a possible contender for the meanest man in Scotland. John met him coming out of the bakery in the town holding two potato scones. He said they were for his and his wife's tea. The following week he was excited to learn that a parcel had been left behind the bar at the club for him. The card with it read 'to ... you have won a meal out for two in the monthly raffle'.

When he tore open the parcel there were two small tattie scones inside.

We decided it was probably time to move over to the clubhouse. There is a wee bar in there, only canned beer, but you can't complain especially if someone else is paying.

John and George

George Leishman bought us a drink and introduced us to the rest of the guys in the bar. Eventually I decided to chance my luck once again and asked them about local rivalries. Surprisingly no one went overboard about their closest rivals just along the road. So I decided to leave them in peace to their pints and moved to the nearest pub.

John: The guys told us the best local bar was '*The Craighead Inn*', and they were right. This is a great bar and the owner Louise Allan is a brilliant landlady; the time just flew in. An interesting Junior Football story she told us was that her grandfather William Boyd had visited every Junior ground in Scotland, and there's 160 at least.

I was told a funny story in the bar by a woman, who I think was called Dorothy Clark. It was about a collie dog. I've forgotten most of the details, but the main bit is that for some reason or other they had to get the dog home, and there was no one to do it as

197

everybody had to leave the house the dog was in, so they just sat the dog outside the door of the house with £2 tucked in its collar and phoned a taxi for McCollie. They say the dog got home fine. If we stayed any longer in the pub, we would have needed a taxi.

Back in the Players Bar, George introduced us to Robert Anderson, John Sanderson, Jimmy McGee and Alan McLukie, the President. Like all Junior clubs, it's the background people and supporters who keep the club afloat.

Robert, John, Jimmy, Allan and George

John Sanderson, who was serving behind, and in front of the bar, was also the Groundsman, and did a great job getting today's game on when so many were off. I'm not so sure he would agree with me as the last we heard the team were getting humped and the goalie had been sent off, probably for banjoing someone with the corner flag!

A sad footnote to the visit was the memorial on the wall of the bar to Graeme Potter, Cumnock's brilliant goalkeeper who died suddenly in 2009 at the age of 29. He had played in the Junior Cup Final the year before he died. A sadly missed young man.

The second half was starting and the bar was closing so we said our thanks and farewell to the guys who had given us such a warm welcome and good time.

Instead of doing the sensible thing and heading straight to the bus station, Craig said we had enough time to nick back into

'*The Craighead Inn*' for a swift one and to say our farewells one last time. The farewells lasted for at least a couple of rounds, and, to cut a long story short, we missed the bus we were trying to get, although we both believe we were on time for it. What time that was I now have no idea.

Craig: Our next pub was the Craighead Inn. John had been knocking back the vodka a fair bit while I had been interviewing the fans, but even so I must say I was a bit surprised when he tried to get into the taxi office instead of the pub. After apologising to the poor woman he had shoved out of his way to get in, I dragged him out of there and into a very good bar. That was a bit of a turn-up for the books as he is quite used to being dragged out of pubs but not so much into them.

Louise, Ian and Bernard

The Craighead is a bright modern pub, but we didn't hold that against it as it was also very friendly. As soon as she spotted us Louise Allen, the barmaid, came over and started chatting away. We liked that. During our long and very humorous conversation she told us that she was really from New Cumnock. I was beginning to think that New Cumnock must be empty with all the people down here working.

It turns out she is married to a chap originally from Auchinleck who not only played for Cumnock juniors but scored the winning goal for them in a game against the Talbot. As you can imagine, he was not the most popular person in his hometown. Even less popular with his dad I would think since he was a bit of a local hero in the town after a career with the Talbot.

At the top end of the bar two guys well on their way to becoming local worthies made their feelings known on the concept of the rivalry. To cut a long story short, and by that I mean deleting all the sweary words, it seems they hold their nearest neighbours in very low regard.

The beer was flowing by this time and very good beer it was, but we had promised to return to the clubhouse for the half-time pies and pieces.

And very good pieces they were. We managed to catch up with George Leishman again and bought him a drink.

The atmosphere in the clubhouse was a bit subdued as 'The Nock' were not doing so well in the game. We therefore decided to retrace our steps back to the Craighead for a last quick drink before catching our bus back.

John: The bus eventually arrived and the next thing I remember was that we were back in Glasgow, refreshed after an hour's sleep. As we had about 25 minutes to kill before our EK train was due, we decided to nick down the stairs, across Hope Street and into one of our favourite bars in Glasgow, 'Denholms'.

After another sleep on the EK train, Craig's Irene picked us up from the station and took us home. I got a slight feeling from the ice forming on the inside of the windows that she was not too chuffed at the time of our return, or the state of her beloved Craig. I was not too bad!!!

So ended our visit to Cumnock. The first of our trips to Auchinleck's rivals. It's a great place with a fantastic crowd of locals, and a great team.

My spends for the day must have been in the region of £40, despite the fact that the drink was cheap and there was some free rounds. I will never learn.

Auchinleck Talbot

Club Name	Founded
Auchinleck Talbot	1909
Ground	**Colours**
Beechwood Park	Gold and Black Stripes
League (2014-15)	**Selection of Honours**
	Scot. Jun. Cup Winners 10
West Super League-Premier Div.	times
Club Nickname	Most successful Junior Club
The Bot	

John: It was time. We couldn't put it off any longer, our visit to Craig's beloved Auchinleck. Without doubt Scotland's most successful Junior club in the last 20-30 years, maybe longer. They have won the Scottish Cup 10 times, a record, and their club badge has 10 stars in a circle to stop anyone forgetting it.

I have discovered during my travels researching this book that almost every club sees Auchinleck as the club they want to beat. This just shows you how successful they are.

I asked Craig how many rivals Auchinleck had. He started going through them before telling me it would be quicker to go onto the SJFA web site. I think he meant every club.

Success is a wonderful thing, but it is not the reason for our book. We are here to meet the fans and the men and women who run their local clubs, always voluntarily, and, to hear their stories, hopefully funny ones.

With all this fame and success, you would think that they would want a more glamorous nickname. The one they have, 'The Bot' after the last part of their name, must have come about because the supporters couldn't be bothered shouting anything longer. How about 'the 10 men'. It's pretty good and would annoy the opposition fans. Probably not, so back to todays visit.

Instead of taking the X16 to Kilmarnock then the X76 to Auchinleck, we had to deliver five books to the Waterstones Ayr shop, not a huge amount, but that's what the job of a famous author is all about, delivering your own books!

I got Craig at 9.30am in plenty of time to get the No. 201 down to EK bus station. Craig wanted to get in the queue early to make sure we beat the rest of the oldies to the few seats available. Ayr on a Saturday is a popular trip for EK's ageing population.

We were near the back of the bus and all we could see in front of us was white perms bobbing up and down. As we were approaching Ayr, Robert Burns country, I felt inspired by the scene in front of me to try and emulate the Bard;

Ayr, a toon that nane surpasses
For white haired oldies waving free Bus Passes

After delivering the five books, Craig had said that instead of going to the bus station, we should just continue up the High Street and pick up the bus in Burns Square. I thought this sounded like a plan bound to go wrong, but today I was thinking of our Bard and a view of his statue in the square may inspire me to improve my writing. Aye right.

A 20 minute wait in a freezing gale followed before our bus, the No. 42, arrived to take us to our destination, although not before visiting god knows how many wee out of the way places. I think I've said before that we call these diversions LB's (the L is for lazy), it would save time, fuel, the environment and let the locals get some exercise if the bus just stopped at the bottom of the road. That's Ayrshire off my Christmas Card list!

Craig: Auchinleck Talbot is without doubt the most successful junior team in Scotland. At the time of writing they have amassed ten Scottish Cup titles and many regional and district honours. This has perhaps fuelled a lot of rivalry, if not deep hatred and resentment, within the ranks of the junior game.

Their closest and most ferocious rivals are of course Cumnock Juniors. In our travels around Scottish clubs people constantly refer to both these teams when the subject of team rivalries is brought up in conversation. The level of hostility attributed to them verges on that of Rangers and Celtic, though it must be said that the East Ayrshire teams and their supporters don't let religion get in the way of a good-going blood feud.

Our journey down to Auchinleck was really part two of an earlier trip. A wee while back we had completed a very successful tour of Cumnock. Unfortunately, on our way home we made the mistake of thinking that we were still fresh enough to get a bit of the Auchinleck trip under our belts.

Unsurprisingly this turned out to be one of our less than sensible ideas. Although by all accounts we had a great time of it, we have little or no evidence to confirm that.

Fast forward a few weeks and we were about to return to the town to put things right. I had devised a fool-proof plan to get us there in plenty of time to visit all the places where we thought the supporters would be gathering.

It turns out that there is no such thing as a fool-proof plan. Although, we somehow managed to miss our intended bus from Ayr to Auchinleck we still had enough time to complete our mission by getting the next one. I was just telling John that we would be coming into the village of Ochiltree in a few minutes when our bus suddenly turned off the main road and headed for the village of Drongan instead.

I have never had too much to do with Drongan. Not because it is a small, out of the way village in East Ayrshire, but because I scare easily. The town is Ayrshire's equivalent of Larkhall. It's the kind of place you frighten your kids with if they misbehave.

I think we must have seen every house in the village as the bus turned into every street no matter how small or narrow. I suppose we should be thankful that the driver didn't find any cul-de-sacs to explore.

John: It was cold but the sun was shining when we got off the bus in the main street. As we were in plenty of time we went into 'The Boswell Arms' for a quick one. The bar was busy and there were lots of people sporting the colours. There were as many supporters in the bar as go to some Junior Club matches. The opposition today was Irvine Meadow, another huge rival, so it was a big match today, a possible league decider. But that is not the important part of our story.

As soon as we got to the ground it was obvious it was a bigger set up than any other ground I have seen so far in our travels, and the playing surface looked great.

Our first call was into the social club. It was absolutely packed with supporters and the atmosphere was great. It was so busy that the girls behind the bar, all decked out in club uniforms, had little time to talk to us, so we said we would return after we had spoken to the secretary. The girls said the bar would be quieter then, although it didn't close during the match. A great idea, in my opinion.

We walked round to the small hospitality facility and were warmly welcomed by the secretary Henry Dumigan who introduced us to the treasurer David Loy and the President Morton Wright. All three were good company and gave us all of their time filling us in with all the information and stories we needed. They were also very generous with refreshments and I can honestly say we had a fantastic time with them and the other people we met. I was warming to this club which is obviously one of the best run clubs in the country, (no wonder everybody hates them).

Kick-off time was approaching and before we went back into the social club, we went over to the stand (where you sit) and found two of Craig's oldest pals Ed and Eugene who were helping out doing a bit of crowd control in the stand, I think!

After arranging to meet up with them in '*The Boswell*' after the match we went back into the social club where it was much quieter than before, but there were still some worthies enjoying the atmosphere.

The girls at the bar were excellent company but were very shy about getting their photo taken. I think Craig eventually managed to get three of them, Maureen, Mary and Liz to stand together long enough to get a photograph.

Three old worthies in particular were great company and were keeping Craig in stitches with their stories. I think their names were Ronnie, George and William, although they all had nicknames. Hope Craig remembers some of their stories.

One tale I remember William (probably Wullie) relating was that one day they were at some away match up north and were passing a wedding. As the groom wound down his window to throw coins out for the children, Wullie took off his cap and caught all the coins. He put his hat back on and wandered up the road, chased by all the children. I think he kept the money. That's his story anyway.

Willie Blane, Jim Goldie, Heather Beatson, Tom Allan

Craig: By the time we actually arrived in Auchinleck John was gagging for a drink so I rushed into the Boswell Arms and bought him an emergency vodka This perked him up no end and we made our way up to Beechwood Park to continue our trip. The social club is probably the biggest and busiest we have come across on our travels around the junior clubs. After a quick pint just to acclimatise ourselves we walked round to the committee room to meet the main men.

Over a nice wee bottle of beer we chatted about junior rivalries and how the Talbot seem to be at the top of the hit list for so many other teams. Club secretary Henry Dummigan, president Morton Wright and treasurer Peter Loy agreed with us that there is only one reason for that. It is a reaction to the level of success the Bot has achieved in the last 30 years. Henry told us that another club secretary had told him that while playing a game up at Glenafton his players were left a bit confused by the chanting of the home support. Instead of laying into their opponents they continually sang songs of their undying hatred for the Talbot. It is a similar story at a number of Ayrshire grounds. Though to be honest, the Talbot support have never exactly been shy about spreading the word about their friendly rivalry with Cumnock Juniors.

Henry, David and Morton

I was on holiday in Blackpool once and overheard a well refreshed Auchinleck man trying to convince a local that the refrain ' If you hate the Cumnock Bs clap your hands' was in fact a traditional Scottish folk song.

At the time of our visit, volunteers were collecting cash for ground improvements although to my untrained eye Beechwood was looking in fairly good order. However, Morton explained that in a dry spell like the present one everything was just fine. But West of Scotland weather being what it is things can go badly wrong if the ground drainage isn't maintained properly.

Peter Loy helped illustrate the conversation with a wee story about an unfortunate incident concerning a Talbot goalie. In a game at Beith in 1993 the Talbot keeper, Mark Thompson, managed to make a bit of an arse of himself. One of the Beith

206

players lobbed the ball towards the goal. It should have been a simple ball for Thompson to catch but conditions were against him. That is to say, the condition of the pitch, and his own physical condition. The goalmouth was a right muck hole and Mark was carrying too much weight. He tried to jump for the ball but he had sunk into the mud and didn't rise an inch. The ball floated unimpeded into the back of the net accompanied by gales of laughter from the Beith supporters.

Back round at the social club we talked to three Talbot stalwarts who were sitting at the door making sure everyone was signed in and had placed an appropriate amount of money in the donation box.

Ronnie McAuley, Georgie McMurdo, William Blake

Ronnie McAuley, George McMurdo, and William Blake are permanent fixtures at their posts. So much so that when kick-off approached and I asked Ronnie if he was thinking about going out to see the game he replied "No, we only go to away games!"

Since we didn't come to see the football either we decided to join the lads in their chosen sport and had some more beer.

The Talbot Club is the only junior social club I know which doesn't shut during the game. This is particularly handy for us non footy types as it gives us more time to talk to other like-minded social drinkers.

I asked Ronnie what his most memorable away game was. He thought for a minute before telling us about the time Talbot were drawn against a team from Peterhead. On the way up there Ronnie's bus was involved in what could have been a major accident. Travelling through Aberdeen the supporter's coach was in collision with a mini bus and tipped over on its side. Passengers were thrown about all over the place.

I had been expecting to hear about all the guys working together to rescue their fellow passengers, but that apparently was not the priority. There was a rescue operation but it centred on getting all of the booze they had been carrying out of the bus and into the bushes before the traffic police arrived on the scene.

Liz Lindsay, Maureen McMahone, Mary Palmer

Today's game was a pretty important one for both teams. Auchinleck and Irvine Meadow were both vying for the West of Scotland Premier league title. A win for the Talbot would almost certainly give them the title. To have any chance the 'Medda' had to win today and also each of their remaining games. At half time the score was 1-1. The tension was so great we decided to find somewhere to have dinner.

John: It was the second half before we said our goodbyes and left. We had about half an hour before we were meeting Craig's pals, so instead of just spending the time drinking, we spotted a Chinese Restaurant, and believe it or not, in we went.

The wee lady who met us inside told us we were just too late for the lunchtime menu, and just too early for the pre-theatre menu. Pre-Theatre in Auchinleck. Who's she kidding? We said we would pay the full price and in we went. It's amazing how quickly you can get in and out of a Chinese restaurant, especially when there's no women with you. By the way, we did have a pint with the meal, which was delicious. An interesting aside is that there were about a thousand things on the menu, but we both picked the same meal, number 23a. It looked to me as if they had missed our meal from the menu but did not want to re-number the whole menu. I told you it was interesting.

Craig: By the time we had finished our Chinese meal the game had finished. We were stunned to find that Irvine had eventually won the game 2-1. Given that the Talbot hadn't lost a home game in two years I was a bit worried that I'd get the blame for jinxing things. Junior supporters are notoriously superstitious and tend to look for omens, especially ones that explain why their team just lost.

We had arranged to meet some of my old pals in the Boswell Arms after the game but it had never occurred to me that it would also be after a defeat.

George, Ed, Alex, Davie, Eugene

The pub wasn't very busy, which didn't surprise me given the circumstances. We decided not to dwell on the result and settled for some lightweight reminiscences.

I recalled one story from many years ago which sort of sums up the thoughts of your average Juniors supporter. The story concerned a new Talbot signing back in the 1970s.

The player in question was what might be described as an enthusiastic tackler. In his debut game he stamped his authority on the proceedings by stamping on the head of an opponent. As he was being sent off I heard a couple of older supporters discussing our newest signing. "That was disgusting, that man is just a monster", one of them said. "Aye but he's oor monster", his pal retorted.

Before we got to the stage where booze and the patter became more important than finding our way home, we left to catch our bus back to Kilmarnock and on to East Kilbride.

John: Back in 'The Boswell' we met up with about three or four of Craig's pals and had a great time. Ed told me a true story about an Auchinleck supporter who had a dog that sat up and clapped its paws each time 'The Bot' scored. Ed asked him what he did if the opposition scored, 'I don't know' was the reply, 'I've only had him three months'. Three weeks later, after being knocked out of the cup by Cumnock, there was an advert in the local paper saying 'performing dog for sale, walks with a limp'. You couldn't make it up.

True stories like this were flying about all the time, but eventually, in order to get the last bus, we said our goodbyes, crossed the road and the X76 took us back to Kilmarnock. We had half an hour to kill, which was killed in the traditional way, before we got the old X16 back to EK. We got off at the stop before the bus station, walked under the Murray Roundabout and straight into 'The Lum'. Have we no had enough?

That was the end of our visit to Auchinleck'. A great club with fantastic people running it. The rivalries between Ayrshire clubs are, as usual, mainly friendly, although Craig would probably not agree with me.

Today I got through about £50. Now about £30 of that was for the meal, Craig had no money on him so I had to pay the lot, that's £15 down the swanney. That meant I only spent about £20 on drink. That doesn't include the fantastic hospitality we had at the ground-so I drank a lot.

Irvine Meadow

Club Name	Founded
Irvine Meadow	1897
Ground	Colours
Meadow Park	Blue and White
League (2014-15)	Selection of Honours
West Super League-Premier Div.	Scot. Jun. Cup winners 3 times
Club Nickname	
The Meadow	

John: I never realized Irvine Meadow considered Auchinleck to be their main rivals. Irvine Victoria was the club I thought would fit the bill as the grounds are near each other, but I was told by a Junior Historian that no, it was Kilbirnie who were now the main rivals. Kilwinning were another club that used to be considered a rival.

Before the visit I phoned the club secretary, a lady called Lynn McFarlane to let her know we were going to visit her club and if she would confirm which of the three clubs I mentioned above were her main rivals. None of them, she replied, our main rivals are Auchinleck, and no one else. So there you go, another rival for Craig's heroes. So it was off to Irvine Meadow to find out about the club and its characters, and their love for Auchinleck.

This trip was a first for us. The season was drawing to a close, the late nights were coming in and this was an evening game.

A seven o'clock kick-off meant that the game would finish about 8.45pm. I wasn't sure if it was still light then (this was the end of April) or if there were floodlights at the ground. Only time and big pylons sticking up in the air would tell us.

We planned to have finished the trip by kick-off time, so any pubs would have to be visited before kick-off. This meant, that by working backwards, which I do all the time, we would have to leave EK on the 3.01pm X16 to get to Kilmarnock at 3.40pm, then get the No. 11 which would get us into Irvine about 4.30pm for the 7.00pm kick-off. Some may say two and a half hours is a long time to fill; if so they have never read any of our books.

'The Medda' is their nickname, another case of laziness by the fans who can't be bothered shouting the whole name. This seems to be the case with many teams in Ayrshire. A team like 'The Medda', who are one of Scotland's biggest Junior clubs and Scottish Cup Winners three times should have a better nickname. How about 'The Garnock Growlers' after the river that flows through the town! Probably not.

The journey as described above went smoothly and we arrived in Irvine just before four thirty. Although the journey was smooth, Craig's attempt at coming down the stairs of the bus as it came to a sudden stop was like a Bull in a China shop. He blamed me for suddenly saying that this was our stop. His humour got worse when we realized we had got off a stop to soon. My comment that the walk will do you good didn't help.

Craig: It was time for us to go back down to Ayrshire to check out another of the big guns in junior football, Irvine Meadow. But it was not the journey that we had originally thought we would be making. While looking at rivalries in the junior football, we had quite understandably thought that the Meadows rival would be the other Irvine team: Irvine Victoria.

Usually rivalries are local affairs. It is surely easier to work up a long lasting grudge with your near neighbours than with some faceless group on the other side of the county. Not so with the 'Medda'. As John has no doubt pointed out the Meadow club secretary insisted that their only rival, on or off the field, was Auchinleck Talbot.

To me this made the whole rivalry thing much better. This might be described as more of a professional rivalry than any of the others we have come across so far. It is just a pity that our own little research team is in no way professional.

John as usual phoned the club secretary the day before we were due to visit her club. Or at least that's what he thought he was doing. I would blame number blindness but it is far more likely that he had been sampling the red wine again but, whatever the cause of his mistake, the outcome was yet another embarrassing incident.

He actually managed to phone the secretary of Irvine Victoria instead of the Meadow. I dread to think what he said to her before the penny eventually dropped but I imagine that she now has the impression that we don't rate her club very highly.

The journey down to Kilmarnock was uneventful but once there John had a bit of a geographical meltdown. When I pointed to the bus we needed to catch to get us to Irvine John announced, with great confidence, that it was the wrong one. The destination board indicated that the bus was going to Saltcoats and according to John that was away in the wrong direction entirely.

I had to draw him a little map showing the location of Irvine and its near neighbour Saltcoats. Even this did little to convince him but since we were running out of time I just bundled him onto the bus. He got his revenge by going upstairs, knowing that I hate going up there.

We then had a discussion on the exact whereabouts of the park. For someone who has never been near the place John thought he was best placed to guide us there. But eventually common sense prevailed and we followed the route I had worked out.

John: Craig recovered from almost falling down the bus stairs, and his spirits lifted when we reached our first pub, 'The Turf', a nice wee old-fashioned pub that I used to visit when Kate's sister Sheila and husband Tom lived there over 30 years ago. The bar was just as I remembered it. At that time of day it was quiet and after a couple we wandered along the road into 'The Crown'. This was another nice bar which had two tables set up for the Poker League match which was on tonight. I had never heard of such a league and would have loved to stay and watch, but time was passing and we only had time for a quick one before heading for the ground.

Craig: The Turf Hotel was our first stop and it is a place that John does know well, or so he said. Perhaps he was just having a laugh when he apparently couldn't find his way into the bar. He couldn't make up his mind which of the two doors led to the bar. As it turned out both of them did. Inside, the Turf is an old fashioned pub with very low ceilings and a long bar. The beer was good and reasonably priced. George the barman was friendly and chatted to us for a while.

He told us that on match days the pub gets really busy with supporters, but midweek evening games were never quite as busy. Since we were the only customers I saw no reason to contradict him. We had a couple of drinks at the bar but it didn't get any busier so we wandered down the road to the Crown Inn.

It wasn't very busy either but we were amazed at the size of the bar. The building isn't overly wide but it is really long, with three separate areas that I saw. It was a good pint again but by now we really needed to make our way up to the ground.

John: You could tell as soon as you entered Meadow Park that this was a big club, similar to its rivals Auchinleck's set up. But size doesn't matter to us, it's the quality of the people behind the team.

Andy Whannel, Brian McNally, Hugh Strain, Stuart McKie and Robert Gibson

We found our way to the bar and met the Secretary Lynn's husband, Tom McFarlane, at the bar working on ticket production, with a pair of scissors which he waved about when he talked. Tom and Jimmy Ryland behind the bar were great company and kept us entertained with stories and the history of the club, although at one point I almost lost an ear. Craig had his recorder with him and will regale you with some of them. One in particular about an old lady who forced the abandonment of a match is really funny. I think I heard it's on You Tube.

Lynn introduced herself, and even though they had just arrived back from holiday that day and were obviously very busy, spent a lot of time with us and were very helpful.

Lynn and Tom McFarlane

We were invited to watch the match and join them at half time for more hospitality, but we would never have made it home if we had accepted, so we had to say our goodbyes to all the people we had met and head for home.

Irvine Meadow (the Garnock Growlers) are a great club with fine people managing it. I know I've said it many times in this book, but the people behind the scenes in Junior Football are an inspiration.

Craig: *We were the social club's first customers. In fact the barman hadn't even had time to get his jacket off before we were up at the bar demanding drink. Once again all the staff are*

215

volunteers and take turns at manning the bar. As we sipped our first drink in the club we were introduced to the club secretary's husband, Tom McFarlane.

Jim Hewitson, Jim Rylan and Graham Somerville

When we explained what we were up to he agreed that Auchinleck was indeed the Meadow's greatest rival. In fact he said that as far as he was concerned they were a few years behind the Talbot in terms of club set-up and team performance but that the Meadow were constantly making up ground.

We pushed him for a humorous story about his team's greatest rival and he came up with one I had never heard before.

Some years back Talbot came into possession of a relatively new grandstand. Apparently Hamilton Accies were moving to a new ground and a deal was done to let Auchinleck have the stand from the old park. The stand was dismantled by the Auchinleck boys, who painted numbers on the various girders as they took them down. This was to help when it came to rebuilding the stand down at Beechwood Park.

Unfortunately, according to Tom they didn't have enough money to rebuild it straight away and so it was left piled up on site at the Talbot's ground. As time went by, a couple of years or so, the girders began to rust. The story goes that some helpful soul took it upon himself to protect them with a good coat of paint.

The chaos this caused when construction eventually began has provided many a laugh for Talbot's rivals over the years.

I have to admit that I did laugh when I heard this but I'm not entirely sure how true this story is.

Once Tom managed to stop laughing at his own story he introduced us to our barman, Jim Rylan. Apparently he had recently completed a 203 mile cycle run from Blackpool to Irvine to raise funds for the club. Amazingly he had done the whole thing in one overnight stint.

To celebrate his heroics we allowed him to pour us another couple of drinks. Of course John did offer to buy him a drink but, knowing he was in training and also on duty, it was a fairly safe offer for him to make.

One of the guys mentioned something about a pitch invasion which halted a recent match. We were suddenly all ears. Parking is a big problem around Meadow Park. We had seen for ourselves that it only takes a few badly parked cars in the cul-de-sac, which ends at the gates of the park, to cause problems.

"Alright, if you don't give us the ball back I'm sending ye off."

According to legend, the referee had to stop the game when an elderly lady marched onto the pitch and sat down in the centre circle. She refused point blank to move until the owner of the car blocking her gate shifted his vehicle. Apparently there is a video of the incident which has become a minor sensation on You-Tube.

Tom reckoned that she might not have been too quick on her feet but, with such a display of determination on the field, the old girl could teach a few of the Meadow's prima donna players a thing or two.

With only about ten minutes left before kick-off we got a chance to talk to club secretary Lynn McFarlane and some of the committee. They were very positive about what they wanted for the future of their club. And once again it was stressed that what they really want is to take over from Auchinleck as the most successful team in junior football. Realistically, they don't see this happening overnight, but they are sure it will happen. With the set up they have put in place they are certainly on the right track.

Stewart Griffiths, Robert Jeffery and Lynn McFarlane

Having left our drinks on the bar when we were summoned to the committee room we thought that it was only right that we go back in and tidy them away.

Somewhere between finishing my pint and saying goodbye to the guys we had met my glass was mysteriously filled up again. What a place!

It was suggested that we take in the first half of the game, thus allowing ourselves to continue enjoying the hospitality of the social club. However, John was getting that glint in his eye, which meant the vodka he had been knocking back like it was going out of fashion was beginning to hit the spot. It was time to leave.

John: As we would be too late for the last X16, I had to plan an alternative route home. This included another trip on the No. 11 bus, this time to Kilwinning, and a train to Glasgow Central.

A couple of interesting things about Kilwinning, (well three actually), apart from being one of Irvine Meadow's old rivals, is that it is also home of Kate's sister Margaret, Scotland's first Masonic Lodge (number one funnily enough), and a great baker across the road from the lodge, that makes brilliant onion pies. Apart from the taste when you bite into them, the only way you can tell them apart on the shelf is by the extra hole in the onion one. Riveting facts eh!

The link up with the train was brilliantly planned by me, and after a quick journey into Glasgow, it was down the moving stair at platform 13, across Hope Street and into our usual watering hole, *'Denholms'* for a quick couple.

We slept on the train back to EK, and as usual, Craig's better half Irene collected us from the Station. I've said it before, but if she didn't pick us up, Craig wouldn't go home. He is one of life's great night owls.

I blew about £25 today. Considering it was a one club visit that seems a lot, but that includes the train home from Kilwinning and a bag of chips somewhere.

Pubs and Clubs Visited;

Cumnock;

Cumnock's social club is a great pub
'*The Craighead Inn*', brilliant bar, worth a visit the next time you are in that area.

Auchinleck

Auchinleck Social Club-fantastic place.
'*The Boswell Arms*'-great bar with restaurant upstairs.

Irvine;

Meadow Social Club;
Great club and great company
The Turf and The Crown;
Both good old-fashioned pubs worth a visit

Cumnock; **How to get there-free with the Bus Pass**
X76 Glasgow to Cumnock

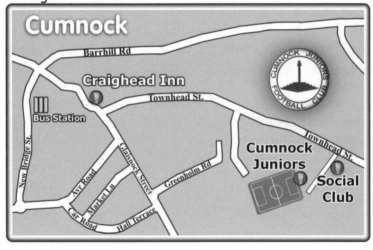

Auchinleck; How to get there-free with the Bus Pass
X76 Glasgow to Cumnock (get off in Auchinleck)

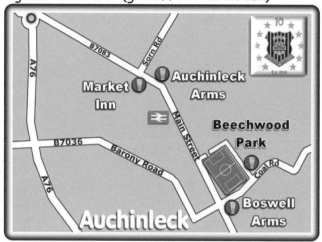

Irvine; How to get there-free with the Bus pass
X76 Glasgow to Cumnock (get off in Kilmarnock Bus Station)
No. 11 to Irvine (get off just passed the Cross)

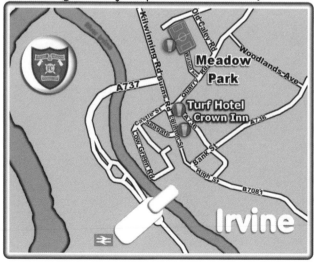

Jeanfield Swifts V Kinnoull FC

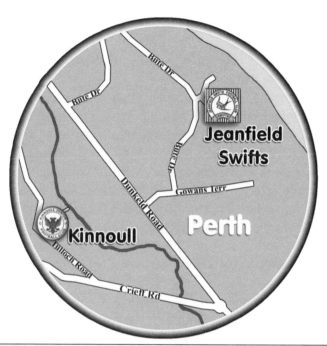

Club Name	Founded
Jeanfield Swifts	1928
Ground	**Colours**
Riverside Stadium	Black and White Stripes
League (2014-15)	**Main Honours**
East Premier League	East Region-Central
Club Nickname	Winners; 2011-12
The Swifts	

John: Perth, today's trip, would take us to the city that is recognized as one of the most desirable places to live in the UK. I think on at least one occasion it has been top of polls to decide that sort of thing. Well done Perth.

Jeanfield and Kinnoull are the only Junior Clubs in Perth. Recently Jeanfield has been the more successful, at least I have heard the name mentioned somewhere, but again I will say that success can be measured in different ways. It's like 'money doesn't bring happiness'. I hope you all know where I'm going with this because I'm lost!

At the time of our Perth visit, I had found it difficult to find a Saturday when both clubs were at home, so we decided that we would make two trips to Perth. Today's trip was to the home of 'The Swifts' and, by coincidence, they were playing their local rivals Kinnoull in an evening game. The light nights were still with us. We would return to Perth at a later date when Kinnoull were at home. It's important that we get a feel of the team's home ground and associated pubs, by which I mean the ones round about the ground.

I usually make some comment on the nicknames of the teams we are visiting. Jeanfield Swifts are called 'The Swifts' and to date I've not found one for Kinnoull. I will ask at the ground when we visit. I hope it's got more imagination than 'The Swifts', though now that I've said that, I suppose I have to come up with a better one.

Here's a real beauty. I don't know if I'm the only one who knows a fact about the bird called The Swift; well seemingly this bird never lands, it does everything, including sleeping, while flying. I got this information from an informed source, so it might be right. How about 'The Flyers' or 'we're up here and we're no coming doon', although I think the latter is a bit long. Never mind, on we go.

It's a lovely run up to Perth, which is just as well as we're doing it twice in this chapter. Being an evening game and with us only visiting one ground, we didn't have to get the Perth bus till 3.00pm. This had to change when we got an order from the Stirling Waterstones Store for some books. As the Perth bus stops in Stirling, it made sense to get the bus an hour earlier and drop the books off before getting the original bus the final bit of the journey from Stirling to Perth. I hope you are all following this.

To stop Craig from panicking, I booked us on all today's journeys, the two buses to Perth and the one back at night. The bus back didn't leave Perth till about half-eight so we would not arrive back in Glasgow till after ten. I'm usually in bed by then-hope I get a sleep on the bus!

We got into Glasgow without any major problems. It was a week or so after the Commonwealth Games had finished but the bus still detoured around the area of the games. The Calton and Parkhead areas seemed back to normal, well, normal to the people who live there.

I was glad that I had allowed an extra half an hour on our journey time into Glasgow to allow for delays, so we got to Buchanan Street Bus Station in plenty time for our bus to Perth, via Stirling.

As always, it was a lovely run up to Perth, and our stop-off to deliver the books in Stirling went without a hitch, and with time for a quick one. Well what else can you do in historic Stirling, sightsee?

We walked from Perth Bus Station to Mill Street and caught the No. 8 to the park on Bute Street.

Craig: Apart from John not knowing which town we were in for a large part of the day everything went rather smoothly on our trip up to Perth. It might seem a bit odd that the person planning the whole trip was so geographically challenged but after a while you get used to John's eccentricities. Besides I knew where we were going and kept him from straying too far off our intended route. The way I look at it I'm just getting in a bit of practice for the day when I become his official carer.

John: The park is fairly new and looks very smart. The club sold their last ground for housing development and used some of the money to build the new ground.

There were still two hours to go to kick-off but when we walked through the main entrance and out onto the park, the Secretary Eric Allan was already there and welcomed us warmly. On commenting on the park which was in great condition and looked a big park, Eric told us that the dimensions of the playing area were in yards the same as the park the World Cup Final was played-on in metres. Work it out for yourselves! It was a great park anyway.

Eric took us inside and ordered us coffee before telling us all about the club. Jeanfield is much more than just a Junior Club. It is set up as a Community Club and organizes football for teams ranging from five years old to Amateur level. It also runs two girls and a ladies team. I think there are about 15 teams in all. An amazing amount of time and work goes into the organization and running of the set up and the committee deserves the highest credit for all their work.

Willie Smith, Sheila Lizanet, Ian Armit, John Souter, Derek Mathieson, Eric Allan, John McErlain, Bob Bissett

The only downside was that when I asked Eric if any youngsters had come through the ranks into the Swifts, he told me that there had been a few, but they had been snapped up by clubs in the senior leagues. The only other downside for us was that there was no bar.

We met the President, Iain Armit, Chairman, John Souter, and Committee man, William Smith. Later on we met the rest of the committee who are a fine bunch of gentlemen, and as you will notice in the photograph, a lady as well, and better off the club are for it.

The rivalry with Kinnoull is intense, but not in the Old Firm way, and after matches the supporters and committee talk to each other, which is just as well because the Swifts Chairman, John's brother Willie, has been involved with Kinnoull for about 60 years including a shift as Chairman, and John's been with the Swifts for about 50 years.

There are quite a few cross-over facts concerning the two clubs. For example; Kinnoull used to play at Jeanfield Park; Swift's sponsors, 'Christies Bar', is located on Kinnoull Street, and so on. I like these wee facts.

Craig: I had checked out the location of Riverside Stadium, home of Jeanfield Swifts, on my computer and was quietly confident that a football team with such a large, modern clubhouse would have a proportionately large social club.

It was only when we arrived at the ground that I noticed something was missing from the wall of the clubhouse. There was no brewer's sign pointing the way to a welcoming lounge bar. I feared the worst. And that is exactly what I got!

Inside the clubhouse we were shown to what in any other club would have been a very well-kept supporter's social club. Unfortunately the strongest drink on offer was black coffee. I declined the offer. John, not one known to ever refuse a drink, especially if it is of the free variety, scoffed his coffee as if it were laced with vodka. As far as I know it wasn't, but I did take my eyes off him for a moment or two so I couldn't actually swear to its contents. He might be getting on a bit but is both fast and devious.

Eric Allan, the club secretary, filled us in on the background of Jeanfield Swifts and their aspirations to play their way to the top levels of the game. When we mentioned our theme of footballing rivalries Allan was quick to mention Kinnoull JFC. But I have to say we were a bit disappointed when he revealed that it was a friendly rivalry between the two teams. Apparently they are only rivals during the game with no real animosity after the final whistle.

Being from Ayrshire I just do not understand this kind of twisted nonsense. If you can't work up a good froth while ranting about your rivals' cheating ways there doesn't seem much point in being a supporter at all.

The rest of the committee arrived and joined in on the conversation. One of them told us that his own brother was actually on the committee of Kinnoull. I had to ask him if he still talked to his brother and was amazed to be told that they were still on first-name terms. In most of the teams I know anything about, having a brother on the opposition committee would very probably lead to a blood feud.

John asked a lot of very pertinent football questions but I'm afraid I was a bit distracted. The only question I managed to ask was, "Is there a pub nearby?"

It would be fair to say that the answer I got didn't exactly thrill me. We had landed in what to all intents and purposes was a dry area. It wasn't planned that way, it was just an unfortunate coincidence. Apparently there had been a pub nearby but it had closed down.

After a quick team photo the committee had to leave us to hold their pre-match meeting. That seemed like a good time to scurry back into town in search of a pint or two. Allan had told us that the pub which sponsors the team was called Christie's and was on Kinnoull Road. I thought that was quite amusing but I dare say the lads have heard it all before, in any event they didn't laugh. Someone told us that we could catch the bus back to town at the stop just fifty yards from the park. It was due in five minutes, according to the timetable. We were not a bit surprised when it turned up twenty five minutes late. When you use buses as often as we do you get to understand that timetables are more of a wish list than a useful guide to travelling.

John: As there is no bar inside the ground, and no pubs nearby, the guys said we should head for 'Christies' when we finished at the ground. So after taking a nice photo of all the committee and saying our goodbyes, we headed back out to the street and caught a No. 9 bus which dropped us off right outside the Swift's sponsor, 'Christies Bar'.

In we went and right away liked the bar, and the barman Dave Lindsay made us very welcome as we enjoyed a good few drinks while listening to his stories about the pub. An amazing story he told us was that in 1437, King James 1st was murdered in the cellar of the bar. It was a different premises then, but the same cellar as is used by the bar today. Even today, his ghost can be seen and felt. Craig has the details. I think, he was talking to John Williams, a local worthy, who was telling him some tales.

Dave Lindsay

Craig: I told John that I could pinpoint Christie's on my phone using the Sat-nav app. He is a bit of a technophobe and refused to accept that such things are possible. I would imagine that the first cavemen had a similar look on their faces when their pal was trying to explain fire to them. He does have a mobile phone, but it is so old that when he texts someone it comes out in Olde English.

Anyway we arrived at Christie's in less than ten minutes and I would have to say we were impressed. It is one of those few pubs which manage to work in modern elements to a traditional bar.

Although that notion took a bit of a dent a couple of minutes later as I was in the middle of complimenting Dave Lindsay, our barman, on the fact that the pub had resisted the temptation to put in-wall-to wall televisions, churning out sports programmes that nobody wants to see, when he admitted that there were seven screens round in the other part of the bar. That was a bit disappointing. But at least there was an area where you could hold a conversation without having to use using sign language.

We met our first Jeanfield fan in the bar. Actually it was a bit more complicated than that. William Smith had been a fan but that was in his youth, which I am sure he will freely admit was some time ago.

He told us that, as a lad, entrance money was collected in a big plate at the turnstiles. Fans were expected to put in what they thought it was worth to see their team play. We agreed that it was just as well that this system didn't catch on with senior teams in Scotland. There would be a lot more part-time players around if it had.

It was about this time that Dave mentioned the pub ghost. I'm not into any of that nonsense but you would have thought that, when asked if anything had ever happened in his pub, the barman would have been a bit quicker to mention that a past king of Scotland had been brutally murdered in the cellar.

Apparently James the First came to a sudden stop in his reigning not far from where we were knocking back our drinks. We speculated that he had been caught getting up to no good down there. It seems that the apparition of the late king tends to appear only to female members of staff. Call me cynical if you must but this sounds like a scam to me. Given that all of the heavy work is done in the cellar it would be very handy if you had a ready-made excuse not to go in there.

John on the other hand reckoned that the ghostly spirit only appeared after a fair amount of spirits has been made to disappear. He could be right.

Since we had only managed to visit one licensed premises so far we decided to leave this very comfortable pub and try our luck in another establishment down near the bus station. Mistake! On the way there we stopped off for some chips. Without a shadow of doubt they were the best chips I have ever tasted. It's just a pity we didn't just call a halt to our day out at that point.

I don't really know what I was expecting from Perth City Sports and Social Club but it certainly wasn't what we got. In fact the writing was on the wall before we even got into the place.

We often complain about the service we receive in pubs but, up until now, we have always been inside the pub before the staff felt free to treat us like dirt. This Social Club obviously work to a different standard.

There was a buzzer entry on the door so we were a bit unsure if non-members like us would be allowed in. Therefore John decided to ask the young lady standing by the door what the score was with entry requirements. She said we could go straight in but we wouldn't be getting any drinks until she had finished her ciggy. It turned out she was the only bar staff on duty that day.

If I had to guess I would say the lassie either suffers from asthma or else she was smoking Superkings as it was ages before she came back into the club. On reflection maybe she had the right idea, staying on the outside of this dump for as long as possible makes a lot of sense. It's just a pity that we didn't go one better and never set foot in it in the first place.

John: Too soon we had to say our farewells to 'Christies', and we made our way back to the bus station, getting a bag of chips on the way. We had time to kill before catching the bus so we took a chance and went into a dingy wee social club across from the bus station for a quick one. It couldn't be quick enough for me.

Our journey back to Glasgow was interesting in the fact that the driver announced, when we left our first stop in Stirling, that he could not stop in Cumbernauld because he did not have enough time left or he would be over the legal limit allowed for bus drivers. As it would only have meant about five minutes extra on the journey, it just shows you how strict the bus companies are with the safety regulations now, or did the driver just want back earlier as nobody on the bus was getting off at Cumbernauld. He had asked us all before making the announcement. We were delighted as it meant a wee half pint extra in Glasgow.

Kinnoull FC

Kinnoull FC	1943
Ground	*Colours*
Tulloch Park	Red and White
League (2014-15)	*Main Honours*
East Premier League	Tayside Prem. Div. Winners
Club Nickname	1982-83/83-84/2005-06
The Noull	

John: It may seem a long way to go twice to complete a chapter, but this is what we do. So it was off to Perth again to visit the other half of the rivals, Kinnoull.

Since our trip to 'The Swifts', I have found out that Kinnoull's nickname is 'The Noull'. Now that's just the last five letters of the team name, and usually I would slag it off for lack of imagination. But I like it, so there you are. 'The Noull' it is.

The run up to Perth is one of Scotland's most scenic, and it was a lovely day, so we both managed to stay awake the entire trip. We passed Gleneagles, which was hosting the Ryder Cup in a couple of weeks' time, so the Grandstands were up and the place looked great. Craig, who's not to the 'fore' when it comes to golf, was less than interested.

When we got off the bus in Perth, Craig was insistent on us visiting 'Kinnoull Social Club', which 'Google' had told him was to be found in Charles Street. Now this is near the Bus Station, and after all, it is Kinnoull's Social Club, so I agreed it was worth a visit. Anyway, we walked around for a bit following the Google map on Craig's new hi-tec phone, got lost, but eventually found it. It was a car park.

As usual, Craig claimed it was not his fault and showed me the 'Street View' of the place with people outside having a smoke.

I think the place had gone up in smoke with them! As most people who have read any of our wanderings will know, this situation is not unusual.

Craig: *Due to circumstances beyond our control it was a good four weeks between our visit to Jeanfield Swifts and Kinnoull Juniors.*

Although the teams are only a mile or so apart we could not manage to visit both on the same day. But since we both like Perth, it wasn't too much of a hardship for us to travel back up there for a pleasant day and enjoy a little refreshment in a couple of the town's hostelries.

As usual, our visit started off with a bit of a difference of opinion. John thought he knew where he was going, though in my opinion he couldn't find his own rear end using both hands and an ordnance survey map of the area. I did go to great lengths to explain exactly where the Kinnoull Supporters Club was. In fact I used my favourite, fool-proof navigational tactic. With many years of experience in the field I have found that if you can locate the main pubs in any given area then you don't really need to bother with street names. In this instance all we needed to do was to wander along the road from the bus station until we reached the Royal Bar. Once there we needed to turn right then second left then left again and we would be standing outside the club. That is not how things worked out. There were two main reasons for that.

Firstly, John decided that we could make better time if we took to the back streets of central Perth. To cut a long story short we got lost. When he at last stopped breenging up and down these roads I took over the navigation. That was when the second reason for our failure became apparent. The social club had been demolished. It was now a small car park.

By the look on John's face I could tell that he wasn't overly impressed by this. I wasn't exactly thrilled myself but decided to make the best of things. There was a pub around the corner which I had noticed while John was charging up and down the road muttering some rather nasty observations about my character.

John: We wandered round the corner and found a pub called *'The Twa Tams'*. It looked nice, if a bit up-markety for us, but we were both gasping for a pint, well especially Craig, so in we went.

It was a really nice pub and the three girls behind the bar, Zoe, Kaya and Siobhan, lovely Scottish lassies with mothers who wanted film stars for daughters. They were great company. Zoe, the gaffer, kept us amused with stories of funny things that have happened in the bar. As usual, Craig recorded the stories, and if his machine is working better than 'Google' he may fill you in with a couple of them. One story I wanted to find out was how the pub got its name. Now, I know none of you will believe this, but seemingly, the pub was named after the two owners who were both called Tom. You can't beat Perth for a bit of originality. If I had been one of the two Toms', I would have called it *'Tu Tams Kum-Inn'*, after the famous Egyptian Pharaoh of a similar name.

Kaya, Zoe and Siobhan

Following instructions from the girls, we said our goodbyes and headed up the road to Mill Street, Stand B, where our next bus, the number two awaited. The driver was very helpful, and told us when to get off; if we had been in some buses in the West, we would have been told where to get off!

Craig: *The Twa Tams on Scott Street was more than a few steps up from your typical supporters club but we desperately required a wee drink. It was rather an odd set-up at the Tams. On* the forecourt area along with seating and tables, there were what appeared to be a couple of garden sheds. Inside it was well laid out and surprisingly big. There was a small stage with a good sized sound-system, indicating possible evening entertainment. In short everything John hates in a pub.

After getting our drinks there was only one question on our minds: where the hell did the Kinnoull Social Club go? Kaya Fraser and Zoe Cooper, our barmaids, quickly solved this riddle. The building was near enough falling down of its own accord but developers had moved in and finished the job. Yet more flats will be built on the site - eventually!

Being disappointed is fast becoming one of the features of our travels lately but we never let it stop us. Instead we just have a quiet drink and talk nonsense to the bar staff. So as not to duplicate our efforts I tend to concentrate on the drinking side of this arrangement leaving John to babble away to his heart's content.

We were joined at the bar by The Twa Tams landlady, Zoe Cooper who, after a bit of encouragement, told us a couple of stories about her pub.

It seems that one of the part-time staff had once had to deal with a rather angry customer who was causing trouble in the pub. Unfortunately for the customer the barman was James Craig who played rugby for Scotland. Once he had been persuaded to go outside, the unfortunate drunk continued his nonsense, lashing out with his fists but only succeeding in tearing James's shirt.

This could be said to have rather annoyed the barman as he proceeded to administer a short but painful lesson in behaviour modification to the ex-customer.

He then ripped his damaged shirt off and walked back into the pub. In most pubs a half-naked man walking through the place might have caused a bit of a stir but, since the whole incident had been watched on CCTV by the staff and customers, all James received was a round of applause.

We probably had at least one more drink than was absolutely necessary but the patter from the girls was too good to *miss. Eventually though, we had to make a move, and we headed up to Tulloch Park.*

John: Our helpful driver made sure we got off at the correct stop. We crossed the road and as we approached the ground, we could tell right away we were going to have a good time, as it just felt right. At the gate a gentleman was sitting, and as we approached he got up and introduced himself. I thought it would be the secretary, Charlie Grieve, whom I had phoned the night before, but no, it was the president, Chris Jones. Charlie had warned him we were coming. I thought he was waiting at the gate just to welcome us, but the regular gate money collector was off and he was filling in. This is typical of the hundreds of jobs the guys who run the junior game carry out to keep their clubs going.

Chris introduced us to Charlie and we had a great time listening to their stories. The lads took us inside to the hospitality room and Craig's eyes lit up at the sight of a bar in the corner. Other characters we met included Graeme Chalmers, who had been the secretary for 19 years, Roddy MacPhee, who was behind the bar, and Christina Steward, who looked after the food and refreshments.

Christina and Roddy

They were all fantastic company and again Craig had the recorder working. But I wanted to know if they had any complaints about their better-off rivals Jeanfield Swifts. Not at all, said President Chris with a straight face. 'Well apart from stealing

236

four or five of our best players each season and two managers in recent years, we get on very well'. Although I know it annoys them that this happens on a regular basis, they know there is bugger all they can do about it.

George Cunningham, Louie Harper, Digger Miller, David Miller, Rab Harris

The men and women who run Junior football almost all get on very well and they are aware of each other's problems. Today's opposition was Bathgate and we had the pleasure of meeting most of their committee. Among them were Hugh (Digger) Miller, his dad was a miner (thank god he wasn't a gynaecologist); George Cunningham, 30 years vice-president and the kit man, David Miller, the secretary, Louie Harper, who videos the games and Rab Harris, the dad of one of the players.

We also had the honour of meeting Jim Walker, MBE, President of Bathgate and a local councillor for 40 years. I bet he lives in a big house!

We had a great day with Kinnoull, and spent some time in the sunshine talking to the lads while Craig took a couple of photos. For the first time in this book, we were watching the match. After about 10 minutes Kinnoull scored with a brilliantly taken free kick. We decided to leave while the luck was with us, so we said our goodbyes to the lads and wandered out to the bus stop.

Craig: From the moment we entered the ground until we left we were treated to some really great and friendly patter. Kinnoull

don't actually have a public bar in their clubhouse but we were invited into the small hospitality room.

As soon as we got in there I started chatting away to the guys who I assumed were Kinnoull committee but, after about five minutes, someone kindly put me right. I was in fact interviewing the committee of their opposition.

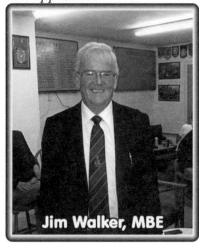

Jim Walker, MBE

Not that it really mattered as everyone was so friendly. It might be the West Coast sceptic in me but I really don't think that level of the committee friendliness happens elsewhere.

Anyway, I eventually got talking to the most important person in Kinnoull's back room staff, Christina Stewart. The food she had prepared was fantastic. Had it not been for my fear of getting a telling-off from Christina I may well have filled my rucksack with some of the goodies she had set out for the after-match tea.

Roddy Mcphee, our barman for the day, was also in good form and didn't even bat an eyelid when I asked for a glass for my can of Tennent's. John thinks it's hilarious that I refuse to drink straight from a can but I have worked in pubs before and know that cellars are far from hygienic. It is a certifiable fact that, as yet, no one has successfully housetrained mice or rats. Until that happens I will continue to wipe the top of my cans and pour the contents into a nice clean glass.

Graeme Chalmers, the club's ex-secretary, told me that Kinnoull Juniors only has three people on its committee. I found that shocking. There is so much to do in the running of a junior football club though I would imagine there is also a lot of satisfaction to be had making sure your community is well represented by their local team. There must be fans out there who could be persuaded to put their names forward to help the club.

We had been talking so much, only stopping to down a drink or two, that kick-off was fast approaching. What we really needed to do was get a story or two from the committee boys. They didn't disappoint.

Chris Jones, the club president, told us about the time Kinnoull was playing a cup game away from home. On the way back from the game the team bus was stopped to allow the lads a wee refreshment. This was something that didn't usually happen, but away cup ties are a bit special.

It was a freezing cold day with the odd flurry of snow, and unfortunately the driver managed to leave the bus headlights on while they were inside enjoying their break. When they emerged from the pub the battery was so flat that the bus wouldn't start. At one point they even tried to push-start the bus but they had to give up.

There was nothing else for it but to go back to the pub and wait for a replacement bus. Because of the weather conditions it was shutting time before that bus arrived.

Chris said there was a lot of explaining to do when they eventually did get home. Apparently the story about the breakdown and the fact that they were all well sozzled didn't go down well with their partners.

By this time the game had actually started and to be honest that was a new experience for us. We generally disappear before a ball is kicked, in the interests of impartiality of course. Anyway, Charles Grieve, the club secretary, told us a wee story which had us chuckling a bit.

During a pre-season friendly against Rob Roy one of the Kinnoull players managed to break his arm. That was bad enough but at the hospital they had to cut the poor boys strip off to tend to his arm. Finances being what they were there was a knock-on effect to this accident. For the rest of the season whoever played in the number six shirt did so with only one sleeve.

We were about to leave the park when Kinnoull scored a goal. This was the first goal we had ever seen scored in all our travels around Scotland's football teams. Just to mark the occasion we both applauded.

Graeme, Chris and Charles

We were still clapping when a supporter wandered over to talk to us. He said that he was amazed that the ref had allowed the goal to stand. Since it looked like a perfectly straightforward goal I asked him what he meant.

It seems that the referee and Kinnoull have a bit of history. Before he had gone over to the dark side the referee had once been the Kinnoull goalkeeper. Apparently, not long after, he stopped defending his goal line he began running the touch line.

In a crucial cup game he gave a devastating decision against his former team mates which put them out of the competition. According to the chap I was talking to, the match referee had *disallowed the goal but his linesman, the ex-goalie, insisted it should stand.*

I got the impression that on bonfire night in this area of Perth it is not an effigy of Guy Fawkes which sits on top of the wood pile.

John: Craig wanted to visit the nearest bar to the ground, which was 'The Tulloch Institute'. We had visited it last year when we were covering St. Johnstone. I told Craig we didn't have a lot of time and that the only way we could manage it was if a bus came right away. It did, and about two minutes later we were outside 'The Institute' trying to talk the two lads on the door, Chris and Graeme, into letting us in. They said we would have to be signed in, so after we told them the reason for our visit, they fell about laughing and let us in.

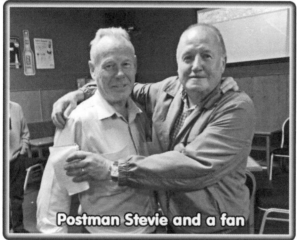

Postman Stevie and a fan

At the bar, we got a round in, and to our surprise, were recognized by a local worthy, postman Stevie, who remembered us from our last visit. We had mentioned him in our last book, but he was disappointed that we had not detailed that he was one of Perth's greatest Junior players. When we told him the two teams in Perth we were visiting, he told us that they were the only two teams in Perth he hadn't played for. Now I was sure that my research told me that there were only two Junior teams in the town, so I challenged Stevie on this point. He told me he played for

241

Luncarty, 'just outside Perth' and another club that is no longer in existence, also just outside the town. Now Stevie's the local postie for goodness sake. Hope he has more idea where the letters are to be delivered.

It was time to go, so we said our goodbyes to Perth's greatest ever postie and headed back out into the sunshine. There was a bus at our stop, and, believe it or not, I waved over to the driver and he waited for us before taking us back into the town. Perth bus drivers are the best!

Because of the quick journey, we had time for a quick one in 'The Burns Tavern', I think it's called. The place was full of mainly lunatics, but we like this. We fit in well.

Craig: After a wee stop off at the Tulloch Institute, we caught the bus back into town. It arrived bang on time which meant that we could manage a quick pint in The Robert Burns Lounge, which is near the bus station.

I thoroughly enjoyed my pint but have to say that readers of a more delicate disposition might want to look elsewhere for a quiet refreshment. There isn't actually a sign to tell you, but I'm fairly certain that tattoos are a requirement if you wish to be a regular in this pub.

John: The old 4.10pm bus will wait for no man, so we headed back to Glasgow. Now, we were back in the city before six, so I was sure Craig would be wanting a session, which I was up for as Kate, the good lady, was away for the weekend with her two sisters. But would you believe it, he had to go straight home as Irene, his better half, is having a bit of trouble with field mice nipping in to their house, and wanted Craig home before dark. The astonishing thing is that Craig agreed. There's something seriously wrong with him.

So I returned home reasonably sober and had only spent in the region of £20 all day. Mind you, the drink was dead cheap at the ground.

Both clubs we visited in this chapter are run by people who are not only great committee men, but some of them should be committed.

242

Pubs and Clubs visited;

Jeanfield Swifts
'Christies'-great bar-worth a visit
Kinnoull
'Kinoull Social Club'-it's no' there-it's a car park
'The Twa Tams'-great bar
'The Tulloch Institute'-old fashioned social club-but good
'Burns Tavern'-handy for bus station

Jeanfield; **How to get there-free with the Bus pass**
M8 Glasgow to Perth Bus Station
Walk to Stop C, Mill Street
No. 8 or 9 to Bute Drive

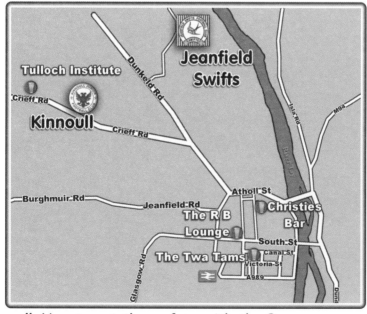

Kinnoull; **How to get there-free with the Bus pass**
M8 Glasgow to Perth Bus Station
Walk to StopB, Mill Street
No. 2 to the Ground
(Same map for both grounds)

243

Beith Juniors V Kilbirnie Ladeside

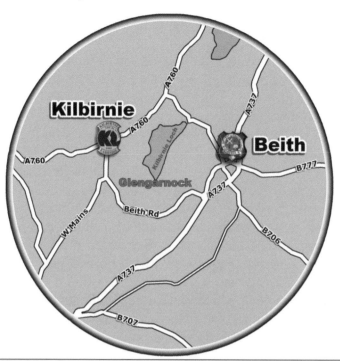

Club Name	Founded
Beith Juniors	1938
Ground	**Colours**
Bellsdale Park	Black and White Stripes
League (2014-15)	**Selection of Honours**
West Super League, Premier Div.	West of Scot. Prem.
Club Nickname	Winners; 2009-10
Cabes or The Mighty	

John; We make no apologies for doing another two Ayrshire rivals. There is nowhere else in Scotland where the small ex-mining towns are at each other's throats quite as much when match day arrives. I've been told the other days of the year are not a lot better.

Both teams are in the West Super League, Premier Division, so we are talking about the crème de la crème, no idea if that is the correct spelling, or the right use of the wee dash things for that matter; anyway, on we go.

Their nickname, 'The Cabes' or 'The Mighty' are both good ones as you can't tell from them how they came about. So they are ok with me.

I try not to talk about our journeys too much as they have been done to death, but I must make an exception for today's trip. We got off the No. 18 in George Square with the intention of walking up the hill to the Bus Station to catch the X34 at half past eleven, but as Craig was complaining about his feet and the hill, I came up with the idea of continuing along St. Vincent Street and picking up the X34 as it comes down Wellington Street. That would mean we might catch the earlier eleven o'clock bus, which would mean time for another pint. I wish I had thought of the idea a few minutes earlier and we could have stayed on the 18 until it went up Hope Street, which is close to Wellington Street. It was just coming up to eleven o'clock, so speed was needed. Now speed-walking with Craig is not an option, so luck was required, and we had none. Just as I was running up to the stop, the bus went right past us. The driver must have seen us as the road was very quiet. I shouted after the bus, 'that was not very nice of you', or words to that effect.

After getting our breath back, we realized that we had half an hour to kill; no discussion was required, we wandered round the corner and into 'The Pot Still'. You wouldn't believe it, they were cleaning all the pipes and there was no lager, so Craig was fuming. We marched out of the place with Craig complaining that pipe cleaning should be done outwith opening hours. He has a point. Another two minute walk took us to Renfield Street and we found 'The Maltman'. The pub is very big and I am sure it will be packed with the younger generation at night. A quick one later we walked back to the stop and caught the bus we were originally going for, the 11.30am X34.

It was a lovely and comfortable big double-decker and fairly belted down the road to Beith. On the journey we both had a couple of our pieces to help us soak up the bevy in the day ahead. Craig was doing his Google Earth bit on his magic phone which showed him where we were. I confirmed his results by looking at the big sign on the road that said Beith. Never mind, it keeps him happy.

Craig: It would seem that the bitterest of rivals, on and off the football field, are to be found in Ayrshire. The two towns we visited today certainly have some history together in the rivalry stakes. Beith and Kilbirnie, being only ten minutes apart by bus, are ideally suited to be deadly rivals. There is certainly enough documentary evidence, often splashed across the front of the local newspapesr or detailed in the court reports of those same papers, to prove there is an unhealthy relationship between the two towns. Unfortunately for both towns' Junior football teams much of that hostility is associated with football.

A few nutters can quite easily earn a team a nasty and long-lasting reputation.

We had decided to visit Beith first as they were having an open day and the committee would be at the ground much earlier than usual. The journey down to Beith was uneventful apart from John getting a bit hyperactive the nearer we got to the town. He wasn't quite at the stage of chanting ' Are we nearly there yet? Are we nearly there?' But it was getting close to it.

He had produced a couple of maps but something had gone badly wrong when he had printed them off. The pages were almost totally black. He must have used up a couple of quid's worth of ink making maps which were unreadable. Once again my smart phone saved the day. The sat-nav is so accurate I could pick out the pub we were looking for and even the bus stop we needed to get off at.

John was not impressed, and claimed that it had been a lucky guess on my part when we arrived at the exact place and time I had predicted. If technology is any more complicated than a pencil sharpener John's technophobia kicks in.

Although I then showed him the exact route we needed to take to get to Bellsdale Park, home of Beith Juniors, he decided it would be much safer to ask a local for directions. Obviously the man agreed with me and my phone and we set off on the five minute walk to the park.

John; We got off in the main street, and a local guy told us how to get down to the park. The two things we noticed right away about the ground were that firstly, it has a lovely setting with a great atmosphere. The second thing, and one of my favourites about the park was the slope; it was amazing. One of the wings in particular is Alpine, Both Beith's wingers have to wear crampons, but it gives them a great advantage over the teams that are under the illusion that football is played on a flat surface. What a load of crap; this was a great park.

Robert McCarter Hughie Cree Mark Sneddon Alan Cree
John Boal and Maggie Jackson

Inside the clubhouse, people were busy rushing around getting food and refreshments ready for an open day that was happening today. When we asked to see the Secretary, Robert McCarter, we were shown through a corridor and into a nice room-with a bar. Craig would have clicked his heels if he could have managed it.

We feel we have to do our bit to help the funds of the Clubs we visit, so the least we could do was buy a round, which we did. This was starting to look like a good day.

Robert joined us and was great company. He answered all our questions, filled us in on the Club and told us some great stories about the rivalry between Beith and Kilbirnie. The trouble is that Robert didn't want us to repeat most of them. You could probably find out about them by reading local police reports. Robert introduced us to the club President, John Boal, plus committee members Mark Sneddon, Hughie Cree and his son Allan. We also met Maggie Jackson, bus company owner and one of the club's sponsors.

Craig was doing his tape recording bit and I heard him laughing at some of the stories he was getting from Martin Dickie, one of Beith's loyal supporters. While he was taping stories I was being entertained by Clem Pott, past treasurer for 32 years. I'll let Craig fill you in with most of the stories, but Clem told me a great one about a player called Ian Aitken who had been signed from St. Mirren. This was many years ago. Well, Ian had missed training one night, and, as missing training was a serious problem, he was called in the next night to explain the reason for his absence. Seemingly he had just bought a flat in Paisley and it was his night to do the stairs. Modern footballers have no idea they are living, or what 'you're turn for the stairs' means, for that matter.

We were having a great time and the drink was flowing. There was great hospitality from our hosts, and behind the bar Sandra Stirra was never still.

As is always the case when you're enjoying yourself, the time flew in and all too soon we had to say our goodbye to Robert and the rest of the team who keep Beith to the fore.

Craig: As we walked down the hill it was hard not to notice that the football ground had a pronounced slope. I said to John that if it had been a pool table every game would finish with the black ball in the bottom left pocket. Even I could pot that shot.Beith were having an open day, and when we entered the park there was a lot going on. In fact everyone was so busy we thought that they might not have time to talk to us at all.

In the clubhouse a huge selection of cakes, sausage rolls and pies were being laid out ready for the celebration. It all looked mouth wateringly good but we maintained our professionalism, headed straight through to the bar and ordered a drink. The function room we were in was a good size and was quite comfortable, more importantly it had a purpose-built bar.

Our favourite tipples were reasonably priced and served by our barmaid, Sandra Stirra. As we were the only customers at that point we made a special effort to keep her from becoming bored. We achieved this by drinking really fast and then ordering another drink.

Sandra Stirra   Martin Dickie Clem Plott

On our travels around Scotland's junior football teams we have noticed how hard the club secretaries have to work, especially before kick-off. Beith Juniors is no exception. We eventually got to meet Beith secretary, Robert McCarter and in between checking various forms and membership applications he managed to talk to us for a little while.

He told us that Beith and Kilbirnie could very definitely be described as intense rivals. But he added that most ordinary fans of both clubs wished that the rivalry was played out on the field and not carried on elsewhere. Both teams have had their fair share of crowd trouble.

Robert is very keen to get the whole community involved in supporting the team. Ideally he wants to see families coming to Bellsdale to enjoy a pleasant trouble-free day out. To encourage this, the club will very soon have their very own mascot, if someone can be persuaded to spend every second Saturday dressed as a giant badger. So far there have been no takers for the job which is quite sad.

Just to be helpful I put John's name forward for the post. He seems eminently qualified for the job as he can often be seen staggering around on Saturday afternoons making an arse of himself.

I'm packing this job in. They Kilbirnie boys keep trying to Cull me!

One solution to the recruitment of the Bellsdale Badger, suggested by Robert, was to make the job the booby prize at the Christmas raffle.

It is not that easy coming up with a funny story on demand but Robert managed to dredge up one from the past.

Apparently the Beith team bus, while on route to a cup game up North, got a bit lost. They had arrived in town but didn't know the way to the park. Robert got off the bus to find someone to ask for directions. Knowing how much of a waste of time it generally is

251

asking the first local you meet for directions (they always turn out to be the village idiot), Robert decided to find a policeman to ask.

Eventually he found one and asked him the quickest way to the football ground. The policeman thought for a few seconds before asking Robert if he was walking or driving. "Driving" he replied. The policeman nodded and said, "Yes, that's definitely the quickest way", then turned and walked away.

We were introduced to the other members of the committee, past and present, and probably enjoyed a little more hospitality than was entirely good for us.

John; Under their instructions, we walked back up the hill to the main street and into 'The Saracen Head Hotel'. The place was packed and the atmosphere was terrific. The girls behind the bar were really friendly and when we told them the reason for the visit, they introduced us to a crowd of Beith supporters who, to a man, were crazy, in a good way. I think their names were Robbie, Jim, Gordon, Ian, Billy and Greg. Craig took a photo of them all outside the pub, and you can see that they are a motley crew. They told us stories of battles between the two towns. The problem with these is that there has been so much intermarrying between the towns, and if you took it seriously, you would be battling with your brother, or more worryingly, your sister.

Robbie Sanderson Jim Calderwood Gordon King
Ian King Billy Jackson and Greg Young

In their younger days I think the brothers Gordon and Ian may have been a bit of a handful. Don't want to say any more as we would like to return to this great bar in the future. They called themselves TOIK, which means brothers 'Take Over In Kilbirnie'. There is another meaning to these letters, but they are unprintable. We had a great time with these blokes, who are fantastic company and god knows how many rounds were bought. Eventually we had to go as we were getting to the stage of not being able to stand. The boys assured us that the good people in Kilbirnie (my words, not theirs) would never notice.

The one important piece of information we got was that there are no pubs open in Kilbirnie anymore. They are all shut, except 'The Glendale', which is not officially in Kilbirnie, well not all of it, but in Glengarnock. Hope you are following this.

Somehow, we managed to get out of 'Sara Head Hotel', go across the road, and on to the local McGills number 904 which took us the 10 minute run into, or almost into, Kilbirnie. The bus stopped right outside 'The Glendale', and in we went.

Craig: The lads in the social club told us that a lot of the fans liked to gather in The Saracen Head Hotel before the game. So that's where we headed next.

Angela Ness and Rachel Manning

The place was crowded when we got there, with just enough room for two thirsty old geezers to saunter up to the bar and order

253

a drink. Rachel Manning, one of the barmaids, told us that the very loud group of drinkers, over by the door were great Beith supporters.

On hearing this I immediately suggested to John that he should go over and talk to them. They looked a bit rough and I decided that, of the two of us, John was definitely the more expendable. Well somebody has to make the big decisions.

Although the pub was quite noisy one guy in the group could be heard above everybody else. For a moment I was convinced that he had plugged himself into the PA system.

Eventually I ran out of excuses to talk to Rachel who, with the other barmaid, Angela Ness, had been keeping the thirsty punters and myself well supplied with foaming ale. I felt obliged to go over to the crowd John was involved with. Everyone was still smiling so I thought it would be safe enough to join them. I'm glad I did as they were a great laugh.

Gordon and Ian King are brothers and in my opinion appear to be dead ringers for the Mitchell brothers out of Eastenders. They had a few stories to tell us about the rivalry between Beith and Kilbirnie but I am fairly sure something bad would happen to us if they ever appear printed in a book. (only kidding lads)

At one point I mentioned another drinking place in Beith that we had been told about, the Masonic. One of the boys we were having a beer with had some very bad news for us.

Not only was the Masonic recently closed down, but another pub owned by the same person had recently been closed in Kilbirnie. According to our informant the owner of these two drinking dens had suddenly shut up shop and left for an extended holiday in Spain. He is not expected back any time soon. We were devastated.

The pub in Kilbirnie was called Ramage's and it was a pub I had been looking forward to visiting. I can only speculate as to what it must have been like on the inside but from the outside it looked rougher than a down market saloon in Dodge City. If I was to be asked for a one word description of the place I would have to say 'intimidating'.

Kilbirnie Ladeside

Club Name	Founded
Kilbirnie Ladeside	1901
Ground	*Colours*
Valefield Park	Black and Gold
League (2014-15)	*Selection of Honours*
West Super League, Prem. Div.	Jun. Cup 1951-52; 1976-77
Club Nickname	
The Blasties	

John; 'The Glendale's a nice wee pub and the barmaid Tracy Ward made us welcome. I asked her about the position of the bar geographically. Now this is interesting. Seemingly, half of the bar is in Dalry, a bit is in Kilbirnie, and the rest is in Glengarnock. I wonder how this affects their rates, if there are any. As I had very little idea where I was, the fact that I was in three different places at the same time made no difference.

Tracy Ward and Del Shannon

One of the locals, well local to somewhere, was called Del Shannon. He promised me he wasn't taking the piss and we had a great time with him and Tracy. I heard him tell Craig a story involving Beith supporters and Police horses. Hope Craig remembers it.

Talking about Police horses reminds me of an old story about an incident involving a Police horse at a match at Hampden. There was a huge crowd and big queues. A lady Policewoman on a horse was doing her best trying to control the crowd. This wee bloke shouts up to her 'misses, your horse is sweating'. Her instant reply was fantastic. 'So would you if you were between my legs for two hours'. I don't care if you've heard this story, it's worth repeating.

Unfortunately, time was short, and we had to say our farewells and leave in time to get the next 904 the rest of the way to Kilbirnies ground, Valefield Park.

Craig: We had to change our plans after hearing the tragic news about Ramage's Bar shutting down. In fact we only had one other option as it seems that Kilbirnie is apparently fast becoming a dry town. The Glendale Arms is the nearest public bar to Valefield Park and it didn't strike me as a natural supporter's pub.

Being on the outskirts of the town home fans would have to travel past the football park to get a couple of pre-match pints. Then they would have to get a bus back for the game. It would cost a fortune in bus fares if the team hit a winning streak since the real fans would feel obliged to return to The Glendale for a celebratory beer or two.

The bar in The Glendale is quite large and fairly comfortable. While we were there only one other customer was enjoying a drink in the place.

The prospect of a wide-ranging debate on the pros and cons of modern football looked to be unlikely but we persevered. The other customer in the Glendale Arms claimed that his name was Del Shannon. Even I have heard of Del Shannon and so I obviously thought he was having a laugh. But he insisted that it really was his name. This gave John the chance to bore us with his alleged knowledge of Del Shannon's back catalogue, most of which I had never heard of.

While we enjoyed our beers we chatted to Del about some of the problems local rivalries can cause in pubs. He had a story to tell us which concerned an encounter with a few angry Beith supporters. Apparently Del -that's our Del and not the long dead American singer- was enjoying a quiet beer when a group of noisy supporters came into the pub shouting the odds. Before he could finish his story John interrupted, asking Del, "Did you run, run, run, run, run away?"

John was very pleased with himself after this little joke. So much so that I thought he might do himself some damage with all that laughing. He's not a young man anymore and perfect bladder control is a young man's game.

We never did get to hear the end of Del's story.

The barmaid, Tracy Ward, told us that the pub did indeed get supporters in on match days but never any Beith supporters. It is always hard to be sure when someone is kidding or not, but the barmaid told us that Beith supporters are barred from the pub.

Given its position, that could be quite understandable. The Glendale is well within walking distance of Beith. Depending on how the grudge match worked out this pub sits on the main road between the two towns and would be an ideal stopping off point to celebrate a classic win or to start the process of sorrow-drowning. It only takes a couple of tanked-up morons to cause chaos.

John; By the way, Kilbirnie also have a great nickname, 'The Blasties', which comes from a poem called '*The Inventory*', which was written by the bard himself, Robert Burns. I know you will want me to quote from it as you are all a pretty sophisticated lot, so here goes.

My furr-ahin's a wordy beast,
As e'er in tug or tow was traced.
The fourth's a highland Donald hastle,
A damn'd red-wud Kilburnie blastie!

I don't have the slightest idea what the Bard was talking about, but he definitely took a bevy!

I hope you will forgive me if some of the rest of today's story is not as word perfect as it should be, it had been a hell of a day so far, and I cannot read some of my notes; I'm amazed I could write at all!

We met the Secretary, Gordon Ronney, who took us into their wee bar, a great place. The girls at the bar, Diane Jeffrey and Carly Johnstone kept the drink flowing. We had a lovely time with them and we met Vice president, Ian McDonald, John Barr, who was the president for 35 years (if my notes are to be believed), Jimmy Madden, who I think does the hospitality, and Allan Madden, the groundkeeper. Like Beith, there are family connections within the club. If you believe the stories we heard from both sides of today's rivals, half of the two towns are related, if you know what I mean. Again, I'll have to let Craig do the recalling of the stories we heard. One thing I do remember was that we were introduced to almost all of the committee and other people, who were all superb company. They are too many to mention, but in the fantastic photograph you will find their names. I think it was Carly who wrote them all down, because I can read them.

John Jeffrey Iain McDonald Ian Johnston John Swindle
Jim Whiteford Mary Johnston Julie Livingstone Diane Jeffrey
Jimmy Madden John Barr Gordon Ronney
Carly Johnstone Allan Madden

Craig: *There is no doubt that the rivalry between Kilbirnie and Beith has often boiled over into violence. In fact we had been told that the teams were once ordered to play a cup tie behind closed doors after a bit of an incident during a previous match.*

It seems that the game was played indoors with only 15 officials from each committee allowed to watch the proceedings. Apparently, because of the confined space available, some rather unconventional rules had to be applied to allow the game to go ahead.

When you consider that one of the most often used tactic in junior football involves 'blootering' the ball as hard as possible up the field you can see how difficult playing indoors must have been for both teams.

Of course Kilbirnie and Beith are far from being the only junior teams to have experienced crowd trouble. In fact they are not even the only junior teams in Ayrshire to have suffered that kind of nonsense going on at their games.

Although 'the Blasties' had been beaten in today's game, the committee were still pretty upbeat. There is a very long way to go in the league after all. One of the guys told us about a Scottish cup game they had once played against their near neighbours up the road which had been rather unusual to say the least. There can be few instances where a goalkeeper ends up scoring a hat-trick but that is exactly what happened in that game against Beith.

It seems the keeper was the designated penalty-taker for Kilbirnie. That might be an interesting way of deciding a winner after extra time fails to provide one. Just have two goalkeepers go to one end of the pitch and take penalties against each other, it could be the best of ten or so. That way it would always be the keeper to blame if things didn't turn out in your favour.

Another of the boys from the committee told us a very sad tale. I would name him but John, who is supposed to take down all the names, lost his notebook, along with any pretence of sobriety later on that day. On the morning of the 1967 Scottish cup final he had just finished an incredible 36 hour shift. Not wishing to waste a minute of that great day he and his pals all headed to Ramage's Bar on Newton Street.

He assured me that he didn't overdo it on the drink, but I was not entirely convinced. Anyway they duly arrived at Hampden Park for the game and took their seats in the stand. Unfortunately, possibly due to lack of sleep, too much booze or more likely a combination of the two, he fell asleep, only waking up after Kilbirnie had lifted the cup. In his own words he " ... never saw a ba' kicked".

The social club at Valefield Park is quite small but from what I remember it was also quite comfortable. The beer was reasonably priced and, as it turned out more than plentiful. We certainly gave it a thorough testing.

The poor barmaids, Diane and Carly, who had to put up with us did so with great patience and had us laughing from the minute we entered the place until we reluctantly left.

Somewhere along the line one of the committee men gave me a club lapel badge. Once again I must apologise for not

Diane and Carly

remembering his name but I think it is only fair that Diane and Carly share some of the blame for my memory loss.

I do remember promising to wear it with pride, which I will do, but maybe not in Beith, or Auchinleck for that matter.

John; The journey home was a bit of a blur, but I must have sobered up, as I finished the night in the neighbour's house for the last of a birthday party. There's no stopping me. Craig, on the other hand, was knackered. He refused to go for a drink in Glasgow or EK on our way home. That's a few times this has happened, it's a worry.

We had a fantastic day and both clubs went out of their way to make us welcome. They may be fierce rivals on the park, but off it they are all Jock Tamson's Bairns, and good ones at that.

Spent a lot more than our £20 kitty, and a few rounds were bought for us, so there you go.

Pubs and Clubs visited today;

Beith;
The Saracenhead Hotel Bar
A great bar-worth a visit

Kilbirnie Ladeside
The Glendale
Another good wee bar-also worth a visit
Both clubs had great facilities for a wee refreshment.

Beith; How to get there-free with the Bus Pass

Stagecoach X36 Glasgow to Ardrossan, or
Stagecoach X34 Glasgow to Irvine (get off in Beith)

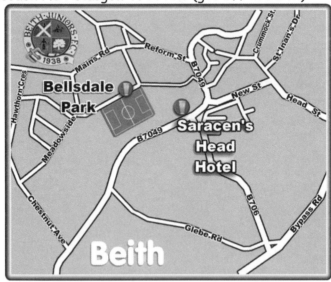

Kilbirnie; How to get there-free with the Bus Pass

X36 Glasgow to Ardrossan
Stagecoach X34 Glasgow to Irvine (get off in Kilbirnie)

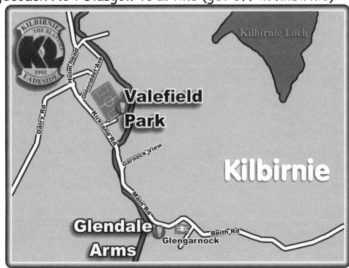

Sunnybank V Banks O'Dee

Club Name	Founded
Sunnybank	1946
Ground	**Colours**
Heathryfield Park	Black and White
League (2014-15)	**Selection of Honours**
North, 1st Div. East	Jun. Cup; 1953-54
Nickname; The Black and Whites	

John: The Northern Lights beckoned, or to put it another way, Aberdeen, here we come. We've visited the Granite City many times researching our previous books, and also delivering books to the good people of Don Land.

We chose what we thought were the two traditionally biggest Junior teams in the Aberdeen area, the only one's who have the distinction of winning the ultimate honour, The Scottish Junior Cup. Sunnybank won it in season 53-54 and Banks O' Dee in 56-57. At the present time one of them is not doing as well in the leagues as they would like, but we are looking at the supporters and committee members who are the backbone of the Junior game, not who's doing best at present.

There are many good reasons to visit Aberdeen, the pubs and people being the main ones. What else do you need? It also means a trip on the 'Gold Bus' with the free tea, sandwiches and tablet: does life get any better? Having said that, as I write this, there have been subtle changes to the Gold Bus, both in physical size and the goodies handed out free!

Double deckers have been introduced on the Glasgow to Aberdeen route, and they look great. We've been on them once before and Craig moaned about the service, and in particular the reduction in the number of goodies they hand out. When you consider they are all free, it's hard to be critical, but Craig is. Recently, Craig has been on them again himself, delivering books to Aberdeen and he said it's getting worse. What a moaner he is. I was still looking forward to today's journey.

Getting to Aberdeen, visiting two clubs, a few pubs, and getting back to Glasgow in the one day takes a lot of organizing, and Craig was worried, as I was doing the organizing. To have any chance of accomplishing this mammoth task, we had to leave early, so I booked us on the eight o'clock Gold Bus leaving Buchanan Street.

I had another worry. This was the weekend of the Ryder Cup, and, as it was being played at Gleneagles, which the bus passes on the way to Aberdeen, I was concerned that there would be delays as we were passing the place fairly early in the morning when fans would be arriving. My only hope was that it is motorway or dual carriageway all the way from Glasgow to Perth and beyond, so even if they reduced the non-golfer transport to one lane, it would not be too much of a delay. That was my hope.

It was about three weeks ago when I realized that our trip coincided with the Ryder Cup, so I booked us seats on the bus as I thought the bus would be packed. It was only last week that I realized that no golf fans would be on the bus as it does not stop anywhere between Glasgow and Aberdeen. What a numpty!

The good thing about passing Gleneagles is that I can bore Craig to death by reminding him that I have played all the three courses in times gone by, hospitality times gone by.

By a strange coincidence, Kate, the luckiest woman in the world, was going to Aberdeen today as well to visit her pal Sandra. She was worried about going with us, or to be exact, she said there was no way she was coming back on the same bus as us. No idea why! Being the perfect husband I booked her on a later bus to Aberdeen, and an earlier one back, so she would not have to put up with a couple of drunks on the bus, having said that, I had phoned the Waterstones store in Aberdeen to see if they would order some books to make the trip viable. They took five of 'Inn Aff the Bar'. Not a lot, but better than nothing. Kate offered to deliver the books to save us some precious time in Aberdeen. What a woman, even if she refuses to travel with us.

Anyway, back to today's trip. As my alarm was set for 5.50am, I had everything ready the night before, including my corned beef pieces. Craig was ready at 6.25am as arranged, and we got the 6.31a.m., No. 18 into Glasgow.

As we were getting into George Square, Craig was complaining about having to walk up the hill to the bus station. I had mentioned in the past that we should be able to pick up a bus round about the square to take us up to the station, so today Craig said we should check the bus stop next to where the 'Open Top' tourist buses leave. By the way, it is amazing the number of people that go on these trips, even when the Commonwealth Games are not on. Kate has said that we should take the trip to find out more about our native city. I've told her that I'm quite happy to be ignorant about what's round the corner in far-flung Glasgow.

Back to today. When we got to the bus stop and checked the timetables on the shelter, we found that there were indeed a few that went up to the bus station, and lo and behold, was one not approaching the stop? We quickly flagged it down and in a couple of minutes we were at the bus station. The only problem was that, for readers who know the bus station, the Gold bus leaves from stand 53 which is at the main end where the shops and things are. This bus, the No. 267, let us off at the other side of the station, which left us just as long a walk as we would have had if we had just walked up from George Square. Craig insisted that it was worth it as our new walk was flat, unlike the mountainous route up from the square. As I've said before, what a moaner.

After getting our papers and crisps, I had a laugh at a wee couple who were last to arrive at the stance but managed to get on the bus first; well I had a laugh, Craig was mad.

We had a great run up to Aberdeen. There was no hold-up at all at Gleneagles, and we got our free tea or coffee, scones and Deans Shortbread, as well as the offer of more coffee or soft drinks. Would you believe it, Craig still complained about not getting a bit of tablet!

As we got near the Granite City, Craig got out his magic phone with the internet in it and found out where the nearest pubs to our first ground were. This discovery necessitated Craig using his phone to plan a different bus from the Station in Aberdeen, which would take us nearer to the pub.

Our new bus, the No. 37, was waiting for us at the bus station and we were able to follow exactly where we were by watching a wee arrow on the magic phone moving about on the screen. I was impressed, but said nothing.

Craig: At last it was time for us to head up to Aberdeen. I had been looking forward to this Junior Football adventure for a long time.

Of course I had forgotten about the early start. We had to catch our first bus at half past six in the morning. It is a fairly well-known fact that I am not a morning person so, as you can imagine, I was less than happy when I discovered that the reason for this early start was John's misguided notion that we would be held up by traffic up at Gleneagles. Not only was there

266

no sign of a delay, but we managed to arrive in Aberdeen fifteen minutes ahead of schedule.

Since it was too early, even for John, to nip into the nearest pub for a quick pint we decided to head up to the Sunnybank area. For someone who travels on buses as often as he does John gets really anxious when he finds himself on a route he has never travelled before.

On the journey up to Sunnybank he was getting positively twitchy. Fortunately I had my magic phone with me. It saved the day and John's sanity. Even he had to admit that it accurately showed us exactly where we were.

John: Unfortunately, the bus did not go exactly where we wanted on Auchmill Road, and we had a good wee walk along to our first pub of the day, 'The White Horse'.

Because all you hear about in Aberdeen is the oil and the plenty of jobs, you imagine that there must be full employment and that everybody must be well off and live in big houses, but this area looked just like a working class, or non-working class area that you get in all cities. It looked a fairly rough place, the kind of place Craig and I like.

We put on our 'we're hard men' walk and went into the 'Horse'. It was just like it looked from the outside, a working man's, or in most other places, a non-working man's pub. We were told by locals we met later that it's an ok place during daylight hours, but late at night you might want to give it a miss, if your'e not as tough as Craig and me.

Craig and I liked it. The guys, who were all hard looking, were friendly and helpful and answered our questions, but nobody wanted to carry on with a conversation as they were either playing pool or watching the TV's, or both at once. To be fair to the locals, they probably had trouble understanding our accent. We did find out from them however that Sunnybank, the club we were trying to find, had a social club which was open for business, and they also told us how to find it. It always amazes me how, in such a tiny country as ours, the accents change so much.

Craig: Our first pub of the day was The White Horse on Great Northern Road. It is a basic, well-run 'man's pub. There is absolutely nothing fancy about the place.

We were served quickly by the barman but he didn't seem to want to chat. Usually when strangers come into a bar they can expect to be quizzed about their reason for being there, their town of origin and, if they are in certain areas of the West of Scotland, what school they went to. But apparently the good folk of Aberdeen are not very curious.

I'll say one thing for the White Horse: it has the cleanest toilets I've ever seen in an ordinary pub. For me that goes a long way towards making up for the lack of pub banter.

One of the locals did give us directions to Sunnybank's park, but before we could engage him in conversation he turned away to watch the football on television. We gave up, finished our drinks and left to find the park.

It had crossed our minds that it might be our accents which were putting people off talking to us, and that certainly proved to be the case on the bus we caught just outside the pub. The driver was Polish.

I imagine he had put a lot of effort into learning Aberdonian and hadn't really had time to explore the intricacies of Lowland patter. He certainly didn't have a scoobie what we were talking about. After a lot of hand gestures and shoulder-shrugging he drove the couple of hundred yards along the road to our next stop.

Although the bloke in the pub had said that Sunnybank had a social club, I wasn't convinced. None of the customers in The White Horse had admitted to ever being supporters of 'The Black and Whites' so their information about the facilities round there might be a bit suspect.

John: So with a cheery 'fit like the noo' we said our goodbyes and, at Craig's insistence, got a bus from outside the pub the two stops to where the ground was situated. It was only a couple of minutes' walk through a dodgy looking scheme, and over a bit of waste ground, which doubled as a football park, to the Sunnybank football ground, and more importantly, the social club.

Inside, the club was like almost all social clubs, i.e. in need of some care and attention, or in other words, money to be spent doing it up. But in today's world most people have other things to do rather than support their local club, which they should be doing. This was a great wee club, and the barmaid Glin Milne was excellent company. We also got into conversation with a couple of regulars who help to keep the club going. Bill Fraser and Dod Ritchie (Dod is short for something) were great company. Dod has been 40 years in the social club, now that's loyalty for you.

Glin, Bill and Dod

I also had a chat with the groundsman, Alan Taylor. We were talking about how some junior clubs will be struggling in the future because the present committees are made up of older people and most of the youngsters today are not interested. Alan told me that the three groundsmen before him had a combined age of over 220 years. I told Alan that I had had a look at the park before we came in and it looked in superb condition, so there's no substitute for experience.

At the bar I met Keith McMillan, who was on crutches. After introducing myself he told me that he was on the committee and had gone through a replacement hip operation that had developed complications, and seven knee operations. It makes your eyes water just thinking about it. I didn't.

Time was getting on and I said we had to meet the Secretary, Yvonne Irvine, a lady! Keith told me she was a great secretary and it was her 60th birthday today. I said that it showed great dedication to the club coming to work on your 60th birthday. Keith's answer was to remind me it was the first round of the Scottish Junior Cup today, which is a big event, and everyone must attend. As I've said before, committee people are dedicated.

John and Allan

One of the lads pointed out Yvonne to me, she was in the car park, so I nicked out to meet her. She was just going away for 10 minutes and said she would meet us in the club on her return.

When she came back, she took Craig and me over to the ground and introduced us to the rest of the committee. You will see in the photo that they are nearly all women. Now there is no reason why this should not be the case, but it is unusual for a Junior club to have a committee made up of burds! And they were all great and hard working. Nobody stopped for a minute, they were all doing something. It took Craig all his time to get them all to stand still for a minute to get their photo taken.

I hope I've got all the girls names correct in the photo. If not, Leslie, Mary, Gloria, Tracy and Yvonne, you are all doing a fine job at the club. I hope you don't mind girls, but I noticed that the car park seems to have been re-designed so you can get in and out without the need to reverse, or it might just be my imagination! Ladies, while on the subject of re-designing things, how about thinking up a better nickname than *the Black and Whites'*? Now I know in today's economic climate there's more to worry about than the club's nickname, but how about a wee competition for the supporters to come up with a better one. We would donate a prize of our book to the winner; the runner up would get two books! My entry would be '*The Sunnydolls*', hope that's not sexist. Your rivals Banks O' Dee have a couple, and one of them, '*The Rechabites*', is a good one. I've no idea how it came about, but that's a good thing. Come on girls, you can do better.

Yvonne, Tracy, Gloria, Mary, Leslie and Jack

We had a great time and we were sad to leave Sunnybank, a great club with fine men, but mainly women, looking after it.

Craig: I shouldn't have worried; there was a social club and it was a good one. It was also very big. There is a large bar area and a main hall. The hall was decorated with banners and balloons celebrating someone's 60th birthday. It turned out that it was, in fact, the club secretary's big day. When we eventually met Yvonne Mearns we made a big thing about not believing she could possibly be that age. For some insane reason John wasted any good will this created by going on and on about how women were rubbish at reversing cars. Personally I think he has a weird form of Tourette's syndrome, or as we would call it down in East Ayrshire, an inability to keep his big sully mooth shut.

271

Every time we go into a new club and ask the folk in there for any tale about club rivalries we always hear a similar phrase. It seems that we are constantly there on the wrong day or at the wrong time because ' the man we really should be speaking to, the guy who knows absolutely everything there is to know about the club, is either away on holiday that day or running late'.

In the bar we chatted to the barmaid, Glin Milne, and customers Bill Fraser and Dod Ritchie. We had a good laugh with them but I'm afraid that phrase came up once again.

Glin told us that, like most junior clubs in the area, crowds had been dwindling over recent years but the social club was holding its own.

We were joined at the bar by Allan Taylor, the club grounds-man. He had ordered a bottle of flavoured water and had to suffer the consequences. Once the mocking had stopped, he told us that he had once been to a game down in the Glasgow area. He said that he couldn't remember the name of Sunnybank's opponents that day, but I think he was just being diplomatic. It seems that, every time the ball was kicked out of the park, instead of it being returned straight away a tennis ball would be thrown back in. I suggested that the ground they were at was probably Pollok's as they were only Glasgow team who were likely to have access to tennis balls.

A few minutes later we met Keith McMillan. He was making heavy weather of walking up to the bar as he was on crutches. You really do have to admire the commitment of any supporter who would make that kind of effort just to see his team play.

Keith is also on the committee of Sunnybank but is having a bit of a break from his duties while he recovers from surgery. I won't go into all of his physical problems, mainly because it makes me feel queasy. But Keith says his grandchildren think it's hilarious when he sets off the alarms when going through airport security.

Just to cheer him up I told him about the time John was stopped at the airport in Tenerife. I had just walked through the metal detector, but as soon as I heard the alarm going off I knew it was John who had been stopped. He had had a hip operation which involved a metal coating on the hip joint. It was quite funny to watch him being questioned by the guards, but when the female guard pulled on a rubber glove I thought John was going to pass out. I very nearly cracked a couple of ribs laughing at him so I felt we had both suffered a painful ordeal that day.

The teams were starting to leave the dressing rooms and head for the pitch. One young boy was pointed out to us as an exceptional player according to committee man George Jack; the boy was only 17 but was proving to be one of their best players.

What was really amazing as far as I was concerned was the fact that the young player was on loan from Sunnybank's oldest and nearest rivals, Banks o' Dee. It seems he played part of last season before being recalled to Banks o' Dee. However he spent all his time there on the bench. Eventually he was allowed back to Sunnybank and has been playing a blinder for them ever since.

I had to tell George that such situation would be unlikely down my way. Letting a good player away on loan to your biggest rival would be a capital offence. The police in Ayrshire would have to set up a committee protection unit and have safe houses for club secretaries in neutral areas of Scotland. Apparently there has always been a flow of players back and forth between the two Aberdeen rivals.

Unbelievably George is seventy years old but still manages keep up the duties of linesman, although he did say that he was only allowed to indicate whether a ball was in or out and didn't get to have a say in offside or penalty decisions.

I'm old enough to remember the time when all junior games had only one neutral official and the lines were run by a member of each competing team.

The situation was worse than useless when it came to grudge match between bitter rivals. Only a suicidal linesman would give a decision against his own team.

Just before kick-off we managed to grab a quick word with the club secretary again. She was really busy getting things in order, but in between signing team sheets and other club *paperwork she told us about her team. Although they had recently been relegated they have high hopes for the future. The only problem the team has is one which is shared by many clubs whose finances are limited. Keeping good players can be very difficult when bigger outfits can just open the cheque-books.*

I don't think there is any resentment from these club officials. They understand that the young men who show potential need to move on to find out if they can make the grade in the higher leagues or even as full-time professional footballers.

Just before we left I got Yvonne to organise a team photo of the committee. I had tried to do this myself but nobody was listening to me. I think John had destroyed our credibility with his constant references to women drivers. Obviously the penny hadn't dropped yet that he was the only person who thought his jokes were funny.

John: So we retraced our steps through the field and housing estate to catch the first of the two buses that would take us to our next port of call, Banks O' Dee.

I can't remember the bus number that took us back to the bus station, as it was not a pre-planned bus, just a spontaneous 'let's just jump on this one' kind of thing. Anyway, we were back in Aberdeen Bus Station in no time and after a bit of jumping about and nearly getting killed crossing Guild Street in front of traffic, the driver of the No. 3 took pity on us and waited. I've said it before, but the drivers up in Aberdeen are great. He even said he would tell us when we were at our stop for our next team, Banks O' Dee.

Banks O' Dee

Club Name	Founded
Bank's O' Dee	1902
Ground	**Colours**
Spain Park	Blue and Dark Blue Hoops
League (2014-15)	**Selection of Honours**
North Superleague	Jun. Cup 1956-57
Club Nickname	
The Rechabites	

John: It was only a short walk from the bus stop to the park, but we had about 45 minutes before the match finished, so we would find the nearest pub for a pint before going to visit the ground at the end of the match. The only problem was that after checking his magic phone, Craig announced that there were no pubs close enough to the ground that would allow us to get to them, have a pint, and get back in time. So the only option open to us was to go to the ground and watch the final 40 minutes or so of the match. This had never happened before, and, as usual, Craig blamed me.

Craig: The journey over to Spain Park was far easier than we thought it would be. That really should have worried us; nothing good ever comes easily.

The bus driver cleverly agreed with me and my phone and let us off quite close to the park. Unfortunately, the area we found ourselves in was very deficient in places of good cheer. That is to say not a single pub was to be found there.

After a few minutes of bitter recrimination, centred on who made the decision to come straight to this place instead of stopping off at the comfortable watering hole along the way, we made our way down to the park.

I had checked the place out on my computer and it looked very modern and well set up. This was a worry. Many clubs we have visited who have very modern facilities don't have social clubs attached. To be honest, the location of Banks o' Dee's park doesn't lend itself to keeping a social club busy. Passing trade would be almost non-existent.

John however was convinced that there would be a bar in the place. He had been told that the club would be opening a brand-new hospitality suite on the day of our visit. I tried to tell him that hospitality didn't necessarily mean access to alcohol, but he was in no mood to listen.

We wandered into the park with about 40 minutes of the game still to go. I think we must have looked like a couple of fish out of water as we were immediately asked if we needed any help. Actually what we were doing was just taking in the fantastic facilities the club has in their ground. A lot of money has been spent there.

John and Kerry

Kerry Berton had been the person who asked us if we needed help. In fact she took us to the brand new hospitality suite for a cup of tea. I could see John was a bit disappointed to find out that there was no bar, but I suspected he was even more disappointed that I had been right about that.

It had been about an hour and a half since John had last tasted alcohol so he was perilously close to getting withdrawal symptoms. I think Kerry must have tuned into this and quickly administered a medicinal vodka. Just to be sociable I had one as well.

Out by the side of the pitch we enjoyed watching the game. I was a bit relieved to find that Kerry's son was quite a good player as I would have felt a bit daft pretending he was doing well while giving away penalties and free kicks.

It was back into the suite after the final whistle. This time bottled beer was on offer and both of us were back in our element. One of the committee men told us that Banks o' Dee did at one time have a social club but, like so many others we have heard of, business dwindled away to such an extent that it had to be closed.

John Irvine, Banks o' Dee club secretary, came over to talk to us and explained that even though his club and Sunnybank remain rivals it's a friendly sort of rivalry. Many of their players have turned out for both teams but, unlike certain teams down south, there have never been any recriminations over this.

Usually when we ask club officials for any amusing stories involving their closest rivals we get a cheeky tale about their opposite number in that team doing something embarrassing and or illegal, but John had another target in mind- himself.

A few years back John had returned home from working up north and took his wife out for a wee drink on the Friday night. Unfortunately he had a bit more than a wee drink and, as a result, he was a little hung-over at the game the next day, which was away to Sunnybank. Due to his delicate condition he decided to sit by himself and quietly nurse his sore head.

The game had been going for about twenty minutes when the referee suddenly stopped play and marched over to where John was sitting. The ref, Billy Christie, asked him if he was alright. What do you mean? asked John. Billy said "Well I'm refereeing a game between Sunnybank and Banks o' Dee, the game's been going for twenty minutes and nobody is giving me any abuse. Either I'm having a great game or big John Irvine isn't here. So am I having a great game?" They don't make referees like that anymore.

All the time we were in the hospitality suite we were regaled by Willie Forrest who seems to have an endless supply of dodgy jokes. John was much amused by them so obviously I didn't write any of them down. This was just a bit of self-protection as when he gets a joke he tends to flog it to death by telling it at every opportunity. However if he has had a few drinks at the time he tends to forget them.

We said our goodbyes after I took the team photo of the committee, and were about to wander back up to the main road to catch a bus when William kindly offered us a lift round to the main bus station.

John: The set up at the ground was very different from Sunnybank. Everything looked sparkling and new. The club, like some other junior clubs, is involved with the 'Local Community' project and they carry out great work with youngsters in the area.

We walked into the ground and decided that as the secretary and committee would be in the new grandstand, which was brilliant, watching the match, we would just stand at the side of the park and do the same.

We must have looked out of place and lost, because within a minute or so we were approached by a lovely lady who asked if she could help us. We introduced ourselves and she told us she was Kerry Berton and was always here, as one of her sons, Mark, played for the team. He was a substitute today, but she was hopeful he would be brought on.

When we told her we would not normally be watching a match, but would be having a refreshment at this time, she insisted on taking us into the club's new hospitality suite, which was just opening today, and we had a cup of coffee. You could have knocked us down with a feather when she said we should have something stronger. So, with a coffee in one hand and a wee Vodka in the other, we enjoyed the rest of the match. Mark came on with about 30 minutes to go, and I can tell you, as a former Govan High FP's star winger, that Mark has a great left foot and I believe he could be a great asset to any club, and I'm not just saying this because of his hospitable mother.

As a wee aside, Banks O' Dee scored with a penalty with about five minutes to go and won the match, so we're not jinxes after all.

Kerry said her husband Federico, an Italian, is a hairdresser, or maybe it was her, I have forgotten. Anyway, she said that Craig had a great head of hair and it was well styled. What a nancy. He wasn't even embarrassed. I hope some of his Auchinleck pals are reading this.

William, Willie, Allan, John, Gordon and Brian

At the end of the match Kerry took us into the hospitality suite and we met up with Secretary, John Irvine, vice president, Gordon Christie, and committee men Tom Ewan and William Faulkener. Craig was getting some good stories from the guys, and I was talking to William about the rivalries between junior teams, and how it's at its fiercest in Ayrshire, where Craig comes from. When he heard this he told me that although he had played for Banks O' Dee for 11 years, he had also played for Sunnybank, the local rivals, for five years. He said that in one game against Ayrshire giants Cumnock, he had played a blinder, Sunnybank had won 3-2, and he had to be escorted off the park and out of the ground by the local police. Craig said that this was just a normal Saturday in Ayrshire.

Craig will fill you in with other stories he was hearing, but time was getting on, and the six o'clock Gold Bus back to Glasgow waits for no man, or woman.

Craig: *We had always intended to visit the Spirit Level on Stirling Street but had been unsure how much time we had to spare. By getting a lift we probably saved about half an hour on travelling time so we felt compelled to spend that time wisely.*

A visit to Aberdeen is not complete for us without a pint or two in the Spirit Level. I don't suppose very many of its regulars ever go to watch either Sunnybank or Banks o' Dee but we had to include it in our tour.

I thought I recognised the barmaid but John said I was talking nonsense. A couple of minutes later Suzanne came over to ask us if we were the two guys who had taken her picture for a book about five years ago. So much for memory man Mackay!

We enjoyed chatting to Suzanne and Gwen, the other barmaid, before making our way round to the bus station.

The trip home was unbelievably quick, for me anyway. I think I was asleep before the bus left the station but I did have a good excuse for this, apart from the booze that is.

A bit of a mistake in checking my watch had led me to be up and about at 4:30 that morning instead of 5:30. By the time I realised my mistake it was too late to do anything about it, but as the saying goes, all's well that ends well.

Once again we had a great day out, meeting a lot of interesting people and having a drink with them.

John: As we said our thanks to everyone and made our way out, William caught up with us and kindly insisted on giving us a lift back to the bus station. This was kind of him, and in just about five minutes we were saying our goodbyes to him and we were now at the bus station with about an hour to kill.

There was no argument about what to do. A one minute walk took us into 'The Spirit Level', our favourite pub in Aberdeen. The girls behind the bar, Suzanne and Gwen told us that the owners Jackie and Julie were away to Glasgow for an overnight to see the show 'Still Game'. This was funny as the two of them call Craig and me Jack and Victor when we walk into the bar.

Anyway, we had a great time in the 'Level' and the young barmaids looked after us well. Suzanne, who is Jackie's daughter, is pregnant, so there will soon be three generations behind the bar. The world, or Aberdeen at least, is being taken over by the fairer sex. No bad thing I hear you say.

At about ten to six we said cheerio to the girls and headed over to the bus station. The Gold Bus was the Double Decker version, but it was not busy and we had a table for four upstairs to ourselves. The service was great, but Craig saw none of it as he slept the whole way back to Glasgow.

We had another great day out at the juniors. Everybody should at some time visit a junior ground to enjoy the fun and hospitality that every club has to offer.

Pubs Visited Today

Sunnybank
'*The White Horse*'; old man's pub-as a visitor to Aberdeen, I have no idea why you should be in this area, but if you are, in you go!
'*Sunnybank Social Club*'-great club, the locals should use it more.

Bank's O' Dee
'*Hospitality Suite at Ground*'-fresh and new, but again it should be used by local people to support the club.
'*The Spirit Level*'- near bus station, been there several times, great bar, a must to visit.

Sunnybank; **How to get there-free with the Bus Pass**
M9 Gold Bus to Aberdeen Bus Station
Stand 6-No. 37 to Sunnybank

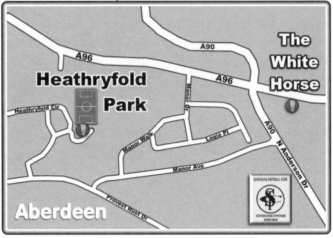

Banks O' Dee; **How to get there-free with Bus pass**
M9 Gold Bus to Aberdeen Bus Station
Stand M1 on Guild Street, No. 3 to Wellington Street

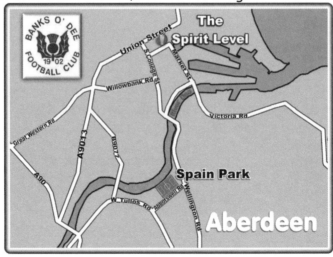

Inverness City V New Elgin F.C.

Club Name	Founded
Inverness City	2006
Ground	**Colours**
Lister Park	Black and White
League (2014-15)	**Selection of Honours**
North Super League	PMAC Group Div. 1
Club Nickname	Winners 2010-11; 11-12; 13-14
The City	

John: Our Highland Capital was calling us, and we had no choice but to reply with a 'yes, here we come'. The bevy merchants are on their way.

There are not many junior clubs in Inverness. Inverness City was the obvious one, being, as it was, in Inverness. It was also close to the city centre. A short walk from the bus station, or so we thought!

Having chosen the first club to visit, the question was what was going to be the other one, and could we find one that was at home on the same Saturday as Inverness City. The first one I checked up on was in Nairn St. Ninians, as Nairn is only about 10 miles from Inverness.

Unfortunately, I could not find a Saturday when both teams were at home in the short time we had left before we had to get the book ready for press. After more research, I found that New Elgin were at home on the Saturday we had in mind.

The problem of visiting Elgin is the distance from Inverness, which is almost 40 miles. The advantage is that there is a Waterstones in Elgin, and, when I phoned them to ask if they needed any of our books, they ordered 15! This was a big plus. The money we would make from this sale would almost cover the first round today.

Now many of you will say that towns with a Waterstones are not a good enough reason for a visit. Obviously not many of you are as skint, or as it tight fisted, as Craig and I.

But, you are right, we should not be governed by our wallets, so before organizing the trip, I phoned the Inverness secretary Laura Pollard. Laura told me she is no longer involved with the club, and to phone the new secretary John Campbell, which I did. John confirmed that New Elgin could be considered as their rivals and we should visit them. This was good news, both for the book and our pocket.

The problem with the time it would take by bus to get from Inverness to Elgin and back, and also have a good bevy, was solved. My young brother Robert, who has a Guest House in Inverness, said he would love to run us around all afternoon on the Saturday in question. By the way, it was his partner Ruth's birthday. Blood is thicker than water, or is it more likely that Robert is as daft as me?

Now, I know we should carry out all trips on buses only, using the legendary 'free pass', but this was a bit of an unusual situation, and I'm sure you will forgive us for this one slip.

So the Inverness and Elgin trip was on. In the interest of giving you all the correct information on how to get to every place by bus, that is still detailed at the end of the chapter. This will help all readers without brothers in Inverness.

As usual, I booked us seats on the G10 both ways, as I've said before, that's another £1 I won't see again.

Even with the help of my brother, the trip today relied on an early start, and all the buses turning up, leaving, and arriving on time. We had a few worries.

When we got on the first bus, our usual No. 18 from just outside Craig's house, at 7.30am in the early morning, the driver told us that their was some sort of running event starting in George Square, and the bus may not get there. So our journey in was a worry. Everything turned out ok, the bus nicked round the back of the square and dropped us off in St. Vincent Place. First worry gone. Our second worry was just about to take over from the first.

There seemed to be hundreds of oldies waiting for our G10 Gold Bus, and it looked sick. Dozens of men in these bright yellow jackets were standing about phoning and touching the steering wheel. As our departure time was passing, a man started going round the bus tightening all the nuts on the wheels. Now Craig gets wound up by the slightest of things. Tightening the nuts on the wheels was a blood pressure event.

About 15 minutes after our departure time, we were told we could board. There was a mad rush to get on. Queue jumping was rampant. It must have been like people desperately trying to get into a bomb shelter during an air raid in Clydebank. Criag's elbows were nearly worn away by the time we boarded. We got the last double seats left, near the back.

Anyway, we were on, and our host for the day, Justin, who did a fantastic job all the way to Inverness, assured us that our driver, Scott, would be able to make up the time on the way, which he did.

It had been a miserable morning, and the rain continued until we got to about Aviemore, where the weather cleared. By the time we arrived in Inverness, it was a lovely day, and stayed that way all day.

Craig's feet, and other parts of him were hurting, but the map I had produced, although almost unreadable, showed that the park was only a short walk from the bus station. To cut a long story, and walk, short, we took a wrong turn or two, and the walk took us over half an hour. It's hard to put in writing the mood Craig was in. But he was in pain, so I forgave him.

Craig: *Without a doubt today's trip was to be the longest one of all our journeys around junior grounds. Even without visiting Elgin it would still qualify for that title. Without cheating it would not be possible for us to do the whole trip in a single day. As it was the entire thing was planned to take almost 17 hours, most of that sitting on a bus or in a car.*

We were at the end stage of our tour, and so far everything had gone more or less to plan. We had been very lucky with both the transport and the weather, and were looking forward to much of the same on this trip.

They do say that pride goes before a fall and from the outset I was beginning to think that we were pressing our luck. When I heard one of the staff at the bus station, say that they were waiting for a mechanic before they could let us onto our bus, I thought that things were beginning to sound a bit scary.

I would be lying if I said that every time we ran over a bump in the road I didn't imagine that one of the wheels had just come off the bus. Given the state of the roads in this country you can appreciate what a traumatic journey this was. By the way there was no tablet on offer aboard our Gold Bus; again!

There was a fair bit of discussion about finding our way to Inverness City's ground, but without a hint of bias, I can categorically state, that I was right John was wrong. I would like to illustrate my point by stating that at no time that day was I ever more than a couple of yards out in knowing our exact position on this planet.

John, on the other hand, spent his day wandering around like a recently despatched chicken. An hour into our fifteen minute walk to Lister Park, even he must have realised we had taken a wrong turn.

Eventually, we spied a large grandstand and well-kept pitch, unfortunately neither had anything to do with the junior football. It was a shinty pitch.

John: At last we found the ground, called Lister Park, which is in the middle of a much larger public park, called Bught Park.

The ground was one of the most basic we have visited. The playing area had a small fence round it, and there were three portacabins that acted as the changing rooms.

We met the secretary John Campbell and president Alastair Wardhaugh, who had been at the park for hours already getting the place ready for today's game.

John Campbell and Alastair Wardhaugh

Although the ground and facilities are basic, everything was set up with the players in mind. The changing rooms had showers installed and the place was spotless. How it would look after the game is another story. But John and Alastair and any helpers they could muster would have the thankless job of getting the place stripped down and cleaned up. These guys are keeping the game alive.

John and Alastair were good company and before we said our farewells, told us a few stories about the club and the rivalries with other, mainly bigger, or richer clubs. As usual, I've went on too long about our journey, so I'll let Craig recall the stories the lads told us.

Craig's main worry was the walk back to town. John pointed out the best way, which was along the side of the 'Ness'. It was a lovely walk in glorious sunshine, but it seemed like a 10 mile hike to Craig. I'll let him go on about it.

Craig: Eventually we reached the park and met up with John Campbell, the secretary of Inverness City JFC. Lister Park is next to the shinty park, and looks poor by comparison.

John Campbell told us that the shinty officials won't share any of their facilities with his football club, even though this pitch is only used about four times a year. The excuse being, playing football on the pitch would harm the grass. It is hard to see how a sport which involves charging around whacking a hard ball with even harder sticks can be gentler on the playing surface than football.

I have to admit that I've never been a fan of shinty. In fact I'm still not convinced that it is actually a sport. I assumed it was an activity which allowed young farmers to let off steam by thumping each other with big sticks.

Anyway, John introduced as to Alastair Wardhaugh, club president, who told us that the shinty stadium was the biggest one in the world. As he said, that is hardly surprising when you realise that Scots are the only people daft enough to play the game.

I would imagine that all of the shinty supporters in the country, possibly even world-wide, could fit into this stadium at the same time.

The only international ever played in this super stadium is against Ireland, and they don't even play shinty. In my humble opinion staging a match between a shinty team and a team of hurlers has all the sporting credibility of a contest between a wrestler and a boxer.

All four of us had a good old rant about lack of support by the local council. Perhaps a bit of council pressure might bring about a change of heart with the shinty authorities. Having a more permanent ground would make a big difference to the football team. As it is John and Alasdair are forced to cover up the advertising boards as soon as their games are over because their ground is in a public park.

While we were talking, Alastair recalled a story about one of their players who decided to further his career by joining a Highland League side. This is a big problem for junior teams in the north of Scotland. The Highland League poaches many of the junior leagues best players.

It seems that this particular young player accepted a signing on fee of £750 to join the Highland team. Unfortunately, the big time was not as good as he thought it would be. In fact he never managed to get his rear end up off the subs bench.

Disillusioned, he decided that he wanted to go back to his old junior team. The problem was, he had squandered every penny of his signing on fee. He had to wait until he could scrape up enough cash to pay it back before he could return.

The one theme in this book has always been inter-club rivalries, but to be honest, they have been a bit thin on the ground so far. Not so with Inverness and Elgin.

John told us that there are always players sent off when the two teams meet. The game was just about to start so I didn't get a chance to ask any further questions about this but I made mental note to bring up the subject when we reached Elgin.

We had been invited to join the City team and committee at the Chieftain Hotel after the game but, time was against us. The Chieftain is actually on the outskirts of the city, and nowhere near the park. There are a few pubs quite near the ground, 'Glenalbyn', 'Ceol-Mor' and 'Tarry Ile' for example. We could only manage a quick pint in the latter of these pubs.

Tarry Ile is a decent wee pub selling a decent pint. There was no time to talk to the bar staff or any of the locals as our walk-about earlier had eaten up all our allotted time in Inverness.

John: My brother Robert was waiting for us in our next port of call, a wee pub called '*The Tarry Ile*'. Craig said he thought we had been in it before, I couldn't remember. Anyway, it's a nice wee old-mans bar, the kind we like, and worth a visit for a quiet pint on a Saturday.

After a quick one, Robert drove us to Elgin. It's a lovely journey, even if you have to go by bus. Craig slept in the back seat most of the 50 minute journey.

First port of call was the Waterstones store, where I jumped (or to be more exact struggled) out the car, and delivered the books.

It was a blessing we were in the car. It took us about four wrong turns to get to the ground. We could see the park 10 minutes before we eventually got to it by driving round the back of a wee industrial estate.

New Elgin F.C.

Club Name	Founded
New Elgin F.C.	1946
Ground	Colours
Nicol-Togneri Park	Red and Black
League (2014-15)	Recent Honours
North Superleague	North Reg. Div. One Champions
Club Nickname	2012-13
The Freestaters	

John: New Elgin's ground is completely different. It has been there for years and has a very settled and very old fashioned look to it. The game was not finished yet so we wandered into the clubhouse and the first person we met was Joyce Rose, secretary

George's wife. She pointed him out and we wandered down to the touchline and introduced ourselves.

We talked to George until the final whistle (Elgin won 2-0). He told us that as they had no real bar in the ground, they were going, as they always did, to the '*The Springfield Bar*', which is owned by two ex-players. These guys kindly lay on food and hospitality in the lounge bar for both teams, after all home games. I'm sure the increase in bar takings will help them.

Craig: John's brother, Robert, had kindly volunteered to drive us to Elgin for the second part of our trip. Fortunately, for all concerned, Robert decided not to depend on John's maps to get us where we needed to go. Instead we used the Sat-nav on my phone, and in no time at all we arrived at Nicol-Togneri Park. Actually it was a wee bit harder than that but at least we got there. Following John's directions, we could well have found ourselves lost in the wilds of Northern Scotland.

The game between New Elgin and Dyce was just finishing as we arrived. Someone pointed out George Rose, the club secretary for us. He was down by the touchline, and after the introductions he suggested that we might like a cup of tea up at the clubhouse while the team and committee got ready to move round to the pub where hospitality was laid on.

His wife, Joyce, runs the kitchen in the clubhouse, so we decided to go up and introduce ourselves. We chatted for a little while but to be honest a cup of tea was not at the top of our list of priorities. In fact it didn't appear at any position on that list.

So, although stopping for a nice cup of tea sounded like a sensible idea, we completely dismissed it. Instead we got directions to the pub, The Springfield Bar. Unfortunately the directions were so complicated that John got an instant migraine. He knew that we could never find the place, but I had an ace up my sleeve, or, to be more precise, a phone in my pocket. In no time at all we were standing at the bar in The Springfield Bar enjoying a drink and a bit of banter with the locals.

John: Using Craig's magic phone, which shows you where the place is and where you are, Robert managed to find the pub. If first impressions were anything to go my, we would have turned round and drove away. The outside area of the building looked pretty rough, even by Auchinleck or Govan standards.

Kay Hastings, Louisa Stevenson

Inside, it was a completely different kettle of fish. The two bars and the girls behind them were fantastic and the locals were great company. We had a drink in the public bar before heading through to the lounge bar where the committees and players of both clubs were arriving.

Bill Thomson, Scott Gilchrist, George Rose, Joyce Rose

George introduced us to all his committee and some of the players, as well as to Norman Mackay, who is the president of Dyce, today's opposition. Norman then introduced us to his committee and some of the Dyce players.

Like most of the committee members we met today, and others in previous weeks, the time and effort they put in to the Junior game is immense. George has been involved for almost 40 years, and Norman 50 years with the Juniors. We were presented with ties and badges from both clubs and had a fantastic time in both club's company. If it had not been for us having to get back to Inverness, we would have been there all night. At one stage it crossed our minds! Again, I am going to let Craig recall some of the stories that were going around.

So it was with real sadness that we had to say our farewells and leave our friends from both New Elgin and Dyce. We have had a warm invitation to visit Dyce in the future, and would love to take them up on it.

I've forgotten to comment on the nicknames of the two clubs, so now I will. The nicknames show a complete difference in the effort put in to produce them. Inverness City's, *'The City'* definitely lacks imagination, but Elgin's *'The Freestaters'* is brilliant. Again, like some other clubs nicknames, I have no idea what they mean or how they came about. I should have asked someone about it today, but I completely forget. I think drink was involved. But it's not important, as all that matters is that it is a good one. Remote nicknames are good. Inverness could call themselves *'The Untouchables'*. The older supporters will get it.

Craig: I mentioned to George Rose that the pitch at Nicol-Togneri Park looked to be in good condition He said that it benefited from good drainage courtesy of the gas board. This sounded a wee bit strange to me but he explained, it seems that the local gasworks was being knocked down and there were hundreds of tons of cinders left lying around where the gas tanks had been. In a process I know nothing about the cinders were used to help with the drainage of the football ground. I was impressed, not just with a very effective drainage system but, with the fact that somebody had got something for nothing out of British Gas.

Outsiders might not realise it, but most football committees get on quite well with their opposite numbers. That was certainly the case with New Elgin and Dyce Juniors. Even the players, who minutes before had been involved in a fierce struggle with each other on the pitch, seemed quite happy to sit and exchange friendly banter. I say friendly banter but, the truth of the matter is I didn't have much of a clue what they were talking about.

Franny More, Seamus Connolly, Stuart Strathdee, Alan Burges

One thing I did learn however is calling someone a loon up in the north of Scotland doesn't lead to anything like the trouble it would down in Glasgow.

Norman Mackay, the Dice President, summed it up when he told me that junior football in the north of the country is all about camaraderie; the teams all get on well.

That is probably true for about ninety per cent of the teams up north but, as I was about to find out, it is not always the case. Elgin and Inverness, for whatever reason, don't seem to get on well with each other. My informant gave his name as Keith. That may or may not be his real name but, for the purposes of this story I am prepared to believe it was.

Anyway, according to Keith, at a game between Elgin and Inverness, not that long ago, tensions boiled over to such an extent that a total of ten people were shown the red card. That has to be a record in junior football surely. In total, Inverness had two players carded with the remaining eight cards being collected by New Elgin.

Keith pointed out that not all of the cards were given to players on the field, with some substitutes gaining the dubious honour of being sent off without ever actually 'being on'. Unfortunately Elgin's manager also attracted a card.

The part of Keith's story which really had me laughing was when he told me that in this single game there were no less than three goalkeepers sent off.

It seems that one keeper from each side had been caught handling the ball outside the penalty box often enough to merit an early bath. Elgin's substitute keeper then committed professional suicide by getting himself sent off for throwing his gloves at the ref because he disagreed with the man's decision to award a penalty against his side.

Lee Shanks, Scott Ross, Louis Garden, Mitchell Braidwood, Andy Munro

I wandered back over to the bar, after listening to Keith's story, just in time to hear John once again attempting to stir things up by telling people that I was from Auchinleck. Happily neither George nor Norman fell for his nonsense.

In fact George was reminded of the time when Elgin managed to get their hands on the Scottish Junior Cup. He told us that his team was down in East Ayrshire in 1986 to play the *holders of that prestigious trophy. After the game one of the New Elgin players asked if he could have a look at the cup. Unfortunately the player underestimated the weight of the cup and dropped it and the base, right in front of the startled Talbot committee.*

I had to ask what they said to him, but apparently no one in the clubhouse was able to speak for quite some time.

Not to be outdone, Norman told me that Dyce had once played a game against Auchinleck. He claimed, presumably tongue in cheek, that if it hadn't been for five offside goals his team would have won 2-0.

All too soon it was time to leave. Actually I was feeling a bit guilty about keeping Robert hanging about waiting for us, since he couldn't have a drink.

Today's Visitors – Dyce F.C.

Although it is not usual for us to include photographs of the opposition, today we had such a great time with the Dyce people we decided to make an exception. So below are the Dycer's

Syd Birnie, Keith McIntosh, Ally Hardy, Dave Gadenhead, Norman Mackay

Ally McGinlay, Scott MacKenzie, Andy Robb,
Stewart McLaren, Jason Coyle, Ryan Stewart

Michael Gunn, Grant Moorhouse, Jorday Morrice,
Mark Bartlet, Stuart Morrison

John: Anyway, back to today. We said our thanks and farewells to Robert when he dropped us off at *'The Phoenix Bar',* just round from the Bus Station.

This is a bar which we have also been in before, and its new owner is making a good job of turning it into a great bar. One thing I didn't like, they charge twice as much for a double vodka and soda as a single. A pint of San Miguel and large Smirnoff and soda (25ml) was well over £9! That's a record, by a long way. Mind you, both drinks can be substituted for other makes which are much cheaper, but nevertheless!

Our G10 awaited us. The bus only had a handful of passengers. It was a double decker, and we had a four seat table upstairs to ourselves. The other good thing was that we got tablet! Does life get any better?

Craig: Obviously going straight home was not in the plan. We had a little time in Inverness before our 7 o'clock bus back down to Glasgow, so we got Robert to drop us off near The Phoenix on Academy Street. It's handy for the bus station, a five minute walk or seven minute stagger, and is a good pub.

I should qualify that statement by saying that it is a good pub if you're happy drinking pints of beer or single measures of spirits. During our stay in the pub John was doing neither of these. He was not a happy man. A logical person would have worked out that since we were, as always, working with a kitty, it would be a no skin off his nose situation, whatever he was charged for his girly wee double vodka and soda. However by this time logic and common sense had left the building.

I managed a couple of pints and once again took upon myself the role of carer, guiding John round to the bus station and home.

This had been our longest journey and, to be honest, not our best. We had once again met some really good and interesting people but, we had always been up against the clock. We had so little time to spend with the guys in Inverness that we didn't get to hear any of their football stories. By the time we got back from Elgin it was too late to catch up with them at The Chieftain, the lads would have been long gone.

John: We were both knackered by the time we got back to EK at about 11.30pm. It's a long day for oldies like us, but we had a great time and met some brilliant folk.

Funnily enough, we did not have a lot of drink today, and were as sober as judges when we got home. Craig was mad as Irene was babysitting tonight and would not see how sober he was, what a wean he is.

Pubs Visited today;

Inverness;
'The Tarry Ile', a nice wee pub, worth a visit
'The Phoenix Bar', a very nice bar, but keep off the proprietery makes and don't drink doubles.

Elgin;
'The Springfield Bar' a brilliant bar, hard to find, but worth it.

Inverness; **How to get there-free with the Bus pass**
M10 Gold Bus to Inverness Bus Station
A 10 minute walk to Bught Park (Lister Park is part of it)

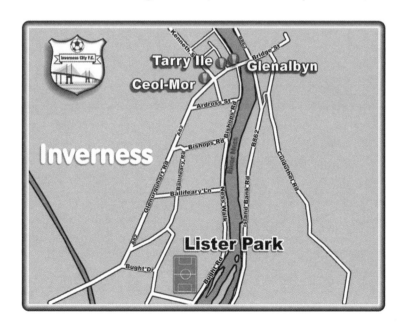

Elgin; **How to get there-free with the Bus Pass**
M10 Gold Bus to Inverness Bus Station
Stagecoach No. 10 Inverness to Aberdeen (get off in Elgin)

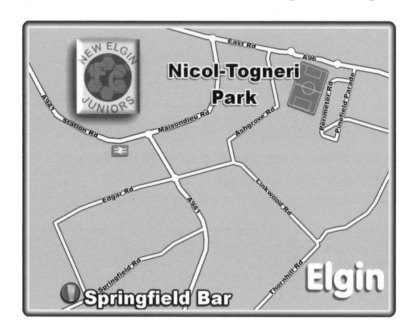

Clydebank V Vale of Leven

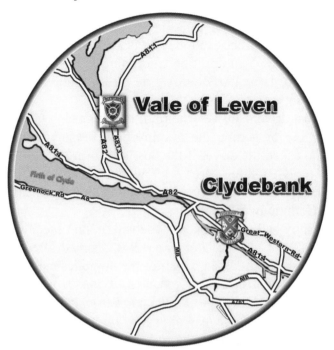

Club Name	Founded
	1899 (orig.); 2003 (present
Clydebank F.C.	club)
Ground	*Colours*
Holm Park, Clydebank	White
League (2014-15)	*Selection of Honours*
West Super League Premier Div.	Scot. Jun. Cup 1941-42
Club Nickname	
The Bankies	

John: The clubs we were visiting today have geography and history in common. Geographically, both grounds are on the North Bank of the Clyde. In previous lives, both were senior clubs, and I'm sure you could fill a book with their past glories. But, as you all know, this book is about the present day, and the trials and tribulations the Junior game is facing, as well as the laughs we have on the way.

But let's get back to today's visit. Clydebank is easy to get to from Glasgow. You don't need to go up to the bus station, just jump on a No. 1 (or 1A/B) on Argyle Street, there's one every 10 minutes or so.

Most drivers are very helpful, but this being Glasgow, you are in danger of getting the grumpy one. Behind us were three ladies who asked the driver if the bus went near the SECC. 'Naw' was the reply, nothing else. I know bus drivers are not travel guides. But a bit of civility costs nothing. Maybe it all stopped after the Commonwealth Games.

Grumpy had us in Yoker/Clydebank in no time at all and we got off right outside the *'Boundary Bar'*, named after its unique position. Thought I'd explain that for the numpties reading this.

Craig: *The last journey of our look into rivalries in junior football was thankfully one of the shorter ones. Clydebank and Vale of Leven are both less than an hour from Glasgow. I am happy to report that nothing of the slightest interest happened on our bus journey to the Yoker area of Glasgow. Yoker JFC and Clydebank share a ground at the moment.*

The area is well served by public transport and public houses, and is therefore a place we have been looking forward to visiting. Two pubs which had been recommended to us were well within walking distance of the football park.

John: From the outside, the *'Boundary'* is an old, run down looking place, and inside is similar. We loved it. It was not long after opening time on a Saturday morning, so the smell of bleach still lingered on the nostrils. At this time of the day it only had a few regulars at the bar and we were warmly welcomed with a look. The locals assumed we were supporters of the 'away' team, which today was Arthurlie. We had just taken our first sip of the golden nectar when we were hailed from behind. Three supporters had come in, and one of them, Robert Burns (no relation) had met us

302

during our visit to his club Arthurlie. So right away everybody in the bar knew the reason for our visit.

Although Robert is an Arthurlie supporter, his two mates Gerry McArthur and Stevie Doogan were Clydebank men. Stevie is Clydebank's official photographer and like his two pals was great company. Being our official photographer, Craig had to take their photograph just to show them how good he was! Have a look yourself and see the result. All that's missing is 'Goldilocks'!

Stevie Doogan, Robert Burns, Jerry McArthur

We were having a brilliant time and the barmaid Laura Allison is a lovely girl. When we told her we were looking for stories, she directed us to the end of the bar where three local worthies welcomed us into their company. These guys were brilliant company and kept us going with their stories. One of them, a unique looking old guy called Lex McLean, had as many stories as his famous namesake, who used to fill the Pavilion theatre in Glasgow, mainly with Rangers supporters, every night during his summer season.

Again, Craig had his recorder out and he will fill you in with a selection. I overheard parts of stories covering topics as remote as balls in the Clyde and Lambretta Scooters! Lex's mates Billy Brannon and Tam Clougharty (what a great name) were just as daft and we were beginning to enjoy ourselves a bit too much.

Another thing that helped our enjoyment was the price of the drink. To give you an example, a half and a half pint was £2.00. This was better than any pub I remember visiting. We were just about sober enough to realize that we had to get out and along to the ground while we could walk, so with great sorrow and slurring of words we left the *'Boundary'* . As I always say, it's the company that makes a pub.

Lex Mclean, Billy Brannon, Tam Clougharty

Craig: Our first pub, 'The Boundary', turned out to be almost next to our bus stop. John thought that this was a wonderful coincidence, but of course I had checked it all out beforehand. In fact I had timed things so well that after ringing the bell, the bus stopped at the exact moment I reached the door.

Due to an early kick-off, we found it necessary to visit our first pub of the day at the ungodly hour of 12.00pm. I wasn't really expecting to find too many customers in the Boundary, but our entrance doubled the total number of thirsty punters in need of refreshment. Things didn't look too promising for any sort of pub banter.

Laura Allison, the barmaid, came straight over to us, asking for our order and enquiring about what we were doing in the area. It's always nice to have a cheery welcome to a pub. We spent a good quarter of an hour chatting away to Laura before the first football supporters came in. Clydebank was playing Arthurlie and we had expected to see fans from both sides at some point in the day. What we were not expecting was for both sets of fans to come in together. Even more surprising was the fact that we recognised one of them. Robert Burns, our old pal from Arthurlie, tapped us on the shoulder and we all had a drink together.

Laura Allison

One of his pals, Stevie Doogan, is a Clydebank supporter and I had to ask how they would get on during the game. Stevie said everything would be fine as he was the official photographer for Clydebank, and would be sitting on the touch line during the game.

At that point, Laura called us over to tell us that one of her customers had an amusing story to tell. At first the chap was a bit reluctant to speak to me, but my natural charm soon won him over. It seems that quite a few years ago The Boundary's pot man was up at Holm Park where his team, Yoker, were playing Irvine Meadow, and not doing very well. He decided it was time to give his team a bit of a hand. So he staged a one man pitch invasion, grabbed the ball and kicked it into the Clyde. In those days there was no spare ball and the game had to be abandoned. Unfortunately for Yoker's saviour, the authorities took a rather dim view of his actions and gave him 60 days in Barlinnie as a reward.

I thought it was a great story, but the bloke still didn't want to give his name. However, one of the other customers shouted over, "Come oan Lex, tell the man yer name".

His identity was further revealed when Allan Grimmond came over to talk to us. He had noticed that I had been talking to his wee pal, Lex McLean, and had a story of his own to tell us. Apparently, about 40 odd years ago, before he had ever met wee Lex, his prized Lambretta 250 GTX scooter had been stolen. Fast forward 20 years and Lex let slip that it had been him who had nicked the scooter. Understandably, Allan was curious as to what had happened to it. Lex explained that he had soon realised that he could not afford the petrol for it and so had thrown the machine into the canal. Amazingly they are still friends.

Who would have thought that in one small pub in Clydebank, early one Saturday in October, we would come across two of the biggest names in Scottish entertainment: Rabbie Burns and Lex McLean.

John: It was only a short walk to the ground. After assuring the wee man on the gate that we were not here to watch the match and had an appointment with the secretary, he was very friendly and pointed out Matt Bamford for us.

Steven McAneney, Ronnie Johnson, Matt Bamford, Bill Abraham

Matt was very helpful and introduced us to his fellow committee members Steven McAneney, Ronnie Johnson and Bill Abraham who are the backbone of the club. I was talking to Ronnie, and asked him what his main jobs were. He told me he was Clydebank's 'Match Day Operations Manager'. He explained that this means he arrives at about seven in the morning to cut the grass. There are no egos in Junior Football.

We had a good time with the guys and they then told us we should go to the upstairs lounge, where food and drink were to be had. He didn't have to tell us twice. We still 'had the taste' from 'The Boundary' so we fairly shot up the stairs into a brilliant lounge bar overlooking the ground.

The sun was shining and the set up of the park was very nice. Clydebank share the ground with Yoker. It is Yoker's park, but Matt had told us that there are moves afoot to move to their own ground in the not too distant future. Mind you, I think ground sharing, especially in the case of two clubs who are very close neighbours, makes sense. I'm sure there are other reasons for separation.

It was good to see that improvements to the ground are being made. I think Craig has more information about how this is being carried out.

The girls behind the bar, Tricia and Joyce were very friendly and Joyce told us that her husband Kevin plays for 'The Vale', our next port of call. We enjoyed a couple of drinks, and I had a pie, before saying our farewells to the girls and the committee.

Craig: Up at Holm Park we met Matt Bamford, Clydebank secretary. As usual, we talked about the club's prospects and past victories. When we mentioned ground improvements Matt told us that there were great things happening around the club. In a deal with the local college and a major building firm, Holm Park is enjoying a period of rebuilding. Materials are provided and young apprentices get practical experience, while the club has retaining walls and terracing upgraded.

We had been told that there was a social club at the park, but didn't like to bring it up in conversation in case Matt thought that that was all we were interested in. It was a great relief when Matt himself brought up the idea of a wee refreshment.

The social club is upstairs from the changing rooms and offers a good view of the pitch. Since the bar remains open all afternoon it would seem to me that it would be the ideal place to do my supporting from, if I was a Bankies fan.

Tricia Hamilton, Joyce Stanley

The bar in the social club didn't have draught beer, so I made do with a couple of cans. The barmaids, Tricia and Joyce, were less than keen on having their pictures taken. In fact they suggested that we come back the next time Clydebank is at home. Hair do's and makeovers were mentioned. However, my whining and pleading soon paid dividends and they agreed to pose for my camera.

Tricia got so carried away that she insisted on buying one of our books. I suggested that she could pay for it in cans of lager, at cost price obviously, but she insisted on making it a cash transaction.

Since the game had already started, we thought it was time to check out another local pub.

John: Although it was almost an hour to Alexandria, we had plenty of time as the Clydebank game was a one o'clock kick-off.

This was because Scotland were playing tonight at five. I can only assume that a lot of Clydebank fans are members of 'The Tartan Army'.

With the time available, we decided to visit another bar for more research. All this research must be damaging my liver! *'The Lovat'* is across the road from *'The Boundary',* so in we went. The noise when we went in was ear splitting. To be fair, the barmaid Donna McPhail was apologetic and offered to show us through to the lounge. We rejected her offer as the noise was from the players of the local amateur team 'Whitecrooks' who were celebrating a victory in their morning game. The players were in fine form and singing and even some solo dancing was being demonstrated. What the dancing confirmed was that, to quote an old film title, 'White Men Can't Dance', (or should that be jump). The singing was just as bad.

Two girls, Leanne Walker and Katherine Coll were doing all they could to keep the boys in check. Leanne was the sister and Katherine the girlfriend of two of the players. We got talking to the boys and they were a really great bunch. They even all sat together to let us take their photograph. You can see what a good looking bevy of beauties they are! The long suffering girls even wrote down all their names for us, but I lost the bit of paper. Hope you all know who you are.

It's hard to say what sort of bar *'The Lovat'* is, but we enjoyed our time there. So, in our opinion, Yoker/Clydebank have two great pubs across the road from each other.

It was time to go, so we left the team to their harmonizing. Talking about harmony, there wasn't much from Craig. I made the mistake of being unsure of which stop our next bus left from. There was a stop across the road, and one just round the corner and up the street. I said to Craig we would have to check them both out. You can imagine his answer! Minor things, especially ones that involve unnecessary walking, are major issues for Craig. I'm sure he will give you his more detailed version.

Leanne Walker, Katherine Coll

Craig: The Lovat is only a hundred yards or so back down the road from The Boundary. It is a fairly traditional pub, but the music coming out of it was anything but.

Personally, I thought that we had made a mistake going in, but it was too late to turn back. That was just as well really, as we ended up thoroughly enjoying our short visit to The Lovat.

There was an amateur football team in the bar, letting a little steam off after their game. In my day that usually meant a couple of pints, a couple of punts and, quite often, a couple of punches.

This lot, or at least some of them, were into solo dancing. To the more mature drinker this is indeed a strange sight, especially at one o'clock on a Saturday afternoon.

Donna McPhail

The barmaid, Donna McPhail, must have the patience of a Saint to put up with the music they were playing on the jukebox. She told us the lads come in every week and spend an hour or so enjoying a couple of drinks before going out on the town later on.

During the odd break in the music we managed to chat to the boys and shared a laugh or two. Someone, I know not who, suggested that I should take a group photo of their team; Whitecrooks. It was like herding cats trying to get them to sit at peace long enough to get them in focus. Incidentally I really hope that their team is named after a local district and is not in fact a comment on what the lads do when they are not playing football.

Vale of Leven

Club Name	Founded
Vale of Leven	1872 (orig.) 1939 (current club)
Ground	*Colours*
Millburn Park, Alexandra	Blue and White
League (2014-15)	*Recent Honours*
Central League, 2nd Division	Scot. Jun. Cup 1953 (current club)
Club Nickname	
The Vale	

John: Thankfully for me, our next bus, the same No. 1A we got to Clydebank, turned up right away and took us through god knows how many wee detours before it got to Alexandria. Things then went from bad to worse. I made the mistake of getting us off the bus at the wrong stop. This resulted in a 15 minute walk along the banks of the river Leven. It was a beautiful walk in bright sunshine. Craig moaned the whole way, he's like a wean. Never mind, we got to the ground and met up with our editor (sounds very professional) Ian Baillie. Ian stays near the ground and is a 'Vale' supporter.

Ian checks all our, or more correctly, my attempts at writing, and does it all for the love of the job, what a guy. The very least we could do was visit his club, 'The Vale of Leven', and glad we are we did.

As a wee aside while we are talking about 'The Vale', it's not much of a nickname. For that matter, Clydebank's 'The Bankies' is not much better. 'The Vale' could be 'The Fast Train', and Clydebank could be 'The Blitzed'. Work it out for yourselves.

But back to today's visit to 'The Vale'. Although the club is in the lower leagues at present, this does not matter to us. The ground is in a beautiful setting, and although the park is in need of some TLC, it is a very atmospheric ground, and the surface itself is on of the best we have seen. Ian told us that up until recently, the Scottish team used the park for training before internationals. It really is a superb playing surface.

A sensationally interesting fact about 'The Vale' is that they are one of only three clubs to have their name on the Scottish Cup. That is rubbish, I hear you say. But no, all the other winners like Celtic, Rangers and the rest have their names inscribed on the plinth, which is the base that holds the cup. That's one for the next pub quiz!

Craig: *After yet another farce, which saw us cross and re-cross the road, trying to find our next bus stop, we headed towards the final destination of our junior football study: Alexandria, home of Vale of Leven JFC.*

The bus seemed to take ages getting up there, but we made our own entertainment to help pass the time. I spent the first part of the journey mocking John's ability to plan simple bus trips.

Later we decided to have a go at the crossword in his newspaper. It was The Daily Mail, so we had a head start, as most of the answers are just variations on the words, socialist, benefits cheat and illegal immigrants. The crossword then developed into a communal activity when the chap sitting in front of us decided that we needed his input.

Even while doing the crossword I was also multi-tasking. I managed to eat my pieces while keeping an eye on my phone sat-nav.

Once again John refused to listen to the information I was giving him, claiming that he knew exactly where and when we needed to get off the bus to get to Millburn Park. Obviously he was again rejecting my high-tech mapping solutions, in favour of his crumpled up, hand drawn, scraps of paper.

I would have called him a Luddite, but since he was struggling with, 4 Down: a three letter word for a public transport vehicle, I decided that it was probably not worth it.

As soon as we got off the bus I knew we were in the wrong place. Not content with this act of sabotage, John compounded his mistake by sauntering off in the wrong direction.

Don't get me wrong, it was a very scenic route, it just wasn't the right one. After a long trek along the riverside, during some unseasonably warm weather, we arrived at the football park.

John: We met up with Angus Wallace, and first of all congratulated him on today's 3-2 win, made all the more amazing in that their goalie was ordered off after 10 minutes. There's life in the old 'Vale' yet. Angus does almost all of the work keeping 'Vale' going on his own. It makes me wonder why guys like Angus can be bothered with all the hassle. But come rain or snow, Angus is at the ground making everything happen.

Angus Wallace, Ian Baillie

I'm sure there must be some supporters willing to join the committee and help out. If you are reading this and are a 'Vale' man, or woman, get on the phone and offer to help. It's a great cause.

After a chat in the sunshine, we left Angus to his chores and walked round the short distance to the *'Laughing Fox'*. Craig was none too chuffed when he saw that the bus stop we should have gotten off at was right outside the pub, only a couple of hundred yards from the ground. I told him that as this was the last trip of the book, a screw up was essential. I reminded him we had had a travel hiccup in the first chapter. Craig's answer concerning my travel screw ups in almost every trip is not for publication.

Craig: Millburn is a really old park and could do with a lot of money being spent on it. That, unfortunately, is unlikely to happen any time soon. Vale of Leven has had its share of glory days, but those have long gone. I doubt that the money generated by the crowd that day would do much more than cover the club's running costs.

We had arranged to meet Ian Baillie, our editor, at the park and he was waiting for us just inside the gate. The game was still in progress, but I had no idea which team was which. I had to maintain a neutral stance and didn't applaud either side's efforts.

As soon as the final whistle went Ian took us over to talk to Angus Wallace. He confirmed that Clydebank were indeed his club's greatest rivals. They have had a series of disappointing results over the last few years, but Angus insists that it is mainly down to bad luck and some very suspect refereeing decisions.

On one occasion The Vale snatched a last minute equaliser against The Bankies, only to see their rivals score again in the last second of the game.

There has been a bit of bad feeling between the two teams, but I got the impression that Angus has a soft spot for Clydebank, albeit a very small spot. He told me that Matt Bamford, the secretary of Clydebank, had followed The Vale in the days after Clydebank's senior team folded. He had even sponsored The Vales team bus.

John: The *'Laughing Fox'* is another old-man's pub, the kind we like. We were made to feel right at home. Mind you, most of the time was spent with Ian going over some of the previous chapters showing me the mistakes I had made. I am dead ignorant about grammar and other English language things. A worry for me is that this chapter, the last, will not be read and checked by him, because of time constraints, so apologies for any mistakes you notice. It's not Ian's fault.

We left the '*Fox*' and walked the few yards to '*The Station Bar*'. This is another old fashioned bar and again we felt right at home. The Scotland match was being shown live on the big flat screen TV's, so we did not get much of a chance to talk to anybody. Amazingly, Scotland scored while we were watching. It was actually an own goal, but who cares, Scotland won 1-0. Who they were playing is of little interest, a win is a win.

Craig: We were all in need of a few beers by this time and headed out to find the Laughing Fox. For the record if you ever wish to visit the Laughing Fox there is a very convenient bus service which stops quite close to the pub.

While we were crossing the road, I have to admit that it did occur to me that it would be highly ironic if the 1A bus came whizzing round the corner and hit John, nothing fatal you understand, just enough to get him airborne. I think that the heat might have been getting to me.

Inside The Fox we found a traditional Scottish pub. For some reason I had imagined a more upmarket interior. The name of the place kind of suggests a middle-class, country pub; all half pints of real ale and quail pies. It was nothing like that. However if you are ever going to the Millburn Park, the Laughing Fox is an ideal watering hole, especially if you take the direct route.

After a couple of reviving pints Ian told us a story about a former Vale manager, Jimmy Brown. Apparently Jimmy was well known for his animated team talks. On this particular occasion the manager was firing on all cylinders, giving his team a rollicking for their lack of commitment in that day's game.

He got so wound up that he lashed out and kicked the dressing room door. It may have been the sheer power of his frustration, a bit of woodworm or a combination of both, but Jimmy's foot went through the door.

Unable to extricate himself from the woodwork, he continued with his high decibel rant. Legend has it that not one player so much as sniggered at his predicament.

It is only a few minutes' walk from the Fox on Bridge Street to the Station Bar on Bank Street.

As Station Bars go this one is pretty good. It feels like a real pub rather than a transit café which also flogs booze. I got the impression that it is well used by locals whether they are using it when waiting for a train or just out for a pub session.

John: All too soon it was time to leave. So we said our farewell to Ian, thanking him again for all his hard work, and instead of getting on the 1A which would have taken us on the one-and-a-half hour journey through darkest Dunbartonshire, we cheated and jumped on the train which is a lot quicker. I hope you will appreciate that at 67 years of age, the bladder would have struggled with an hour and a half without a toilet in sight.

I had a laugh on the train as Craig could not find his ticket. He was wearing his new jacket for the first time. It is one of these new all-weather jackets with dozens of pockets in strange places.

The ticket lady on the train felt sorry for Craig and said to explain to the person at Queen Street what had happened. Craig was convinced I had not given him the ticket. He found it just before we reached Queen Street. He still said it was my fault!

We wandered down to Central Station. I was sure Craig would be all for stopping for a nightcap in *'Denholms'*, but no! The new Craig wanted to go straight home. There is definitely something wrong with him.

Kate collected us from EK Station, and our last trip was over. Ah well, on to the next book. Is there no end to this?

***Craig:** We had always planned to travel back from Alexandria by train. Not just because we wanted to end our travels around the 32 junior clubs we had selected to visit in style, but because we thought there might be an element of celebration involved. As it was that didn't really happen mainly because of all the wandering around John had included in our itinerary: we were both knackered! Maybe for the next book I'll take over the planning.*

317

Clubs and Pubs visited today;

Clydebank;
The *Boundary Bar*-brilliant
The *Lovat*-great as well
Clydebanks lounge- great food, drink and view

Vale of Leven;
The *Laughing Fox*-good man's bar
The *Station Bar*-another worth a visit

Clydebank; **How to get there-free with the Bus Pass**
Walk down to Argyle Street (at Hope Street)
No. 1 (A or B) from Argyle Street to Yoker/Clydebank

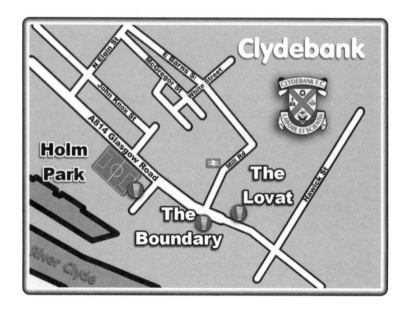

Vale of Leven; **How to get there-free with Bus Pass**
No. 1 (A or B) Alexandria to Glasgow

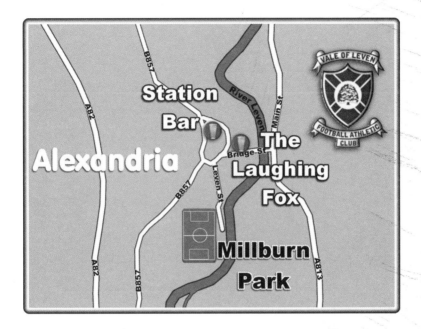